Lost Restaurants of SACRAMENTO and Their Recipes

Lost Restaurants OF SACRAMENTO AND Their Recipes

MARYELLEN BURNS & KEITH BURNS

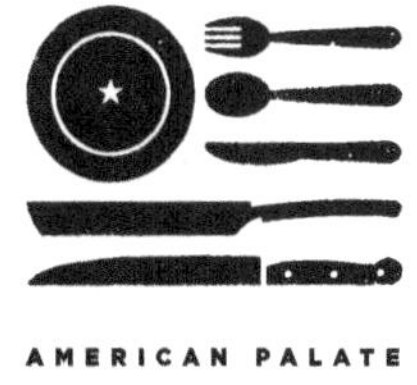

AMERICAN PALATE

Published by American Palate
A Division of The History Press
Charleston, SC 29403
www.historypress.net

Cover: Images provided by Sacramento Public Library, Center for Sacramento History and Bob Miller.

First published 2013

Manufactured in the United States

ISBN 978.1.60949.973.0

Library of Congress CIP data applied for.

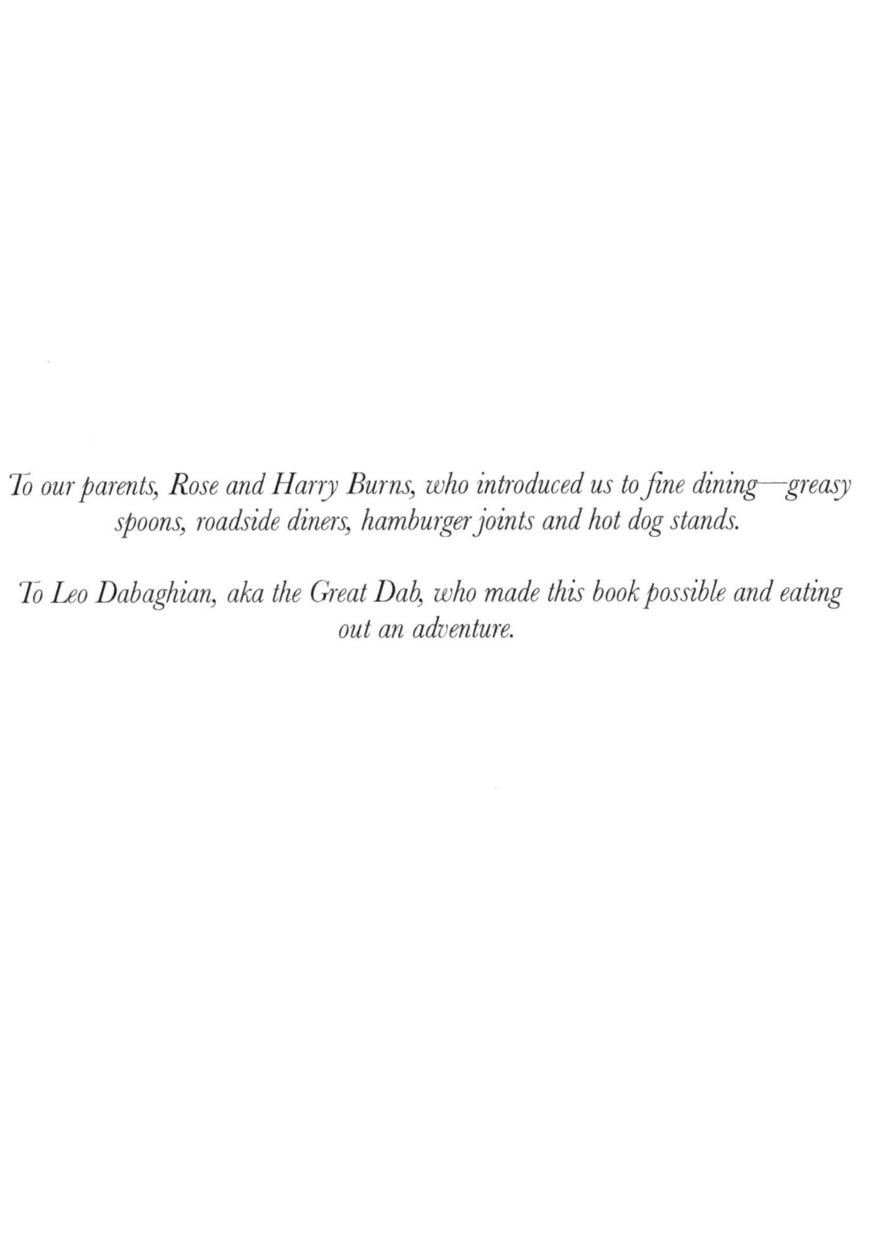

To our parents, Rose and Harry Burns, who introduced us to fine dining—greasy spoons, roadside diners, hamburger joints and hot dog stands.

To Leo Dabaghian, aka the Great Dab, who made this book possible and eating out an adventure.

Contents

Acknowledgments

This book could not exist except for a lot of help from friends, family and colleagues who helped research, edit and interview; provided anecdotes and essays; and endured endless talk about Sacramento's lost eateries. Our heartfelt thanks to Scott Burns, Sister Sheba, Joy Gee, Arianne Laidlaw, Francis Ng, Lawrence Fox, Connie Geffert, Rick Castro, Stephanie Georgieff, Isaac Gonzalez, Emily DePol and Kelley Woodward.

Leo Dabaghian, Maryellen's spouse, could claim co-authorship. He slaved over each word, chauffeured and took out his wallet when we got a whopping bill for photo permissions. Also, as the deadline approached, he slogged and flogged us onward. Now that's true love.

Bob Miller generously supplied the watercolors gracing the cover and interior. He captures, in a way words never could, the character, texture and essence of Sacramento's gone-but-not-forgotten places. Our profuse and heartfelt thanks!

We are deeply indebted to the staff of the Sacramento Public Library, in particular the Sacramento Room. Amanda Graham, Tom Tolley and James Scott gave us unlimited access to a treasure trove of materials—books, maps, pamphlets, postcards, photographs and old city directories from Sacramento's earliest days. Tom and James deserve special thanks: Tom, a former bartender at the Coral Reef, provided a firsthand account. James shared his work on early Sacramento saloons. Our Sacramento Public Library card opened up vast treasures of information via online databases.

The Center for Sacramento History has a dedicated staff, knowledgeable beyond measure. We spent most Thursdays there researching this and other food- and history-related projects. Archivist Pat Johnson is irreplaceable. Ruth Craft, a volunteer and friend, tracked down obscure and vital material.

Our colleagues at the Sacramento County Historical Society are inspirational. Each deserves mention, but a special nod to William Burg, consummate Sacramento author and historian; Pat Turse, who kindled a passion for history; Tom Herzog, book store owner and Delta historian; and Dr. Bob LaPerriere, who opened his rare (and valuable) Sacramento history and cookbook collection to us.

We are grateful to the food reporters at the *Sacramento Union* and the *Sacramento Bee* from the 1850s forward. A special note to Elaine Corn, former *Bee* food editor, now friend and colleague. Elaine's husband, David SooHoo, is a walking encyclopedia. Sacramento's dining scene probably suffered its biggest loss when the two of them closed their last restaurant.

A special nod to eateries that fed us when we stopped cooking, letting us write at their counters or tables for hours: Market Club, Willie's Hamburgers, Waffle Square, Pancake Circus, Fortune House, Afghan Kabob House, Casablanca, Blackbird, Temple, Kebab House and the many others we cherish. Thanks to the staff of Taylor's Market and Corti Brothers, past and present, suppliers of top-quality meats, fruits, vegetables and wines to many small restaurants and caterers (including In Any Event, Maryellen's original entrée into the world of food). To Gary, special thanks. He'll know why.

Our editor, Aubrie Koenig was a delight. She made the process run smoothly, given we took it on with only a few months of research/writing time.

Lost Restaurants of Sacramento has many contributors. Their voices tell the story much more authentically than we could. Thanks to Joan Alby, Thom Allen, Albert Breck, Martha Breck, Don Burns, Scott Burns, Clarence Caesar, Rick Castro, Leo Dabaghian, Bonnie D'Alessandro, Josie D'Alessandro, Paul D'Alessandro, Jeannette Davis, Susan De La Cruz, Lawrence Fox, Howard Frasinetti, Joy Gee, Mary Gee, Louise Gonsalves, Randy Grenz, Tom Haseltine, Thomas Herzog, John Hull, Arianne Laidlaw, Toni Lane, Bob Miller, Elaine Nakamoto, John and Kathy Newman, Myron Owen, Maurice Read, Gail Robbin, Craig Rutledge, Ken Saunders, Norm Sayler, George Sullivan, Gordon Takamoto, Maury Temple, Mavis Temple, Tom Tolley, Socorro Zuniga and all the others who shared their stories.

Introduction

Sacramento is situated at the confluence of the Sacramento and American Rivers, an area full of natural bounty. With its rich stew of hard-working immigrants, it became, early on, a major crossroads for food, wine, beer and many other agricultural products that flowed to the nation and the world. Along the way, it begot a unique and rich culinary history.

It provided the finest American restaurants with caviar from Sacramento River sturgeon. Our canneries, food manufacturers and bottlers produced Sacramento Tomato Juice, Libby's Peaches, Campbell's Soup, Kraft Cheese, Coca-Cola, Hostess Cupcakes and Wonder Bread and sent it off by rail, sea or roadway to towns small and large. A&W Root Beer popularized drive-ins, carhops and fast food franchising. Shakey's gave us a hankering for pizza. Our test markets for new food products and chain restaurants changed eating habits worldwide.

When immigrant Chinese workers finished building the railroads, reclaiming Delta farmland and building our levees, they turned to the restaurant trade, as has every new immigrant group since. Innovators such as Theodore Judah utilized improvements in cold storage on trains to allow restaurants nationwide to feature our bountiful agricultural products—fresh, canned and frozen.

Our "gilded age," the growth of our local breweries, the emergence of counter culture, Prohibition, the Depression, the war years and drive-in mania mirrored cities around the country. But in Sacramento there was something truly awe-inspiring about the political watering holes, from the shenanigans that moved the legislature here permanently in 1854 to the rough-and-tumble politics of Jesse Unruh and Willie Brown a century later.

So, where are we after almost 175 years of eating out?

Boston gave us baked beans and clam chowder. San Francisco is known for sourdough bread, crab sold fresh off the wharf and innovative hotel creations like Celery Victor and Green Goddess Dressing. Does Sacramento have a signature dish? Well, no and yes. Most signature dishes began as a specialty of a particular restaurant. Nevertheless, they define Sacramento. Frank Fat's banana cream pie, Americo's fettuccini with asparagus and mushroom and Merlino's Orange Freeze present a taste of who we were and are.

We've also exported some great chefs. Chef Caesar Cardini, creator of the Caesar salad, did a stint in Sacramento. Jack Cardini (no relation) was one of our first television chefs. Adam Pechal, homegrown boy from Tuli Bistro, lasted for weeks on NBC's *The Taste*, although Tyler Stone was sent home on day one of Food Network's *Top Chef*. The face of that network, Guy Fieri, trained at the American River College culinary academy. Our chefs have cooked at the French Laundry and other four-star restaurants across the country.

Of course, women have guided our decisions of where and what to eat from the beginning. They've staffed our kitchens, drawn up our menus, served our meals, washed the dishes and almost invariably kept the books. Though there were early pioneers, they came of age in the 1980s. Biba Caggiano, Lina Fat and Mai Pham created successful restaurants and penned nationally respected cookbooks. Biba had a nationally syndicated cooking show on television. Journalist Elaine Corn worked alongside her husband, Chef David SooHoo, at Bamboo, Nine Doors and Neptune, while also writing award-winning cookbooks and has received Julia Child and James Beard awards.

Sacramento has a long history of eating out, ranging from crab shacks and oyster palaces along the river, peanut butter and steak in the Delta, to dozens of Asian eateries running the length of Little Saigon off Stockton Boulevard. We've also had mermaid bars, pasty shacks, rathskellers, dim sum houses and, recently, coffeehouses on almost every corner.

This is a brief glimpse into some of their stories. In these few pages, we share a tapestry of treasured recollections, images and historic and memory-evoking recipes. This bare sampler gives a glimpse of restaurant culture from John Sutter's rough fort kitchen and the bakeries, saloons, hotels and fruit pie vendors of the gold rush to the delicious history of small cafés, ethnic restaurants, funky eateries, country kitchens, soda fountains, creameries, lunch counters, speakeasies, drive-ins and fine eating houses that closed with the twentieth century.

Maleville's Coral Reef, *the* place for a first date, family reunion or to get sloshed on Polynesian drinks; the Rosemount Grill, more than seven decades of "fine food to fine families"; and the Ram, a restaurant with wild game on its menu long before there was an endangered species list, are just three eateries that now exist only in our collective memory.

We've concentrated on the iconic, classic places remembered by a fair number of Sacramentans. A smattering of places survived, some for almost one hundred years.

A survey of all the eateries that have come and gone would have run into the thousands. We feature places that gave more than sustenance, drawing crowds, decade after decade, creating lasting memories, like the Milk Farm, Buggy Whip, Aldo's and Harvey's Hamburgers. We explore the food on the plate and the plate itself, from the square milk bottle patented by Henry Hart to the china used on Sacramento-bound railroad dining cars.

Not every beloved spot could be included. For every restaurant mentioned, ten more had to be excluded. An abundance of neighborhood diners, breakfast houses, lunch spots, burger joints and ice cream parlors warrant their own book. Had we tried to cover every neighborhood of the city and county, it would have filled an atlas. As it is, we couldn't resist driving out into the county to sample eateries slightly beyond the city limits.

We've tried to capture a taste of what it was like to dine out—lush-red banquettes, long-legged and scantily dressed carhops and the smoky din of after-hours jazz clubs. We wanted to celebrate Sacramento's culinary scene at its best, collecting stories before dimming memories fade away.

We have wandered into back rooms, basements and closets of restaurant owners, employees and patrons to uncover fading memories—evocative photographs, restaurant receipts, bills of fare, menus, matchbooks, posters, advertisements and other memorabilia—plus tried to gather delicious stories and recipes before they vanish forever. We talked to foreign-born and homegrown chefs and visited regional archives, libraries and museums to fill in the missing pieces.

There were hundreds of restaurant stories told. It quickly became obvious that many cherished the same places, reminiscing about favorite bartenders who dispensed wisdom as well as whiskey, passed on rumors about legendary characters who frequented popular eateries or shared salacious tidbits about local celebrities or politicos too risqué to share here.

Most of the owners and chefs we talked to don't have recipes written down—these cooks carry their recipes in their hearts and in the muscle memory of their hands. A few, however, had amassed a treasure trove. They gave us recipes from long-gone restaurants from the mid-nineteenth century to now, recipes for dishes that would have been lost if a great-grandparent, aunt, uncle or mother hadn't passed it to the next generation. Many were simple recipes, dishes like a wedge of iceberg lettuce with Thousand Island dressing or Les Petits Pois à la Parisienne, an item popular in the 1860s. We also managed to get some of the most popular recipes from Antonina's, Wulff's, Ding How and even Woolworth's legendary ham salad sandwich.

We also wanted to tell a personal story. These are the restaurants we came to love as children, places our parents, Rose and Harry Burns, took us (along with brother Scott) or we explored on our own as young adults and later with husbands, wives, friends and family.

Like most children of the 1950s, eating out was a treat, a once-in-a-while thing that made the experience special. Now that we can afford it, we try to explore new dining experiences weekly. Still loyal to our favorites, we also go to the same wonderful places we've been eating at for more than fifty years.

We hope this book gives you pleasure. Take a small bite at a time. Savor the stories, essays, images, menus, memories, excerpts, recipes and snippets scattered tantalizingly throughout. Then make a reservation at your favorite eatery, invite friends to join you and keep the places you love in business. As hungry as we are for the favorite places of our past, no one can eat a memory.

A Taste for History

A heroic figure he was not, although his romantic position as pioneer in the great valley made him seem so to many travelers and historians...his fate was the ordinary one of the persistent and unteachable dreamer.
—Sutter's Friend, *I.S. Tichener (1866)*

We might say that the first restaurant, bar and hotel proprietor in Sacramento was Captain Johann Augustus Sutter, "the persistent and unteachable dreamer" who envisioned building an agrarian empire in the West.

Sutter's repeated business failures and the specter of debtor's prison prompted him to flee Switzerland to seek his fortune in America. In August 1839, after a several-year odyssey, he landed with an ensemble on the American River. William Heath Davis, his guide, noted, "It was the first echo of civilization in the primitive wilderness so soon to become populated and developed into a great agricultural and commercial center."

To qualify for a land grant from the Mexican government, Sutter needed to become a Mexican citizen and to recruit new settlers. To protect his investment, he started work on a fort, relying on the labor of Indians, allowed him as subjects by Mexican law. They began work on a large trading post and on the construction of a landing on the Sacramento River that he would call the Embarcadero. By 1853, more than twenty steamboats would ply the waterways between Sutter's Embarcadero and San Francisco.

In the fall of 1839, he hosted his first visitors, a group of eight men from Oregon, and in August 1840, five more arrived. Soon, his fort had become a place to rest and eat for all who came through. The following year, he got his formal grant of land, naming it New Helvetia, after his homeland. Having recognized the Sacramento Valley's agricultural potential, he now commenced in earnest to build the empire of his dreams.

A distillery, flour mill, bakery and brewery arose. Merchants opened shops at the fort trading in staples, cured meats and dried foods. Soon a boat launch ferrying freight and passengers between Sutter's Fort and the San Francisco Bay brought more guests.

All this effort took many hands. Sutter used the indentured Indians and took on employees, offering opportunity to anyone who wanted a job. All had to be housed and fed. Sutter employed overseers, whose job was to secure provisions and supervise the Indians, who most likely did all the cooking and serving.

Sutter wrote, "We lived very simply in the main—roast beef mostly and vegetables when we had them. Many times we had neither sugar nor coffee. We found that peas were a fair substitute and acorns still better. Indeed it was difficult to tell acorn coffee from the real beverage. Rations of beef and bread were given daily to the Indians; also a mush made of flour was cooked for them in a huge kettle. I paid them their regular wages in my tin money."

Historians have amended his account, noting that the Indians were fed once a day, at breakfast time, in large wooden communal troughs. Beef they received rarely, usually when there was excess from cattle slaughtered for their skins and tallow. The others were fed three times a day, boardinghouse style, in a room housing up to thirty men at a time.

Julian Dana, in *Sutter of California*, recounts the story of a breakfast he encountered at the fort in 1843: "Breakfast was announced for the white employees. It was served in an outhouse adjoining the kitchen. There was wholesome corn bread, eggs, ham and excellent venison and coffee, surprising fare for the wilderness."

For his settlements, Sutter recruited immigrants from the United States, Switzerland and Germany, providing them with housing, food and drink, usually without recompense. His agricultural domain extended from the American to the Feather Rivers.

Sutter began to spend more time at Hock Farm, near present-day Marysville. Successfully, after several failed attempts, he planted peach, fig and pomegranate orchards; citrus trees; peas; vineyards; and wheat fields and grazed cattle.

The fort occupied one of the most strategic locations in Northern California. It became the natural destination for parties crossing the Sierras, especially during the winter. Most came hungry. Sutter fed them all and the ones that followed after, including the now infamous Donner Party.

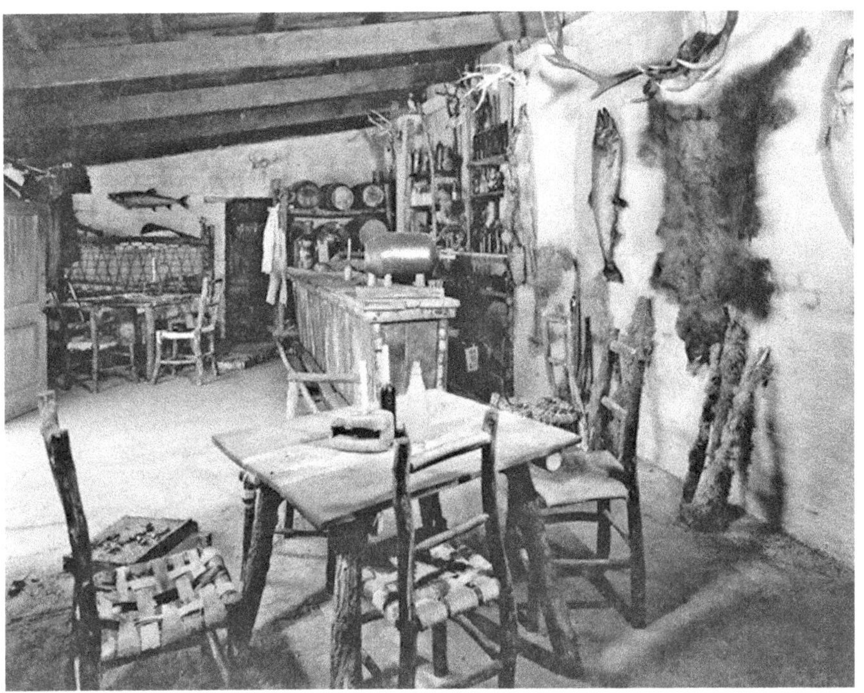

Sutter's rough kitchen could produce food for about thirty men. *Sacramento Public Library, Sacramento Room.*

A garrulous and welcoming host, he enjoyed sharing his liquor and his table. The following article in the January 1964 issue of *Sacramento County Historical Society Golden Notes*, adapted with permission, tells of a particularly memorable Christmas Dinner in 1845, as seen by a cooking assistant.

> *Sutter was a gourmet, having lived in Paris where cooking is an art. In his new empire he made every effort to hire the best cooks he could find. Usually a ship's cook from some sailing vessel in the bay, lured to his employment by the promise of liberal inducements. Recently Sutter had hired an English cockney, who had deserted some ship some years before. In the interim he had lived among the Spanish and Mexicans in southern California.*
>
> *He approached his chef and broached the subject of a special Christmas dinner for John Bidwell, P.B. Reading, S.J. Hensley and two or three others.*
>
> *In spite of the limitations in supply he assured the Captain a feast for the most royal of palates. "Leave it to me and you shall have a feast unlike any ever seen in these wilds."*

Sutter agreed, but he was doubtful as the commissariat consisted wholly of beef, frijoles (brown beans), unbolted flour and Mexican panoche sugar, about the color and consistency of beeswax. There were no fresh vegetables, but an abundance of the ever-present chile colorado (red peppers), plenty of salt and black pepper and a little coffee and tea. Even more incredible was the cook's promise: "And, I'll top off the meal with a real John Bull plum pudding."

Plum Pudding! There was mouth-watering appeal in the very sound of the word. But how could the fellow manage it? There wasn't an egg in the place, no spices, butter, milk, eggs or raisins. To be sure the river was lined with a profusion of small black, wild grape, a little more sour than concentrated vinegar.

Finally the big day arrived. Sutter was in high spirits as he greeted his guests. All took their places at the long redwood table with expectancy, and no little curiosity.

The first course was beef soup, garnished with frijoles, chili colorado and garlic; the second course was roast beef; the third course was baked beef pie; the fourth course was stewed beef; and the fifth course was fried beef, accompanied with black, unbolted flour bread. All these dishes were garnished with the same condiments as the first, but the chili colorado dominated over all the others, and our bodies were aglow with heat, and our stomachs were like a boiling cauldron. We were all very anxious for the plum pudding, to counteract the artificial heat created by the red peppers. He soon brought it in with an air of self-gratulation. And such a pudding! It is doubtful if another, to compare with it, has been or ever will be concocted. In its construction the cook had used common beef tallow liberally, and filled it with the aforesaid sour grapes and seasoned it unsparingly with chili colorado, black pepper, salt and garlic. He also made a sort of sauce with the panache sugar and tallow, and he had also doused that liberally with chile and black peppers.

All of the guests had been helped plentifully, but after taking a mouthful or two were as perplexed as the Captain. They gazed at each other and at the dish in silent astonishment until Reading broke the silence by asking. "Cook, what is it? "Why sir," said the cook, "it's a regular Christmas pudding, Mexican style."

Captain Sutter was a singular man about his food. He would partake of anything set before him without a remark, but this dish bothered him.

Though seen by all as benevolent, Sutter had long-term ambitions. Like the "free lunch" that saloons offered in later years to entice people to purchase more drink, he offered these inducements hoping to profit later, through the sale of land and provisions to a burgeoning community.

By 1847, fields of wheat, a bounty of vegetables and fruits and herds of cattle, sheep and pigs had placed Sutter at the verge of an empire. In 1841, Sutter had purchased Fort Ross. Russians now provided a hungry market for caviar harvested from sturgeon growing fat in Sacramento's rivers. Salmon, hides and tallow, wheat and fresh produce now made their way almost daily to market.

Sutter contracted with millwright James Marshall to help construct more facilities and a sawmill on his land near Coloma. It was here in 1848 that Marshall spotted the "glisten of gold" that would inexorably lead to an overwhelming population explosion and eventually to Sutter's ruin.

The rumor of gold wound its way around the globe, luring thousands who would risk life and what little else they had seeking their fortune. Swollen with miners, merchants, workers and seekers, a dirty, makeshift, canvas-and-cloth town mushroomed up to feed and house them. Most entered the engorged city at the Embarcadero, immediately making their way to coaches taking them to the mines or nearby boardinghouses, rooming houses or hotels. Along the way, they would be assailed by a cacophony of sound and stink—the clap of hooves against cobblestone, manure everywhere, shouts from hack drivers vying for their attention, rotting fish and decaying vegetables, fruits and trash thrown into the streets.

The first Argonauts had found Sacramento City free of gambling houses, saloons and hotels, but by late summer of 1849, one couldn't make his way without being assaulted by drunks, con artists or young women perched in doorways lauding the wares and delights inside.

In this era, men did not cook. The frenzied rush to the gold fields, overwhelmingly male, created a bonanza for those who did.

Finding food and shelter wasn't easy. What few physical structures existed were crowded and uncomfortable. Finding a single room was almost impossible. Men often slept on storeroom floors, on a heap of straw under a wagon or in the open air. If they were able to find room at a boardinghouse, the bare meal could cost twenty-five dollars a week, and meals were served "family style" with boarders seated side-by-side at big communal tables. Diners passed around platters piled high with meat and potatoes. Come late to the table, and there was nothing left to eat. You paid for room and board whether able to make your way back to eat or not.

No need to seek a meal elsewhere unless you were flush with gold, bored with repetitious fare or didn't have a long enough "boardinghouse reach." Most eating houses catered almost exclusively to those who worked nearby and lived in rooming houses, which housed them overnight but didn't feed them.

Local restaurants were, by and large, unsavory: smoky in winter from coal stoves, and flies and dust everywhere in the summer heat.

There were exceptions. Poet Bayard Taylor wrote of eating in a tent restaurant in Sacramento, where the floor was uncovered, the tables made of planks and the food bountiful, "salmon-trout that when made in a chowder or stewed in claret would have thrown into ecstasies the most inveterate Parisian gourmand."

If a miner were flush, he'd come to town and order Champagne and oysters, items that almost every hotel dining room offered. Oysters were so much a part of the Argonaut diet that, by 1851, the oyster beds of San Francisco were tragically depleted. Lucky miners relied on canned oysters while waiting for a schooner to arrive from Oregon or even higher up the Pacific Coast.

In the 1850s, Sacramento's eating, drinking and sleeping proprietors gambled that the allure of gold would keep men—and hopefully some women—coming. They built large hotels and permanent structures. Fire and flood often destroyed them, but they just built them again. The gamble paid off, producing a wealth few had anticipated. It came not from the gold fields of the mother lode but also from the golden fields of the Sacramento Valley.

Sacramento City: The Second Wave

Merchants, tradesman, shopkeepers, laborers and workhands comprised the second wave of gold seekers, drawn by the beckoning economic opportunities. They had no intention of struggling in the mines: the wealth they sought was from commerce.

These young, single men entered the city in droves, bound for jobs in the banks, offices, warehouses and wholesale fruit, meat and vegetable vendors near the wharves. They settled in nearby boardinghouses and rooming houses located between J and K Streets.

Sacramento City was bound by A and B Streets to the north, Thirty-first Street to the east, Y Street to the south and Front Street to the west. Most activity in the early days was near the Embarcadero, at the foot of K Street. As the population expanded, so did the city. Restaurants, hotels, saloons, gambling halls and businesses took up an area of barely five square blocks, exploding from 150 people in 1849 to 10,000 a short time later.

Those were the free-and-easy days. At night the city was full of boisterous, rowdy men frequenting gambling halls, city saloons and theaters, looking for excitement. During the day, quieter streets belonged to working residents.

Each neighborhood supported its own eating-places. The Embarcadero favored large hotels, restaurants, coffeehouses and bakeries close to the steamboat landing and the railroad. Workingmen ate mostly at their boardinghouses or at cheap restaurants near their jobs. Most of these restaurants were on the lower part of J Street or on Front Street.

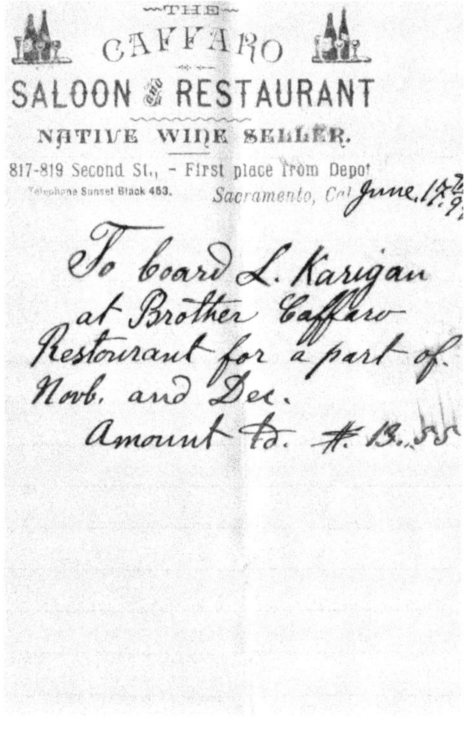
—THE—
CAFFARO
SALOON and RESTAURANT
NATIVE WINE SELLER.
817-819 Second St., - First place from Depot
Telephone Sunset Black 463. Sacramento, Cal June 17th

To board L. Karigan
at Brother Caffaro
Restourant for a part of
Novb. and Dec.
Amount Pd. # 13.55

Boarders paid for room, board and sometimes drink. *Center for Sacramento History.*

Men ate whatever was plopped down in front of them, subsisting on fried and overcooked food intended to fill the stomach with little concern for taste.

A "restaurant," a freestanding establishment that served meals to customers from a fixed or rotating menu at any time of the day, was a new concept. The term, a French word meaning "restoring place," arrived in America in 1845 with Delmonico's in New York. Until then, there were "eating houses," almost always attached to saloons, usually to encourage drinking.

The *Placer Times* of April 7, 1849, ran an advertisement for one of the eateries in Sacramento, the American Hotel on Front Street, run by Orland McKnight. Although there were earlier saloons in the town of Sutterville, a few saloons on the waterfront and roadside taverns on the roads heading out to the mines, it was the first restaurant of any permanence.

At least one known cannibal opened a restaurant during the rush. Lewis Kesborg had a place on K Street. The last man to survive near the lake where so many of the Donner Party suffered ignominy, he claimed he never killed anyone but boasted of eating meat from every corpse he could get his hands on. Some women, among the few survivors, claimed that of all the meat, the flesh of two Indians sent to retrieve them was the best.

Cooking conditions were not much better than cooking under the stars. Mary Ballou, who ran a boardinghouse in Negro Bar, wrote a letter to her sons on October 30, 1852, detailing the primitive cooking conditions.

> *All the kitchen that I have is four posts stuck down into the ground and covered over the top with factory cloth—no floor but the ground. This is a Boarding House kitchen.*
>
> *Sometimes I am making mince pie and Apple Pie and squash pies. Sometimes frying mince pies and Donuts. I make buiscuits* [sic] *now and then Indian jonny cake…and then again I am Stuffing a Ham of Pork that costs 40 cents a pound.*

Restaurants articulated status and prestige. While some catered to the affluent, most served the workingman. The successful ones served either one type patron or the other—men seeking a cheap midday meal near work or those with fortune enough to frequent the city's luxury hotels.

A few tended to businessmen who commuted to the commercial district and were too far from home to return for the midday meal. If they were entertaining clients, the meal could be served leisurely, possibly over distilled spirits, thus was created the "business man's lunch."

Restaurants were chiefly masculine concerns, and customers, cooks and counter and table help were all male. Women made up only 8 percent of California's new population. Before the 1900s, only women of ill repute would accompany a man to dinner. Women were served privately in "ladies' ordinaries" (private dining rooms), or family rooms if they had children, while the men gambled the night away in the saloon.

Although a few women owned restaurants or ran boarding or rooming houses, it was late in the century when women were hired first in the kitchen and then as waitresses. Only when ice cream parlors and "ladies' ordinaries" restaurants became the norm did attitudes toward women dining out really change.

Unless they hired a town crier, advertised in the daily newspapers or became the talk of the town when they succumbed to fire, flood, murder or robbery, most eateries in early Sacramento existed for a time and then simply vanished. They unpretentiously served ordinary, everyday all-American meals: bacon and eggs, soup, stew, steak, roast beef, chops, potatoes and almost always oysters, at reasonable prices. A few lasted more than one hundred years. The Saddle Rock even laid claim to having stayed open from 1849 to the early 1990s.

Restaurants could pick and choose from a wealth of ingredients purchased from local farmers and ranchers, at auctions or wholesale warehouses on the Embarcadero. In 1849, auctioneer J.B. Starr would meet incoming boats at the wharf and hold an auction on the spot. Everything was on offer—fish, fruits, vegetables, meat, sugar, chocolate, caviar, oysters and exotic canned goods from international markets. Eventually, the rapidly growing railroad linked Sacramento markets to city shoppers nationwide.

By the 1860s, most restaurateurs never had to leave their establishments to get foodstuffs to cook. Door-to-door delivery became the norm. Truck farmers and vegetable, fruit and fish peddlers displayed their wares early each morning at restaurant kitchen backdoors. Some forged contracts with suppliers—not unlike today's farm-to-table movement. Usually, most restaurants were owned and operated by family members working a long day from early breakfast to late night supper.

Construction of the Sacramento Valley Railroad accelerated the city's geographic spread. Sacramento had been a walking city, or the affluent could rent carriages or "hacks" that would transport them to their residences. Now, fire and flood caused many to move farther out of town. Restaurants moved with them.

Completion of the Transcontinental Railroad in 1869 altered the complexion of the city. Workers poured into the area to work in the shops. Specialty restaurants flourished, catering to their tastes with quick, inexpensive food. Some began staying open all night. Sacramento became more and more a twenty-four-hour city.

Population continued to grow, and the economy flourished. Trains delivered agricultural bounty eastward and brought back barrels of iced oysters from New York, beef from Chicago and fresh shrimp from New Orleans, ready for restaurant kitchens. Cheap processed foods like Kellogg's and Post cereals made eating on the go easier still.

Early railroad cars were not outfitted with dining compartments. The train would arrive at a way station and disgorge the human cargo into dilapidated eating rooms or saloons serving substandard grub where they would be given twenty minutes to eat. The rail terminal had a lunchroom that offered quick bites.

In 1893, a number of themes emerged all at once. Tamales and hot dogs appeared, and the first delicatessens, serving cold meats and salads, began luring in casual diners. Sacramento developed a "sweet tooth."

Bakeries began to locate alongside restaurants. The aromas wafting from yeasty breads, chocolate cake and flaky pastries tempted passersby. A popular treat, the Charlotte Russe, was sold in push-up cones by street vendors. Much more luscious desserts with Caffé mit Schlag—coffee with whipped cream—were served at the Vienna Bakery.

The same year, former Delmonico's chef Charles Ranhofer published the *Epicurean*, a cookbook listing daily menus, which suggested recipes depending on what was in season. It had 3,500 recipes, many of which showed up in Sacramento more than fifty years later in offerings by the Sutter Club, a private men's organization. Some restaurants offered verbatim Eastern restaurants' menu cards taken from trade journals. Others mimicked menus from fine San Francisco hotels. Most cooks worked by taste, feel, smell and memory, relying on supplies readily available in season at the markets.

Petits Pois à la Parisienne

Recipe adapted from the Daily Union, *August 17, 1867*

2 cups fresh peas (or 2 10-ounce packages frozen petits pois)
2 tablespoons unsalted butter, softened
1 lemon, zested
1 teaspoon fresh thyme
Salt and pepper to taste

Bring 1 cup water to a boil, add the peas, and return water to a boil. Simmer covered, until they are tender (3 to 4 minutes for frozen peas). Drain. Toss with butter, lemon zest, thyme and salt and pepper to taste.

Charlotte Russe with Raspberry Petals

Inspired by Rose Burns. This was her favorite dessert growing up.

16 or more ladyfingers, split (could take more, depending on size of your pan)
2 envelopes gelatin
¼ cup cold water
⅔ cup sugar

4 egg yolks
1⅓ cups milk
1 teaspoon vanilla extract
1 cup whipping cream, whipped
½ cup sour cream
2 teaspoons finely grated lemon zest

Line a nine-inch springform pan with ladyfingers around the edge of the pan. Next lay ladyfingers in a single layer on the bottom. Trim ladyfingers if needed. Dissolve gelatin in water. Add sugar, egg yolks, milk and vanilla and cook over medium heat, stirring until consistency of a custard sauce. Pour in bowl over ice bath. Stir occasionally. In a large bowl, whip cream until fluffy. Gradually beat in sour cream. Fold in lemon zest and cooled custard mixture. Pour into ladyfinger-lined pan. Spread evenly. Cover loosely with plastic wrap. Chill about two hours, until filling is firm enough to slice. To serve, remove outer ring of pan. Mound whole berries in middle of Charlotte and dust with powdered sugar or make a raspberry sauce and drizzle.

Raspberry Petals

2 pints raspberries
¼ cup sugar
1 tablespoon lemon juice

Combine raspberries and sugar in a saucepan. Cook until raspberries are broken down, about 10 minutes. Remove from the heat and strain through a chinois to eliminate seeds. Cool completely. Pour over the Russe.

Consider the Oyster

All along the waterfront fragrant wood smoke filled the air, beer flowed, fresh-shucked oysters sizzled in oil, and live music played in the background.
—Joseph Conlin

Oyster frenzy hit the nation in the mid-nineteenth century, and Sacramento was no exception. The delicacy was brought in fresh from San Francisco and Oregon. Canning and refrigeration allowed East Coast oysters to be delivered to the West by train. Brined in barrels, or shelled and packed in milk containers, they'd be put back into their shells before serving.

They were plentiful…and they were cheap! Even the poorest could enjoy oysters from the many stands littering the wharf. Saloons offered them—along with caviar, clams and mussels—free to anyone who purchased a five-cent drink. Street vendors hawked them door-to-door. Oyster palaces served the briny mollusks raw, baked, steamed or roasted and in soups, stews and pies.

In 1850, oyster merchants boasted that there were billions in natural beds near San Francisco that could NEVER run out. However, high demand and nasty pollution from mining severely damaged the beds. Some historians claim the beds were depleted a swift decade later. On January 31, 1868, the *Daily Union*, however, reported: "A schooner loaded with oysters as large and fine as any found in the Chesapeake has arrived in port. It is rumored the bed is situated a few hours sail of the Golden Gate, and was discovered in 1851, by Captain Tyler, who returned here recently, after seventeen years absence,

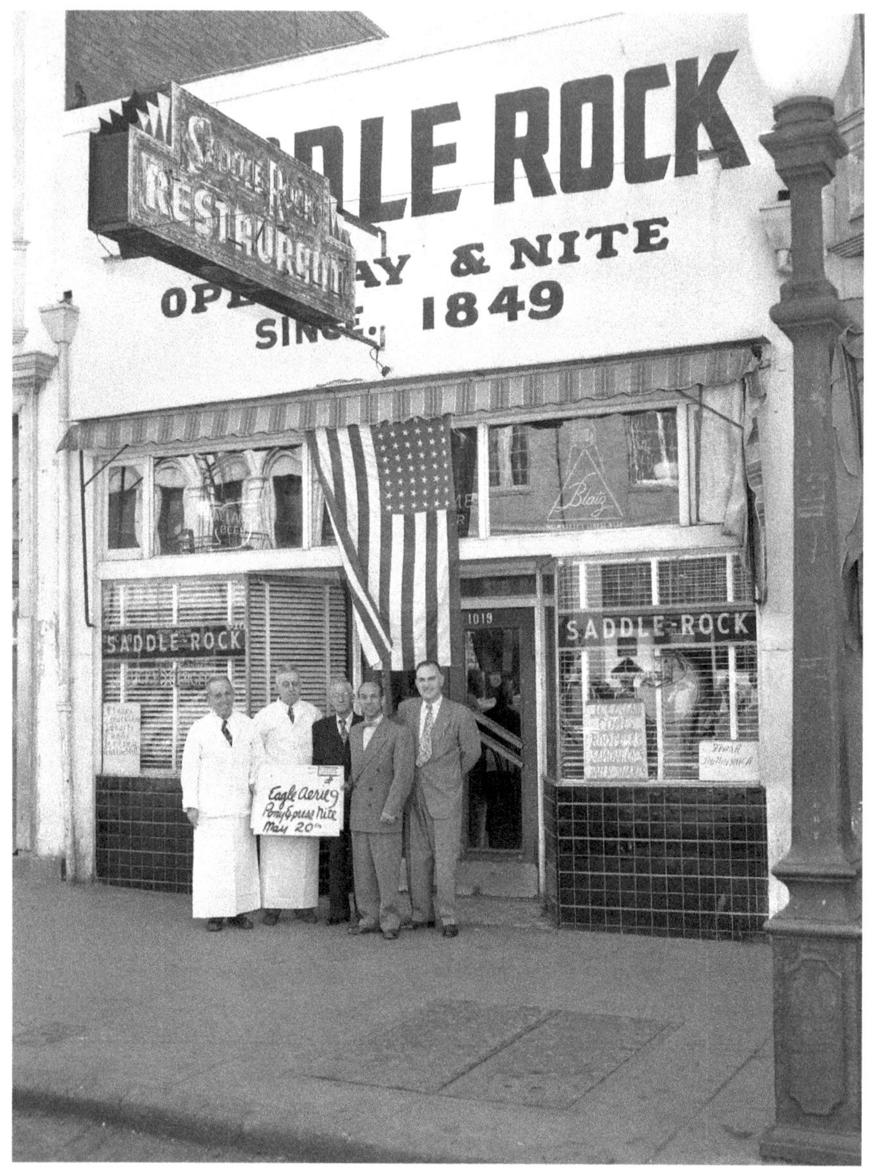

The Saddle Rock stayed open until the 1990s. It served oysters every way imaginable. *Center for Sacramento History.*

and fitted out the schooner for the trip. It is said there is an inexhaustible supply there."

During December 1878, the *Sacramento Bee* and the *Daily Union* reported that an oyster company had successfully transplanted eastern oysters into

Sacramento's river waters. Most of the spawn died, but younger oysters, no larger than a ten-cent piece, survived to grow to full size. In all, some 300,000 were successfully transplanted. Twenty-one boxes, containing about 300 each, were shipped daily to market. Attempts to stabilize the new "beds" were only marginally successful.

The *Sacramento Bee* reported, "As soon as the Sacramento River commences to rise and bring down its flood of fresh water the company will remove all their oysters from here."

Many restaurants opened expressly to sell oysters, along with caviar and champagne considered to be exotic and decadent. The famous "Hangtown Fry"—a mix of oysters, bacon and eggs invented at the Cary Hotel in Hangtown (now Placerville) by a Chinese cook—stayed on bar, hotel and restaurant menus until the 1990s, when the last holdouts, Posey's and the Saddle Rock, closed.

Restaurant Reviews and Recipes

Then, as now, restaurant and business reviewers informed readers about new restaurants or changes in staff or location and published recipes for popular dishes. The *Daily Union* of February 9, 1878, published this recipe: "Oyster toast is the term. It is made thus: Scald a quart of oysters in their own liquor; take them out and pound them in a mortar; when they form a paste add a little cream and with it pepper and salt. Have ready some nice piece of toast, spread the oyster paste upon them, and place them for a moment in the oven to heat."

Special "oyster trains" crossing the nation to satisfy ever-growing demand stopped in towns large and small, their arrivals listed in daily papers. A few, with extra cars for passengers, might stop long enough for people to eat. The *Sacramento Daily Union* reported on May 10, 1875:

> *The oyster train arrived last evening and continued on to San Francisco. Arriving at Courtland at 11 o'clock, boats were secured and a row was taken on the river as an extra appetizer for the chicken dinner that was being prepared for them. At 12 o'clock at the sound of the bell, all lined up "Oyster soup?" "Certainly." "Will you have roast chicken, fricassee chicken or roast beef?" One answer from all: "A little of both, with plenty of chicken on the side." "Strawberry shortcake?" "Yes, but make it as long as possible." And then, "Black coffee?" and then, "Yes," as usual.*

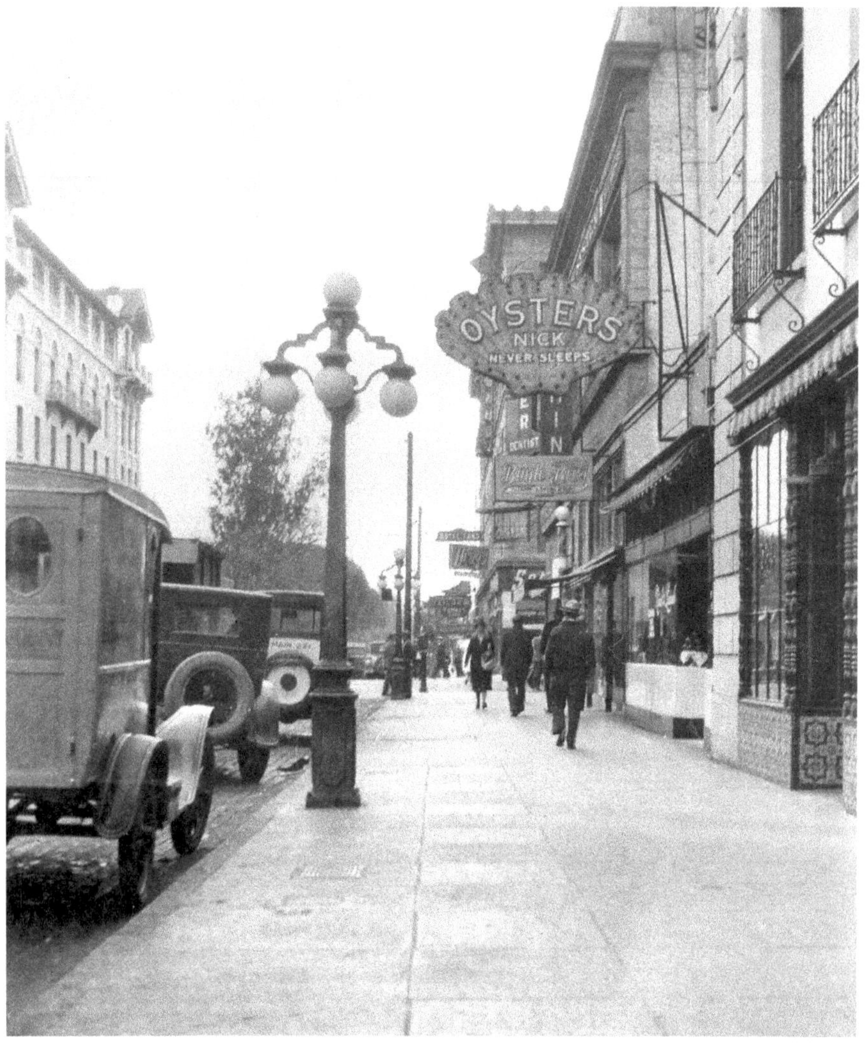

From the earliest years, oysters were a big craze, served day or night by eateries like Nick's. *Author's collection.*

Sacramento's *Daily Union* of January 4, 1884, reported on a remodel of Senatz's Mississippi Kitchen on Third Street. This article gives a rare glimpse into a typical restaurant kitchen.

> *The kitchen is open to the street, and the large show-window looking from it affords an unobstructed view from the public walk of the interior of the kitchen. In this part is a fine French cooking range and a broiler*

hood. Opposite these is a long, broad counter, on which all uncooked food is constantly displayed. The whole section is overhung by a huge iron hood, from which capacious ventilating flues lead to the roof. On the opposite or south side the bread, pastry, etc. is also open to view and examination, while against the section partition and facing the street is the oyster stand, where the bivalves are opened and the supply for cooking kept.

Numerous diners reported finding rare pearls in their oysters. On May 21, 1894, the *Daily Union* wrote that one of three men indulging in an oyster supper found two pearls, valued by competent judges to be worth $500 to $700.

How to Open an Oyster

The *Sacramento Bee* of October 8, 1895, instructed its readers in this art:

There is a correct way for doing almost everything, and generally the correct way is the easiest, as in this matter of opening oysters. The way to open an oyster so as to save all the liquor, which, to connoisseurs, is a valuable part, is not to smash it and murder it, as most of your oyster-openers do, nor to "stab" it, as they do in Boston, Baltimore, Washington and other places. And then your oyster-openers always lay out the oyster on the flat or convex shell, so that by the time your plate of "raw on the half shell" comes to you, what little juice that was not spilled in the slaughtering has all run away. The live oyster opens and closes its shells at will by means of a tough little membrane, or "hinge," about a quarter or a third of an inch in length. This hinge is at the small or narrow end of the oyster. It follows that all that is needed to be done to separate the two shells, whether the oyster is alive or dead, is to sever this little hinge. It is invisible when the shells are closed, but those who understand the business (and anyone can learn it in five minutes) know exactly where and how to find it. I have showed this little trick to scores of oyster-openers, but, because it is a little difficult at first, they go on with their mauling and stabbing.

THE SADDLE ROCK RESTAURANT

The Saddle Rock Restaurant and Oyster House boasted a sign claiming it opened in 1849 and never closed its doors. Like many early Sacramento stories, it might be a wee bit of a tall tale. Most Sacramento hotels and restaurants were regularly destroyed by fire or flood and had to rebuild. But why quibble?

As one of the most popular restaurants in Sacramento for more than one hundred years, it served oysters every which way, as well as mussels, clams and lobster, plus premium prime steaks and chops. Large banquet facilities made it a popular place with benevolent societies and women's clubs.

Maury Temple used to go with his father, who worked in the Southern Pacific (SP) shops nearby at night, and his mother to the Saddle Rock.

> *Mom and I would go in and have a full dinner once a week or so. Dad would come by during his dinner break and down a full dozen fresh oysters served raw on the half-shell, with cocktail sauce (basically Heinz ketchup with horseradish), and Mom would order them with mignonette sauce—shallots and champagne.*
>
> *I loved oysters so I'd order them everyway they cooked them, well almost every way. Somehow the addition of eggs made me gag—but give them to me fried, roasted, steamed, fricasseed, stewed, on a skewer, and even in an oyster loaf or pie and I was in heaven.*

A look at an old Saddle Rock menu from the early 1900s shows Champagne and Ruhstaller Gilt Edge Lager, both for twenty cents a pint. The bar served single shots of scotch, whiskey or bourbon, not fancy mixed cocktails.

The Saddle Rock, though still popular all through the fifties and sixties, was situated in skid row, a bit of a dicey location. The SP shops no longer ran a night crew and eventually stopped all together, so the customers who'd kept the place going faded away.

> *When my dad passed we had a kind of wake for him there, all the old guys from the crew and some of the old waiters, who remembered him fondly. I guess they stayed open kind of late and he'd pop in almost every night on a quick break and down a quick half-dozen of the easterners. I'm kind of sentimental so I saved all the oyster shells we ate that night and keep them in my garden.*

OYSTER STEW

Courtesy of Recipes Tried and True Compiled by the Ladies' Aid Society of the First Presbyterian Church, Marion, Ohio, 1894

Wash one-quart oysters and place on the fire. When they boil, add one quart of boiling milk, and season with salt, pepper, and plenty of butter. Serve with crackers or toast.

FOOD, DRINK AND LODGING

Sacramento's finest hotels sprang up to serve the gold rush titans, then the enterprising merchant class who built the city and, when the legislature settled here in 1854, the political crowd that wheeled and dealed in opulent surroundings with sumptuous food, elegant dining rooms and lavishly extravagant lifestyles. For the businessman and solons, the heavy meals served in hotels featured abundant meat and alcohol.

The state legislature headed to Benicia in 1854, but three hundred Sacramentans got there first and rented all the available hotel rooms. Lawmakers, forced to bunk in saloons, state offices and even stables, decided to look for a home with better accommodations. Sacramento won.

Nevertheless, until mid-1849, Sacramento hotels were little more than tents or rough shacks lining the riverbank. Most lodged in rooming houses, usually with saloons, pool halls and less-than-stellar restaurants attached.

Mid-1849, more recognizable hotels began appearing. John S. Fowler and Samuel Brannan partnered to build the first purpose-built hotel on Front near J Streets. With an elegant parlor, dining room and flowing fountains in its courtyard, it still was no match for the splendid Orleans, THE place where glitterati gathered to make merry.

Large hotels boasting private rooms and separate entrances ensured a steady stream of politicians when the legislature was in season. Each catered to a particular clientele. The Golden Eagle Hotel was headquarters of the Republican legislators and bitter rival of the Capitol, which housed Democrats.

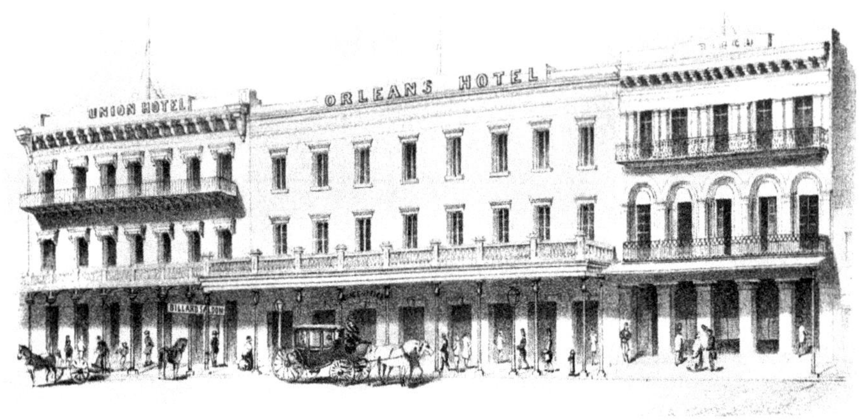

Lola Montez, the shapely dancer, performed in the Orleans Hotel in 1854, the year the city became the state capital. *Center for Sacramento History.*

The Western Hotel (215 K Street), built in 1854, was one of the most popular gathering places for miners, theatrical people, tourists, drummers and the outer rank of politicians. St. George was the most popular home for prominent families who preferred hotel life to the care of their own establishments. The American Eagle Hotel at 829 D Street was a workingman's boardinghouse until it was torn down in 1945. It housed a steady stream of boarders, mostly Southern Pacific workers.

Travelers during the mid-nineteenth century sought hotels with restaurant options. Accustomed to European hotels, where meals were served to order and paid for individually, they objected to the American Plan prevalent in almost all Sacramento hotels. A pattern established in taverns, menu offerings were table d'hote. Meals took place at set times and were included in the price of lodging. Diners ate precooked selections family style, rather than choosing from a menu.

As hotels switched to the European Plan, some hoteliers opened freestanding restaurants to serve both their own guests and those of other establishments. One of the first proprietors to do so was August Lismond Isidore Mouton. He opened a French restaurant on Second Street between J and K next door to his French Hotel. He also owned the finest French bakery on N Street.

Attaching bakeries to hotels was commonplace during the heyday of these restaurant/hotel combos. The Miners Hotel and Bakery on Mormon Island was a favored stop.

Hotel dining rooms and kitchens offered job opportunities that "people of color" were encouraged to pursue. In 1861, well more than a third of

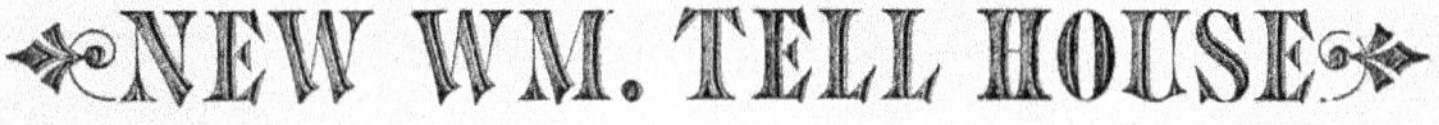

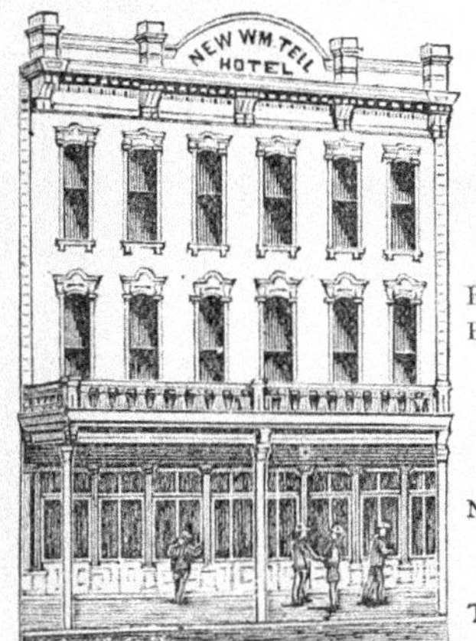

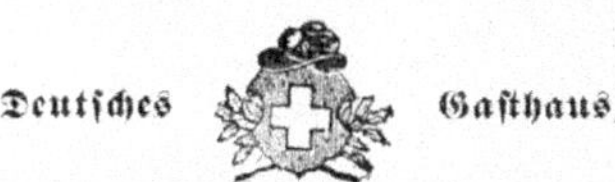

B. STEINAUER, Proprietor.

Board and Lodging, per week, - - - $5 00 to $7 00
Board and Lodging, per day, - - - - 1 00 to 1 25
Single Meals, - - - - - 25 Cents.
☞ Families accommodated on reasonable terms.

NO CHINESE EVER EMPLOYED IN THE HOUSE.

The Bar is Well Stocked with Choice Liquors and Cigars.

814 and 816 J Street, between Eighth and Ninth,
SACRAMENTO, CAL.

This advertisement from the William Tell House clearly displays the common bias of the time: "No Chinese Ever Employed In This House." *Author's collection.*

the black population worked in the food industry as stewards, waiters and cooks. We would have starved to death had it not been for Chinese cooks and waiters. Surprisingly, after the Civil War, when it might be expected to see even more liberality in the hotel/restaurant trade, hotels began advertising "all white staffs." Many signs read: "Chinese Never Employed Here."

Census data indicates that more hotel and boardinghouse operators likely came from extended families than did operators of other businesses. The restaurant industry was one in which respectable women could find employment. Thomas Van Dorn noted in his diary, "Any industrious woman can make here $12 to $15 a day, aside from ordinary vocations. If she is a good cook, all the better."

Golden Eagle Hotel

Steeped in the early political history of Sacramento, the Golden Eagle Hotel was the gathering place for the most powerful men in the country. It began as a rooming house in 1851 presided over by D.E. Callahan. By the mid-1850s, it was among the most highly regarded hotels and restaurants in the city, maintaining an Oyster Saloon and by most newspaper accounts, some of the finest food in the city. Only the Orleans, residence of luminaries like Mark Twain, Lola Montez, Horace Greeley and Bret Harte (when they were in town), could claim more prestige.

Like other hotels, it offered multiple dining rooms, an exclusive dining room for hotel residents and another for non-residents. The Golden Eagle Oyster Saloon operated from 1869 to 1878. Other restaurants later took its place. Oysters stayed on the menu through the lifetime of the hotel.

In 1852, Callahan had one employee: a servant named Enos Ceaser, born in Manila. The first Golden Eagle cooks arrived in 1859: T. Ashburn and James Hunter, both from Massachusetts. The next year, George Dupree, later associated with the French Restaurant, may be the first chef to offer continental dishes to the pleasure of hotel guests. After his departure, an Irish chef, an English cook and a Mexican-born epicure named Quo Rassiadh prepared cuisine Dupree had inspired. By 1869, a barkeeper, three stewards, three cooks and eleven waiters, almost all Irish, had joined the staff.

For more than a century, the Golden Eagle escaped the countless fires plaguing the city. Alas, it could not escape the flames on November 14, 1956. Because the hotel stood in the path of redevelopment, it was torn down. An era had ended.

This menu from an annual banquet provided to the Sacramento Medical Society gives us a glance at the food enjoyed as a matter of course by Sacramento's elite. Dr. Samuel Morse, grandson of Sacramento's pioneering doctor, bequeathed this menu to his son. Passed down through the generations, along with a few of its recipes, it has come to us.

Eastern oysters on the half shell
Mayonnaise of chicken a la Italienne
Lobster salad a la Russe
Boned turkey with truffles
Ornamented cold patties of chicken
Smoked tongue en Bellevue
Eastern ham with aspic jelly
Pressed corned beef al Anglaise
Roast turkey stuffed with oysters
Chicken, Beef, Veal, Lamb
Olives and Assorted relishes

Five changes for pastry
Macaroni pyramids
Pastry pyramids and eleven changes of cakes and pies
Dessert—five changes of fruits
Champagne jelly and ice cream
Wines—Heidsieck, White Claret and Port
Tea, Coffee and Table beverages to order

Lobster Salad à la Russe

Boil a fresh lobster. Remove the meat. Chop and mix with a generous quantity of mayonnaise. Boil beets until very tender. Cut into a dice and stir into the mixture. Heap the salad upon lettuce leaves, and garnish with Russian caviar.

Orleans Hotel

The Orleans Hotel, Sacramento's most elegant hotel during the early gold rush years, hosted many literary men. Mark Twain complained that he paid five dollars for a single meal when he stayed there during his lecture tours or brief sojourns in the city working for the *Sacramento Union*. Notable guests included newspaperman Horace Greeley and Lola Montez, notorious stage star, who stayed for two weeks in July 1853 on her honeymoon (with her third husband—unfortunately, a short-lived but tempestuous affair).

When the legislature was in session, the Orleans was "Political Headquarters." Excerpts from *The Genial Showman: Reminiscences of the Life of 'Artemus Ward'*, by Edward Peron Hingston, elucidate the character not only of the hotel and free lunch but also of Sacramento.

There is a daily spread at one o'clock, a table professing to bear upon it a luncheon gratis, the eatables exhibited consist of the leavings of yesterday, which now reappear in some shape or other. A number of people flock in at this time, and in ten minutes it is difficult to find a vacant place, so eager is the unpaying community to avail itself of this opportunity of dining gratis.

The proceedings of this great body amused me: it consumes voraciously; its members seize a slice of meat, dip it into the salt-cellar and salad mixture and then bite the end so rendered palatable off, continuing to dip and bite till the whole slice is eaten. Others moisten their forks, not being particular as to the source of the moisture, thrust them into the salt or pepper and so carry away a certain portion, and wipe it on the slice of meat in their possession. There is method in this system—it brings some large number of the community to the hotel; and though these visitants pay nothing for consuming the rubbish, yet they are expected to take a "drink" at the bar, which is close to the luncheon table. This they all do with much fidelity, and the "drink" cost twenty-five cents. Now one "drink" almost uniformly suggest another, and many have found that the gratis reputation of the luncheon is but a fiction after all.

City of Saloons

During much of Sacramento's history, saloons, bars, taverns and drinking places—whatever moniker a place of alcoholic refreshment used—were much more numerous than restaurants. Early Sacramento often boasted four per block. Nearly all offered some sort of food, even if just as an enticement. For many years, providing food was a requirement for getting a city license to operate.

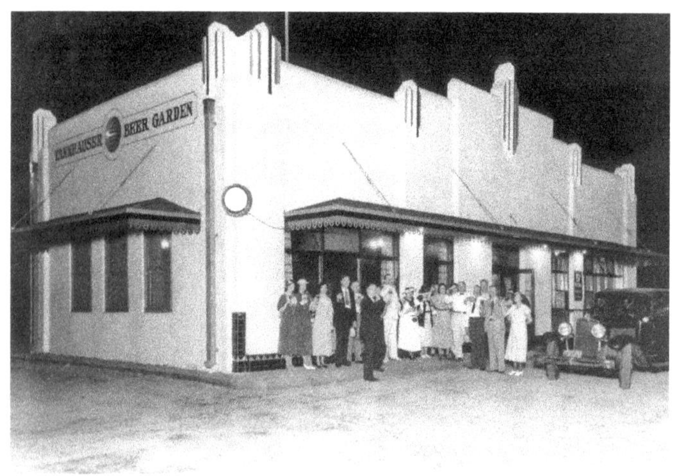

Tannenhouser Beer Garden was a spot for Germans and others who liked to drink local lagers. *Center for Sacramento History.*

As the city grew, so did the saloon. Many saloonkeepers would order stunningly ornate wooden bars shipped from around "the Horn," red tufted wallpaper and magnificent artwork displaying women in various positions of repose and undress and would fit the place out with furnishings costing up to $30,000. Little differentiated one bar from the next. Most served beer, from local breweries, if possible. Hard liquor was nothing fancy: whiskey, rye, bourbon and scotch. What really made a bar stand out from the others was the bartender. Good ones knew how to pour a good drink, how to be a good referee during a fight and how to stop the bleeding when the inevitable happened.

Free Lunch

Although "free lunch" has often been credited to San Francisco in the 1880s, Sacramento had free lunch from its foundation and continued the practice in cocktail bars, taverns, saloons, lounges, beer halls, gin joints, blind pigs and cocktail lounges, evolving into today's "happy hour."

Free lunch was always a misnomer. Saloon patrons had to purchase drinks in order to partake of whatever edibles were on offer. Often, free lunch might consist only of crackers and cheese, but competition from other saloons quickly drove the evolution of sumptuous repasts of roast meats and delectable side dishes.

Hubert Howe Bancroft writes "a free lunch of roast mutton, which never masqueraded as lamb, and stiltonized cheese awaited the early comers."

"Lunch free" or "free lunch" was not a noon-only thing. Some saloonkeepers put out a spread as early as 9:00 a.m., hours after most working people had eaten their breakfasts.

Bancroft also recalls, "At ten in the forenoon and nine in the evening the most fashionable dandy saloons furnished roast beef, pickled cabbage, crackers and cheese, etc., for their patrons, with the order of at least one drink."

J. Gruhlers Saloon on Sixth street, between J and K Streets, advertised cold cuts, cheeses, celery, smoked herring, dill pickles, potato chips and pretzels.

The surrounding woodlands yielded many varieties of duck, goose and other wild game, as well as bear meat, wild turkey, venison, antelope and elk—all in all, a cheap food source.

By the 1880s, upscale saloons were calling themselves cafés. Later, some adopted a small charge for a "merchant's lunch." Businessmen liked these

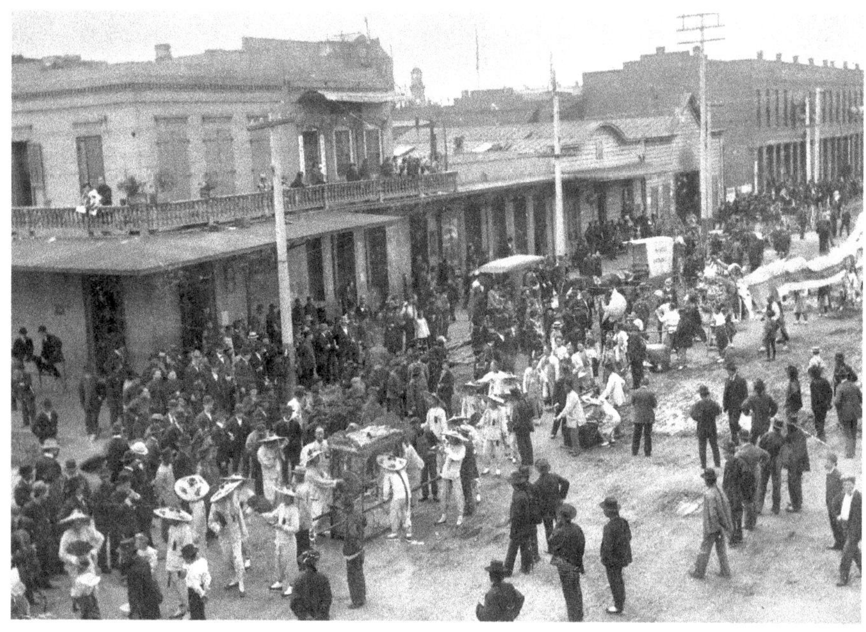

Chinese New Year was a time of celebration. Food carts, a dragon parade and free-flowing liquor connected cultures. *Center for Sacramento History.*

lunches. They were quick. Food was ready, no tipping was necessary and little ceremony was observed. Often you could eat standing. In fact, there were few tables and chairs. Loss of customers induced restaurateurs to repeatedly try to abolish the free lunch practice. Temperance advocates wished there could be cheap but respectable restaurants, which could compete successfully with saloons for the workingman's money. The average saloon usually charged only five cents for food and drink, a price most restaurants couldn't meet.

Coffee Saloons

Not all saloons served drink. Coffee stands and saloons differed from bars only in that they didn't serve hard alcohol. They did serve beer. On April 1, 1853, M. Elias opened a coffee saloon on the east side of Second Street, between J and K Streets, where he served his visitors an extra good cup of coffee, tea, chocolate, all kinds of cakes and German lager beer.

39 FASHION 39

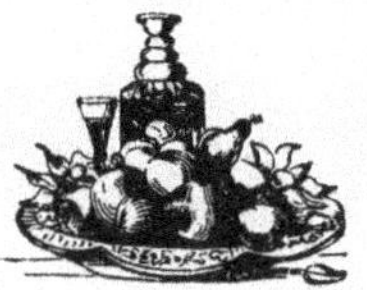

The above well known SALOON, situated in the most central part of the city,

No. 39 J street,
BETWEEN SECOND AND THIRD STREETS,
SACRAMENTO,

Still continues to be kept by the undersigned, who supervises every department of the house personally, and who has spared neither pains nor expense in placing the

FASHION

in rank with the very FIRST CLASS HOUSES of the kind in the country.

THE BAR,

As heretofore, will be found at all times supplied with the most choice

Liquors and Cigars.

served up in the most proper manner. EVERY TASTE SUITED.

LUNCH

Is served up every day at 11 o'clock A. M., and 9 o'clock P. M.

Thankful for the very liberal patronage extended, he trusts by undivided attention to merit a continuance.

JNO. C. KEENAN, Proprietor,
39 J street, between 2d and 3d,
SACRAMENTO.

Politicians, murderers, prostitutes and tourists bumped elbows at the Fashion Saloon. *Center for Sacramento History.*

This also was a business women could enter, as explained in the *Sacramento Daily Union* of January 19, 1877:

> *Know all persons by these presents, that I, Margaret Trestler, the wife of Vincent Trestler, of the city of Sacramento, having this day, January 17, 1877, bought all the interest of Adolph Albrecht in and to the furniture, fixtures, in and belonging to the Saloon on Third street, between J and K streets, Sacramento City, known as the Vienna Coffee Saloon do hereby make this my declaration of intention to carry on business in my own name and on my own account, as a sole proprietor according to the provisions of the Act of the State of California, entitled "An Act to Authorize married women to transact business In their own names as sole traders," the said business to be that of keeping the said Vienna Coffee Saloon, for the purpose of serving up coffee, oysters and such other matters as are generally kept and furnished in saloons.*

There were other inducements. The William Tell Bar and Restaurant was known for the best Limburger cheese in town and the Sazarac Saloon for its delicacies from New Orleans. The Fashion Saloon had an extensive menu that included all kinds of raw fish, tongue and tripe.

Mark Twain, known to be a voracious drinker and eater, reportedly liked the Apollo Saloon. Author Joan Didion's great-great-grandfather owned a saloon on Front Street.

Architect M. Madden built the Old Tavern, now the site of Biba's, on the corner of Twenty-eighth Street and Capitol Avenue, in the 1870s. Originally, the building was a warehouse and distillery, eventually becoming the Sacramento Brewery. Prohibition closed it. In the 1920s, it housed residential apartments on the second floor atop a tavern. One of our former mayors (we'll not say which) reported that the Old Tavern would serve lavish feasts in the "residential" suites and, if you paid for something other than drink, pleasurable activities too illegal to mention in print. Old Tavern moved to Twentieth and O Streets.

Saloonkeepers, fearing that their freewheeling days were numbered, began to take out restaurant licenses. The authorities suspected that many did not actually serve meals but wanted to evade liquor laws. Nevertheless, the trend would grow exponentially, and bars would be turned into lunch counters and soda fountains.

Counter Culture

In Sacramento it is fiery summer always, and you can gather roses, and eat strawberries and ice-cream and wear white linen clothes, and pant and perspire, at nine or ten o'clock in the morning, and take the cars, and at noon put on your furs and your skates and go skimming over frozen Donner Lake.
—Roughing It, *by Mark Twain*

More and more, wives and families joined their menfolk in Sacramento. As families grew, so did objections to rowdiness and public drunkenness. Temperance societies sprang up. They advocated strongly for more "family friendly" establishments and distributed pamphlets with recipes for non-alcoholic drinks.

One popular "receipt" was for the "soda drink," carbonated water blended with flavored fruit syrups. Eugene Rousse, a Philadelphia perfume dealer, created the original formula, which was printed and reprinted in newspapers and magazines.

Pharmacists started mixing pharmaceutical concoctions that served medicinal and commercial purposes, using lemon, ginger and grape syrup, regularly used for nose and chest relief. They ordered highly ornamental dispensing apparatuses for tables and countertops called soda fountains and created counters and tables for customers to sit at and stay. They advertised the "soda drink" as a solution to heat prostration, a disease that overtook almost every man, woman and child, who habitually overdressed in Sacramento's scorching summer heat.

Other quick service restaurants complemented the "soda fountain," filling the need for a casual drinking place serving ladies, families and sober gentlemen. Many citizens came increasingly to believe that saloons and public spaces in hotels were not conducive to civil society. Eventually, soda fountains became almost universal in pharmacies, department stores, confectionaries and railroad stations. How to encourage folks to come to your place? Advertise in local newspapers, like this one from the *Daily Union* of September 23, 1893:

> *Sackamentans always appreciate the efforts of a first-class and reliable caterer, as is evidenced in the case of J. Ernst, manager of the now well-known and established C'reamerie. Since its location at 612 J Street, the patronage has exceeded the most sanguine expectations. Mr. Ernst was for years connected with the Maison Dore, San Francisco, and is thoroughly in accord with the principles of that famous establishment. The bill of fare presents all the market affords for every meal, and ladies and gentlemen will find the C'reamerie the most popular lunch house in Sacramento.*

During the 1880s, many businesses with soda fountains began to offer sandwiches, soups, pie, doughnuts, ice cream, desserts, coffee and other light fare. With the advent of counters for customers to sit at, the "luncheonette" was born. The typical layout was either straight or U-shaped, surrounded by stools. Counter men prepared the food on one side, and diners sat opposite.

Launching a full-scale, fine dining establishment took tremendous capital and staff. During the early days of the twentieth century, Sacramento's influx of new immigrants could carve out a living by opening up delis and markets, lunch counters, sandwich shops, creameries, soda parlors and other small establishments staffed by family members.

Most were set up near downtown workplaces close to the Capitol, the growing industrial area near the wharves and retail stores. They served breakfast and noontime meals to working men and women who had to watch both pocketbook and time. Some stayed open late or around the clock to serve swing-shift and night-shift workers.

Many had counters as their principal feature and advertised "lunch." Lunch did not mean noontime, as it does now, but simply a light, fast, meal.

DELICACY STORES

"Delicacy" stores proliferated during the 1880s. Small grocers, who sold cooked and prepared foods, by the end of the decade had become full-fledged delicatessens (from the German word, *delikatesse*), offering counters and tables as well as take out. Workers brought lunch pails to work or stopped by a deli to pick up a cold lunch in a basket. The basket was returned at their next visit, much like we used to return bottles for soft drinks and milk. The Sacramento Delicatessen, 814 K Street, opened in 1895, advertised in local newspapers.

> *The proprietors have on hand always, all dainty dishes; such as salads, game, poultry, and roast meats, besides the finest of imported English, German and Swedish delicacies in the way of cheese, sausage and the like. The place is a model of neatness, and businessmen will soon find it convenient to take their noon lunches there, where they can be supplied with almost any toothsome dish imaginable. In a compartment in the store are tables, where lunch will be served at any time. Cold lunches in baskets are put up at any time.*

Although many believe Sacramento delis were German or Jewish, they were, by and large, Italian affairs. Exceptions were Brother's Deli in Town and Country Village and a kosher deli downtown in the 1940s. Otherwise, if you wanted lox, bagels and cream cheese, you had to go to Pennisi's Deli or Corti Brothers Grocery. La Colomba Ravioli and Tagliarini Factory offered French and Italian delicacies. Mazzucco Brothers, Italian Importing Company and the Meda Brothers at 914 Eighth Street were also extremely popular.

Frank and Gino Corti, brothers who worked in the wholesale grocery business, took over Meda Brothers in January 1947. An old-fashioned store with wooden floors and refrigerated cases, the brothers began offering delicacies and wines not available anywhere else in the region. With son (and nephew) Darrell and other family members, they grew it into an institution known worldwide. In 1952, it became a full-fledged supermarket, expanding to four locations. Most closed, but the flagship store at Fifty-ninth and Folsom is still vigorous. Colman Andrews, former editor of *Saveur Magazine*, once said, "Darrell Corti knows more about food and wine than anyone else in the world." The Corti's first introduced Sterling Caviar, Parmigiano-Reggiano, Brie cheeses, extra virgin olive oil and dozens of other products, now all commonplace, to eaters around the country.

Prohibition, the Depression and War Years

Sacramento's saloons and restaurants, and any business that served liquor, suffered greatly during Prohibition. A deluxe dining room especially had a hard time. Saloons found it easiest. Their long wooden bars made convenient counters for soda fountains or ice cream parlors. The Depression brought tough times. Cost savings were imperative. Folks fortunate to have jobs barely made enough to put food on the table at home; they could ill afford to eat out. Nevertheless, on occasion, they'd grab a quick bite at the drugstore or five-and-dime lunch counter. Women either displaced from the workplace or forced to enter it for the first time found the lunch counters, with their single stools, a convenience. Housewives or society ladies might meet friends for tea or lunch at local department stores.

Their menus were pretty simple: soup, sandwiches, meatloaf, liver-and-onions, roasted turkey, spaghetti, fried chicken and pie.

Strict nationwide government rationing during World War II affected availability of almost everything. Americans were restricted to twenty-eight ounces of meat per week and limited amounts of sugar, butter, milk, eggs and coffee. Restaurants, also on rations, often had to limit hours. That opened up more possibilities for alternative eating places.

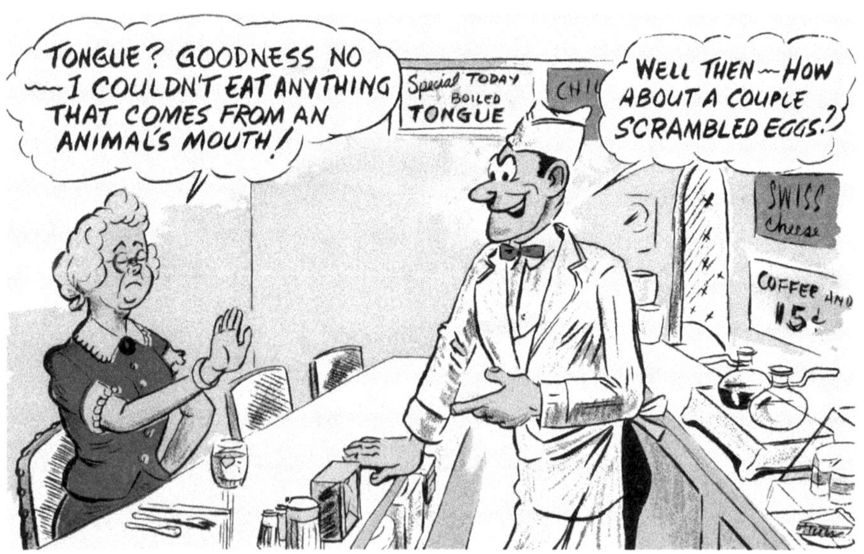

Variety stores, pharmacies and drugstores sold novelty postcards and dispensed sodas. *Author's collection.*

SODA FOUNTAINS

Most neighborhoods had a soda fountain within walking distance. Many pharmacies or drugstores added soda fountains or full-service luncheonettes to their businesses. Pedroni, Fletcher's, Zarett's, Ouye and Owl Drugs also offered candies and confectionaries, sundries, gift products and greeting cards. Tametaro Kunishi Soda Fountain, 1230 Second Street, also had billiard tables.

In 1938, Clayton Solomon opened Tower Cut-Rate Drug Store on Broadway and Sixteenth Streets. He added a soda fountain, penny candy and a jukebox featuring big band–era records. It soon became a popular hangout for teenagers who would come in for a soda, root beer float or sundae and to play their favorite tunes. When the distributor came to upgrade the records, Solomon offered to pay for the old 78s. They cost him three cents, and he sold them for a dime. His son Russ, sixteen, suggested adding listening rooms. After fits and starts, the Tower Record dynasty became the most influential in the world.

Mary Gee grew up on Thirteenth and V Streets, a few blocks away. "What most young people don't know," Mary said, "is that when he built the store on

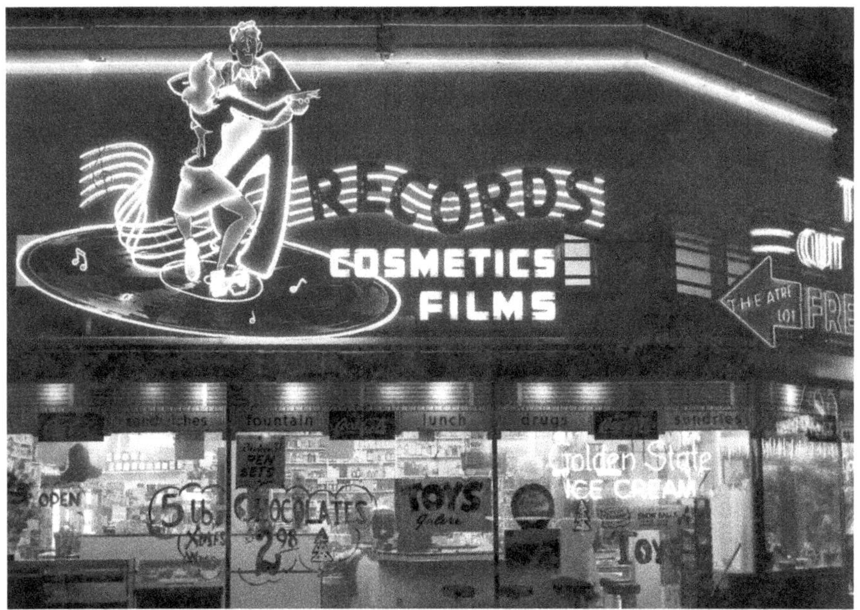

Tower Cut Rate Drugstore, in the Tower Theater complex at Sixteenth and Broadway, was everything: movie palace, drugstore, record shop and soda fountain. *Center for Sacramento History.*

Broadway, most of the area heading towards the river, just beyond Edmonds Field, was still vegetable gardens tended by Chinese." She used to frequent Ouye Pharmacy on Tenth Street, though can't remember whether it had a soda fountain or not. (It may not have, but the original Ouye Pharmacy in the West End did.)

Mary continued, "K's Café at 9th and V Street is where we went for sodas. Kiyo Kato used to run it. He was Japanese but served a mix of Japanese and Chinese food. Miso soup came with every lunch, Hamburger Royal or a stir-fry of whatever was in season. He'd buy vegetables the old Chinese ladies would bring him." Like many other West End businesses, K's Café was forced to relocate during 1950s redevelopment. Joy Gee, no relation, remembers it as Mary's. Now it's June's Café, with an almost identical menu.

When Franke's Drugs closed, in 1991, it was the last pharmacy in town with a soda fountain. Recognized by its red neon sign *Franke's Drugs*, it served cherry Cokes, phosphates, meatloaf sandwiches on white bread, chipped beef, chicken salad, macaroni and cheese and ice cream. Regulars kept their own coffee cups on a rack behind the fountain. In April 1944, Edward Ludwig Franke bought the building, formerly a Walgreen's. In 1945, he added a griddle, nicknamed Gertrude, a small oven that cooked two

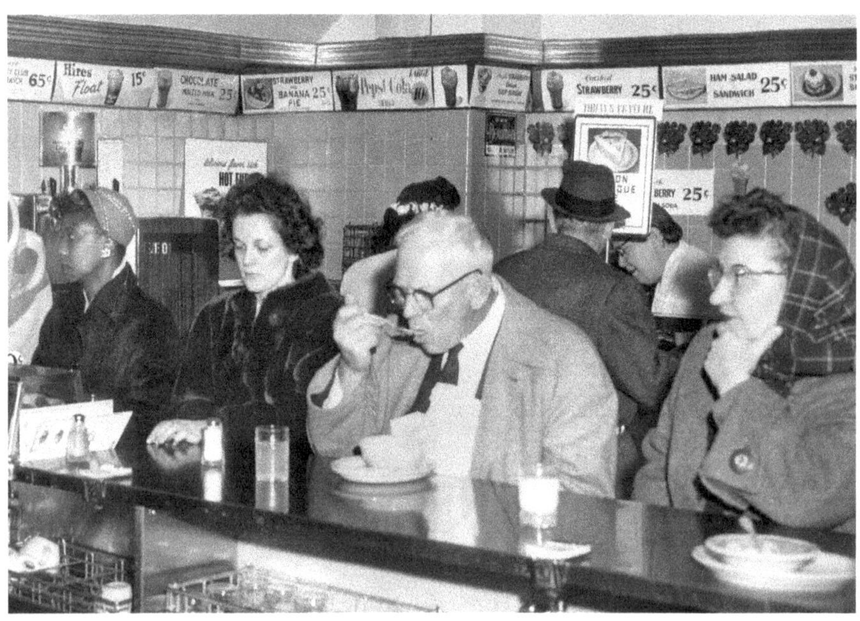

Woolworth's lunch counter was a popular place for a quick bite. Note the prices. *Author's collection.*

burgers at a time, perfectly greasy with a buttered sesame bun. Twenty-nine years later, he sold the business to Ron Kumasaki, who kept the name and traditions, until it was no longer profitable. Everything was sold at auction when Franke's closed, including Gertrude.

Two historic pharmacy soda fountains still exist just up the road a bit in Placer County that capture the texture, taste and character of the old places. Gordon Takamoto and his wife, JoAnn, own the Main Drug Store in Loomis. Gordon's father, Hiroshi "Doc" Takamoto, opened it in 1945, serving only three ice cream flavors. A neighborhood institution, it still serves milkshakes, banana splits and ice cream sodas, along with favored fare like grilled cheese, egg salad and tuna melt sandwiches. "We don't serve hamburgers or hot dogs because we don't have a large hood," Gordon Takamoto explained. "The original had a stainless steel counter. When my dad moved from our old location I was told they placed it on metal pipes and rolled it down the center of the street."

At the Auburn Drug Company, founded in 1896, customers still order phosphate sodas and milkshakes, resting elbows on the old marble counter or swiveling round and round on the stools while drinking them.

CREAMED CHIPPED BEEF ON TOAST
(Also known as SOS)

Recipe courtesy of Thom Allen, who said, "This is what we ate all during the war, because it was cheap and could serve up to twelve people."

½ pound of dried beef or jerky
½ cup butter
Salt and pepper to taste
6 tablespoons flour
Quart of milk
Toasted bread

Shred beef into strips. Melt butter in a sauté pan. Brown meat. Add salt and pepper to taste. Sprinkle with flour. Stir. Add quart of milk and gradually stir until well blended. Cook until just this side of a boil. Let simmer for a few minutes. Pour over toast.

Woolworth's Ham Salad Sandwich

1 slice baked ham, one inch thick, diced
¼ cup celery, finely diced
Sweet pickle relish to taste
Miracle Whip salad dressing
Salt and pepper to taste
2 slices bread, white or whole wheat
Lettuce
Potato chips

Dice the ham, add celery and then add pickle relish and salad dressing to suit taste. Season with salt and pepper. Mix well. Spread on one slice of bread. Top with lettuce. Add other slice. Serve with potato chips.

Cafeterias

As John Mariani points out in *America Eats Out*, the cafeteria struck just the right balance of formality and tradition to serve a solid outpouring of old-fashioned cooking—fried chicken, turkey and dressing, meatloaf, mashed potatoes and ready-made salads. Customers could avoid tipping and enjoy lower prices.

Swannell's Cafeteria and Hart's Cafeteria led the way. Customers slid trays along elongated counters, assembling individual meals while they moved along the line. Trays and silverware first, next desserts, salads, side dishes, entrees and finally drinks. With assembly line speed, a full repast could be obtained, paid for and consumed in relatively little time.

These large-scale operations dramatically boosted profits. Hart's Cafeteria claimed to serve three thousand meals a day, while Swannell's Cafeteria did a mere seven hundred. Swannell's was owned and operated by forward-thinking William Laurence Swannell. To make his cafeteria more efficient and profitable, he converted it to all electric in 1916, the country's first. *Electrical*

World ran a story about the newly renamed Quaker Cafeteria, explaining, "It uses electricity for every possible process in preparing the food served to its customers. Vegetables are peeled and meat chopped by motor power; electric ovens cook the food, the food is kept warm by electricity, awaiting the customer's selection and finally the dishes are washed by electricity."

From the late teens forward, William and Henry Hart operated a number of inexpensive downtown eateries: Hart's Lunch, Hart's Cafeteria and, during the 1950s, Hart's Hamburgers. They expanded to Stockton, San Francisco, Fresno and Salt Lake City.

An engaging feature remembered by Arianne Laidlaw was constantly flowing ice water and carbonated water in fancy soda fountains for the adults and a smaller version for children. Hart's vivid napkins, pie boxes, place mats and other advertising materials flaunting its logo—a big red Hart inside a heart—were a special delight.

The Hart's restaurants main attraction—classic home-style food served twenty-four hours a day, seven days a week—pleased those who needed a quick bite and old-timers who liked its home-away-from-home environment. Famous for fried chicken, mashed potatoes and gravy, bread pudding and baked apples, it also served standard cafeteria fare including meatloaf, ham, turkey, Jello and puddings.

Selling so much milk led to buying an interest in the Blake Dairy. Henry H. Hart and Irva J. Blake patented the first square milk bottle, designed so more milk bottles could fit into a metal or wooden carrying case.

One night a week, Hart's sponsored a live orchestra and broadcast semi-classical music on local radio. Musicians from nearby nightclubs stopped by after work and often gave impromptu performances. *Life* magazine featured Hart's on April 30, 1945. "It takes a ton of potatoes to meet the daily needs of the folks who dine at the Hart's cafeteria in Sacramento, California. Since it first opened up thirty years ago the restaurant has served over 150,000,000 meals." Richard Hart, the son who later went upscale with the Ram, says the business closed because no one wanted to carry their own tray anymore.

HART'S BAKED APPLES

From the collection of Mavis Temple, adapted to serve four

4 large baking apples
½ cup brown sugar, firmly packed

⅓ cup raisins
½ teaspoon cinnamon
¼ teaspoon nutmeg
1½ tablespoons butter

Wash and core apples, then remove a 1-inch strip of peel around the middle of each; place in a shallow baking dish. Combine brown sugar, raisins, cinnamon and nutmeg in a small bowl; fill the center of each apple with the filling and dot with 1 teaspoon of the butter. Add just enough water to baking dish to cover the bottom of the dish and bake, uncovered, at 350° for about 30 minutes, or until apples are tender. Baste with juices occasionally.

George Dunlap's cafeteria lasted for forty-one summers at the California State Fair. La Fiesta Mexicatessen on Ninth Street near Broadway served homemade tortillas, fresh salsas, enchiladas, rice and other traditional fare.

In 1951, Aerojet provided an employee cafeteria that featured roast prime rib of beef (seventy-five cents) on Thursdays, New York steaks (eighty-five cents) on Wednesdays and lobster (seventy-five cents) on Friday.

Writer Raymond Carver used to argue passionately about poetry with Gary Snyder in the Hornet Cafeteria at Sacramento State College.

School cafeterias provided kids with a hearty meal for breakfast and lunch, hiring "lunch ladies" from the neighborhood who brought their own family recipes with them. "Christmas was the best because you knew the lunch lady would make dessert tamales, with banana and cinnamon," posted Sylvia Hernandez on a Facebook page devoted to the Mark Twain Elementary School. Centralization of school kitchens coupled with federal regulations turned school cafeterias into reheating centers.

Slow Braised Cuban Pork

The Capitol Cafeteria, in the basement of the Capitol, still feeds visitors, staffers and legislators alike. This Slow Braised Cuban Pork recipe came from 1959, when Fidel Castro wasn't yet our enemy and a Cuban contingent came to visit California legislators. Recipe courtesy of Cass Thomas.

1 pork butt or shoulder
5 cloves garlic, crushed

½ ounce dry oregano
½ bunch parsley, chopped
1 each lime, lemon & orange
1 teaspoon cumin
¼ cup extra virgin olive oil
4 green onions, sliced
1 onion, thinly sliced
2 cups chicken broth

Mix dry ingredients with extra virgin olive oil to make a coarse paste. Rub all over the pork. Place into a roasting pan. Add the green onions, sliced onions and chicken broth. Cover with foil and braise in a 350-degree oven for about two hours or until really tender. Let rest and then slice. Serve with mashed potatoes and the leftover sauce.

FROZEN CONFECTIONS

To beat the summer heat, Sacramento eatery owners have sold ice cream since the 1850s, when it was sold by stands, coffee saloons (saloon is a term that indicates a spacious room) or ice cream parlors. The growing local temperance movement's efforts to limit saloon licenses created a market for alternatives. In 1925, only 19 percent of ice cream was sold by grocery stores; the bulk of it was marketed through confectioners, drugstore soda fountains, wayside stands, restaurants and lunch counters. A 1931 report in the *Sacramento Bee* referred to Sacramento as an ice cream capital. Ice cream peddlers rode their bicycles, ringing bells to get attention. Peerless Ice Cream Company, the Crystal Cream and Butter Co. and seven other factories produced a total of one million gallons of ice cream each year, more than ten times as much as today.

Popular places for made-on-the-spot ice cream included the Shasta Ice Cream Co. at 2814 Broadway, Borden's at Tenth and B and Country Maid Creamery at 1030 J Street. Ice cream wasn't just a summertime favorite. During holiday season, Shasta Ice Cream supplied a popular Egg Nog Ice Cream, which was served as the base for a frozen drink. West Irwin, owner of the Shasta on Freeport Boulevard, served extra-thick milkshakes, malted milk, sundaes topped with cream and black and white sodas, a little pricey at thirty cents.

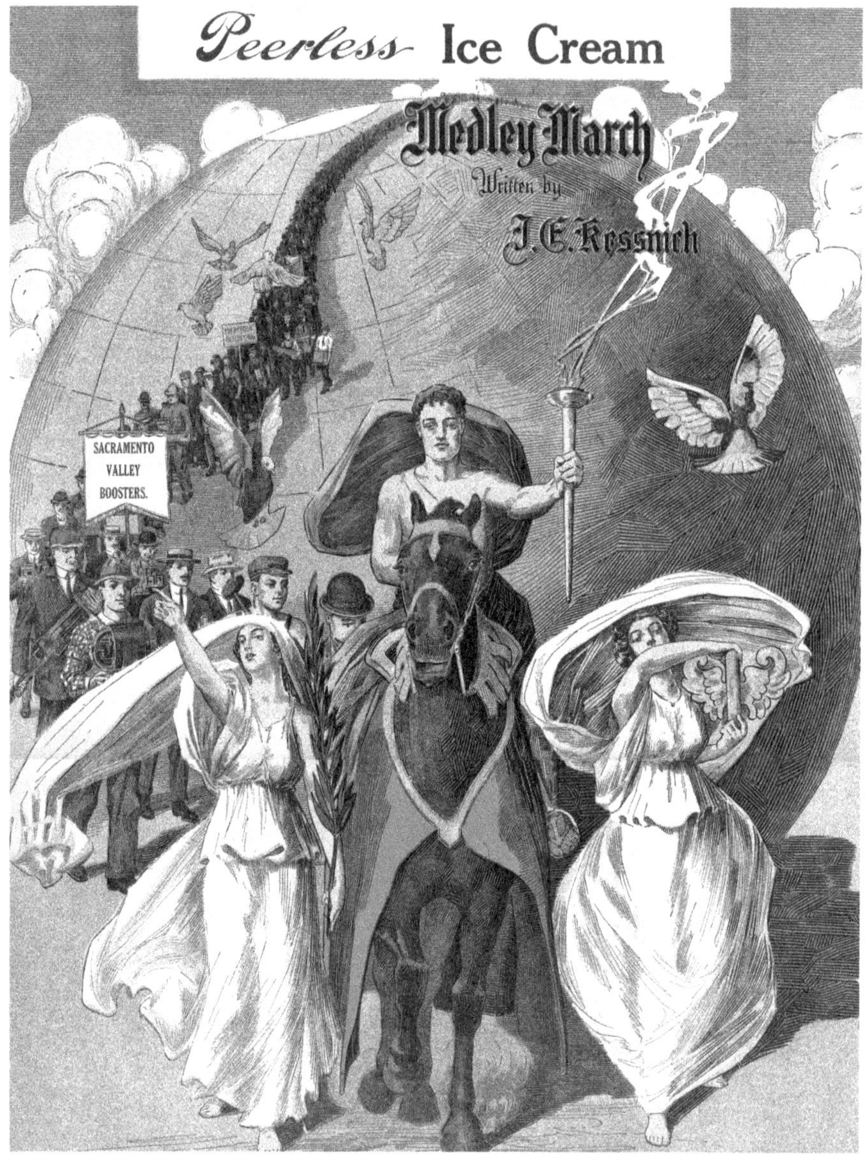

Peerless Ice Cream Company, one of the largest ice cream makers, had carts running throughout the county selling its frozen treats. *Author's collection.*

Opposite: Former Mayor Burnett Miller and other Sacramento notables frequented Wilson's Restaurant for its sugary confectionaries and ice cream treats. *Center for Sacramento History.*

SHASTA DAIRY EGG NOG

1 quart Shasta Frozen Egg Nog
2 quarts milk
½ cup sugar
1 quart brandy or whiskey

Mix well and serve in chilled glasses with a dash of nutmeg.

Most ice cream makers purchased a "base" (cream, milk, eggs, sugar, emulsifiers and stabilizer) from either Crystal Cream and Butter Company or Sega Milk in Galt. They'd add their own flavoring to create unique flavors.

A few made ice cream from scratch, using real cream, pure vanilla, cocoa, nuts and fruits. Gunther's and Vic's, the oldest operating ice cream parlors,

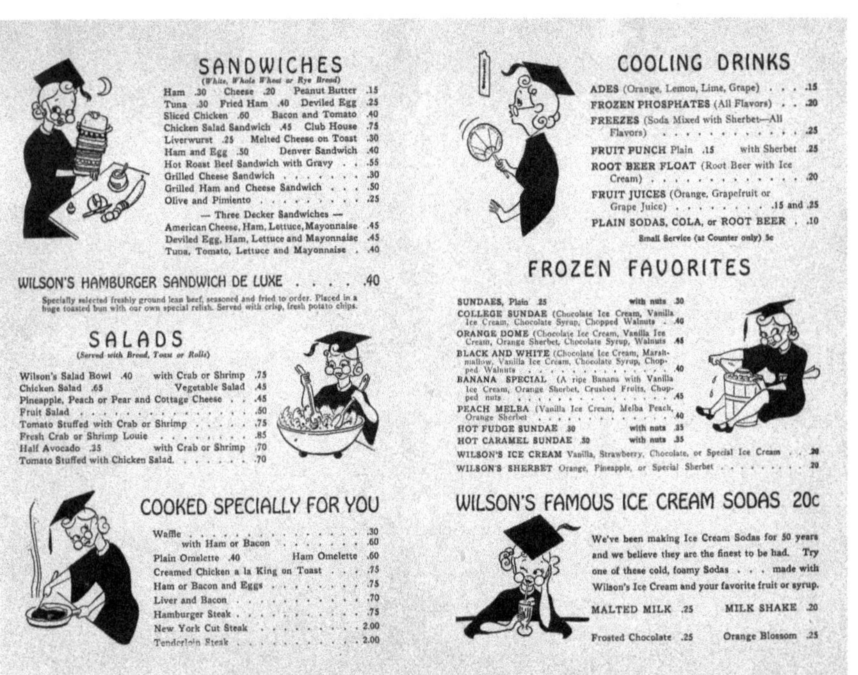

SANDWICHES
(White, Whole Wheat or Rye Bread)
Ham .30 Cheese .20 Peanut Butter .15
Tuna .30 Fried Ham .40 Deviled Egg .25
Sliced Chicken .60 Bacon and Tomato .40
Chicken Salad Sandwich .45 Club House .75
Liverwurst .25 Melted Cheese on Toast .30
Ham and Egg .50 Denver Sandwich .40
Hot Roast Beef Sandwich with Gravy . . .55
Grilled Cheese Sandwich 30
Grilled Ham and Cheese Sandwich 50
Olive and Pimiento 25
— Three Decker Sandwiches —
American Cheese, Ham, Lettuce, Mayonnaise .45
Deviled Egg, Ham, Lettuce and Mayonnaise .45
Tuna, Tomato, Lettuce and Mayonnaise . .40

WILSON'S HAMBURGER SANDWICH DE LUXE 40
Specially selected freshly ground lean beef, seasoned and fried to order. Placed in a huge toasted bun with our own special relish. Served with crisp, fresh potato chips.

SALADS
(Served with Bread, Toast or Rolls)
Wilson's Salad Bowl .40 with Crab or Shrimp .75
Chicken Salad .65 Vegetable Salad .45
Pineapple, Peach or Pear and Cottage Cheese . . .45
Fruit Salad 50
Tomato Stuffed with Crab or Shrimp 75
Fresh Crab or Shrimp Louie 85
Half Avocado .35 with Crab or Shrimp .70
Tomato Stuffed with Chicken Salad. 70

COOKED SPECIALLY FOR YOU
Waffle 30
with Ham or Bacon 60
Plain Omelette .40 Ham Omelette .60
Creamed Chicken a la King on Toast 75
Ham or Bacon and Eggs 75
Liver and Bacon 70
Hamburger Steak 75
New York Cut Steak 2.00
Tenderloin Steak 2.00

COOLING DRINKS
ADES (Orange, Lemon, Lime, Grape) 15
FROZEN PHOSPHATES (All Flavors) . . .20
FREEZES (Soda Mixed with Sherbet—All Flavors) 25
FRUIT PUNCH Plain .15 with Sherbet .25
ROOT BEER FLOAT (Root Beer with Ice Cream) 20
FRUIT JUICES (Orange, Grapefruit or Grape Juice) . . . . .15 and .25
PLAIN SODAS, COLA, or ROOT BEER . .10
Small Service (at Counter only) 5c

FROZEN FAVORITES
SUNDAES, Plain .25 with nuts .30
COLLEGE SUNDAE (Chocolate Ice Cream, Vanilla Ice Cream, Chocolate Syrup, Chopped Walnuts . .40
ORANGE DOME (Chocolate Ice Cream, Vanilla Ice Cream, Orange Sherbet, Chocolate Syrup, Walnuts .45
BLACK AND WHITE (Chocolate Ice Cream, Marshmallow, Vanilla Ice Cream, Chocolate Syrup, Chopped Walnuts 40
BANANA SPECIAL (A ripe Banana with Vanilla Ice Cream, Orange Sherbet, Crushed Fruits, Chopped nuts 45
PEACH MELBA (Vanilla Ice Cream, Melba Peach, Orange Sherbet 40
HOT FUDGE SUNDAE .30 with nuts .35
HOT CARAMEL SUNDAE .30 with nuts .35
WILSON'S ICE CREAM Vanilla, Strawberry, Chocolate, or Special Ice Cream . . .20
WILSON'S SHERBET Orange, Pineapple, or Special Sherbet 20

WILSON'S FAMOUS ICE CREAM SODAS 20c
We've been making Ice Cream Sodas for 50 years and we believe they are the finest to be had. Try one of these cold, foamy Sodas . . . made with Wilson's Ice Cream and your favorite fruit or syrup.
MALTED MILK .25 MILK SHAKE .20
Frosted Chocolate .25 Orange Blossom .25

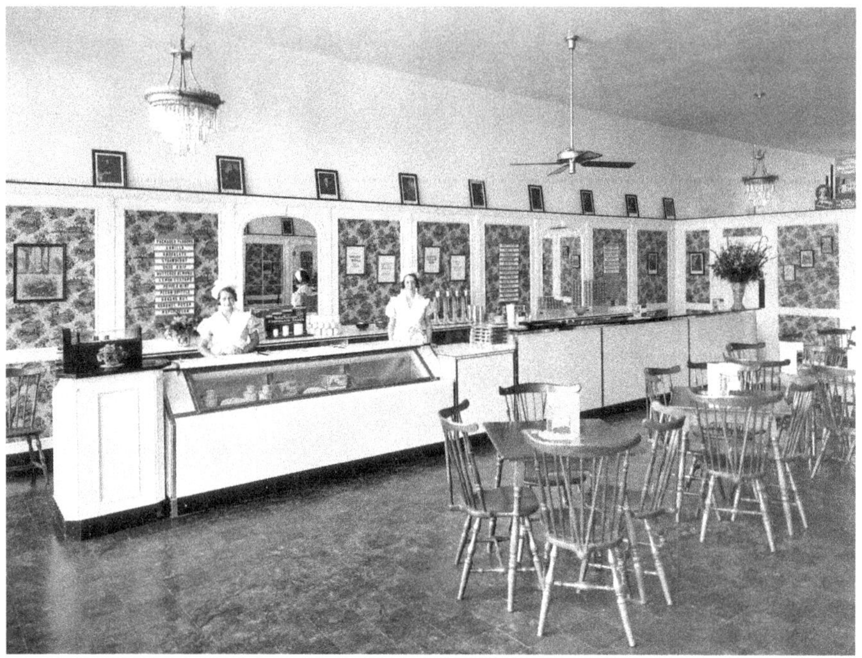

Martha Washington Candy Store at 3130 J on its first day of business, May 4, 1934. The design was a nod to pre–World War I America. *Sacramento Public Library, Sacramento Room.*

still make their ice cream and sherbets in decades-old batch freezers, using a 14 percent to 20 percent butterfat mix, with an "overrun" (additional air beaten in to make it creamy) of 50 percent or less.

Every neighborhood had its own creamery, ice cream parlor or soda fountain. Wilson's on K Street, serving a wide array of ice cream concoctions and sandwiches, provided a much-needed respite from the heat and was one of the first businesses to offer air conditioning. Martha Washington Candy Store, at 3130 J Street, was a large producer of milk, cheeses and ice cream. In the late 1960s, Lorraine's Ice Cream took over the spot. Paul D'Alessandro made the ice cream. Later he opened Americo's Italian Trattoria with his mother, Lorraine, father, Americo, and friend Jackson Leong.

In 1957, a short stretch of Broadway had four ice cream joints: Fehr's Drive-In, Tastee Freeze, Harvey's Drive-In and Foster's Freeze. Foster's Freeze, a popular fast-food chain, came to Sacramento after the war and featured the first soft-served ice milk in a cone, dipped in melted chocolate. The back of all receipts read:

Drink Milk for Health—Mug of Milk 5 cents.
IT'S FUN TO BE HEALTHY
Bulk ice cream

Country Maid Creamery, at Eleventh and J Street, had an extensive breakfast menu and then switched to a lunch menu until midnight. It offered ice cream sodas, root beer floats, milkshakes, malts and banana cream pies. It also had a pastry case for Danish pastries, doughnuts and cookies.

George Sullivan, a former legislative staffer, frequented the downtown Country Maid late at night, after drinks at the Elks Club or a big meal at the Sacramento Hotel, usually a lobbyist's treat.

> *I was usually a little tipsy and needed something sweet to sober me up, so I'd stop by and order a drink called "Doctor's Orders." Now I can't remember what was in it, besides club soda, but it was the most expensive soda on the menu.*
>
> *KCRA radio used to have a studio upstairs. D.J.'s came off shift wanting breakfast. Breakfast formerly ended at 10:30 in the morning, but Lorraine, one of the night waitresses, might let you sneak in some bacon and eggs.*

George has fond memories of buying nickel ice cream cones at Thrifty's, near Corti Brothers on Folsom. "Chuck Winterberger made an incredibly good ice cream, at the Magic Dasher on Eastern Avenue. He boycotted anything that wasn't natural. Truffle Framboises was a flavor I've never seen anywhere else. His best were suffused with fruit and had a rich, tart, quality. For upscale gelato and other creamy treats there was Gelati Robi on J Street."

Until at least 1965, what is now Burr's Fountain on Folsom Boulevard was Zarett's Pharmacy. Neighborhood residents remember it had a soda fountain and a neon sign. Later, Vicki Marie's Ice Cream moved in. Her honey-based ice cream quickly endeared her to neighbors, who turned her business into a neighborhood hangout. Maurice Read, who created *Maurice's Guide to Sacramento*, a whimsical collection of what's best in Sacramento, particularly liked a coconut ice cream called aka punna. Finances forced Vicki to close up shop, and she moved to the Bay Area. Jim Burr, after twenty-five years with Vic's Ice Cream, took it over in 1989. He added a large outside dining area, which still fills up in warm weather.

Sacramento's Best

Norm Sayler, born in Sacramento in 1933, grew up near Twenty-eighth and Broadway. White Spot's Ice Cream Parlor was just down the street, or he could ride his bike to Vic's or Gunther's. German immigrants Herman "Pop" and Iva Gunther opened Gunther's, the oldest still-operating ice cream parlor, in 1940 at Fifth Avenue and Riverside Boulevard. Wartime suspicions about German loyalty, rationing of cream and milk products and curtailed operating hours failed to diminish their business. They succeeded and later relocated to 2801 Franklin Boulevard, in 1949.

"Old man Gunther looked like Ichabod Crane. I would order a pint of banana ice cream, regular as clockwork, and he would have it ready by the time I got there. I'd sit outside and just wallow in it."

Gunther's has one of the now rare animated neon signs in town. "Juggling Joe," tosses a scoop of ice cream in the air and catches it in a cone in his other hand. Rick Klopp, a soda jerk at the Shasta Ice Cream Parlor for sixteen years, eventually moved on to Gunther's as a manager before purchasing it outright in 1974.

Vic's Ice Cream, in Land Park, is its close rival. The oldest, original family-owned ice cream parlor, it dates to 1947. World War II buddies Vic Zito and Ash Rutledge served together in the Coast Guard with Earl Swenson, who returned to San Francisco to create Swenson's, an ice cream empire. Ash, who'd worked in a drugstore fountain before the war, talked Vic into joining him in Sacramento. Together they bought some old-fashioned soda equipment and opened Vic's Ice Cream next door to a pharmacy with no soda fountain.

Vic's provides old-fashioned service, grilled sandwiches with potato chips and pickles, sherbet freezes, ice cream sodas, frappes, milkshakes, phosphates and sundaes. An ancient griddle (purchased in the early 1950s) cranks out their popular sandwiches. The family always hires high school kids from the neighborhood, mostly good-looking boys who keep the neighborhood girls in a giggle. Vic's prepares its own sauces, roasts whole turkeys, beef and ham for sandwiches and always uses the best quality ingredients.

These recipes are taken from *Ice Cream Confections*, a 1921 publication given free to customers of Peerless Ice Cream.

Simple Chocolate Sauce

1 cup Ghirardelli semisweet chocolate, shaved or broken into small bits.
¾ cup whipping cream
1 teaspoon vanilla

In a small saucepan, over low heat or in double boiler, heat chocolate and whipping cream, stirring constantly. Continue to stir sauce until blended and smooth. Stir in vanilla. Serve over ice cream.

No-Cook Apple Butter Ice Cream

¾ cup seedless raisins
¼ cup rum
2 cups heavy cream
½ cup sugar
2 tablespoons fresh lemon juice
8 ounces apple butter

Soak raisins in rum. Dissolve sugar in heavy cream. Add lemon juice and apple butter plus drained raisins, and stir well. Freeze in an ice cream machine according to manufacturer's instructions.

Blackberry Ice Cream

2 cups freshly picked blackberries
1 cup sugar
2 cups heavy cream
2 tablespoons fresh lemon juice

Puree berries and remove seeds by forcing berries through a fine strainer. Add the sugar to the cream and mix until dissolved. Stir in the berry puree and lemon juice. Freeze in an ice cream machine according to manufacturer's directions.

Other Places We Encounter Counter Food

Five-and-dimes, the Sacramento Public Market, the Greyhound Bus Depot, department store lunch counters, coffeehouses, doughnut shops, Merlino's Orange hut across from the fair, the fair itself…wherever we encountered counter food, we liked to sit down or stand up and eat it. The food was simple, unforgettable, fast to make and even faster to eat. In some places, though, the food was so good, or the company such a pleasure, that you wanted to linger.

The Public Market at Thirteenth and J Street was just such a place. It had permanent facilities, coffee shops, butchers, grocery stores, fishmongers, bakeries and specialty produce. One day a week, local farmers and antique dealers or flea market vendors could rent stalls. Our dad was in the antique

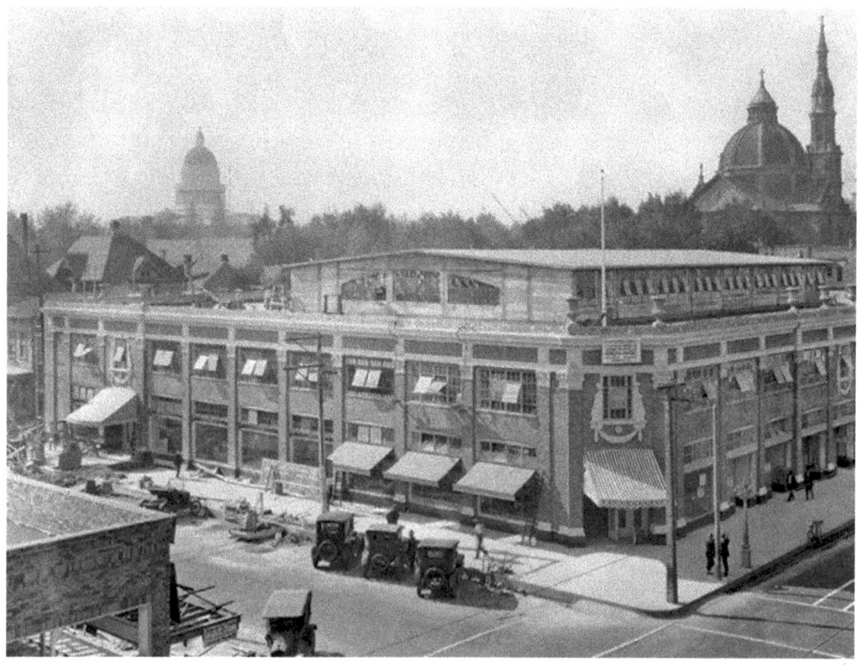

The Public Market featured Falor's Coffee Shop, produce, butchers and five thousand chickens on the roof. *Center for Sacramento History.*

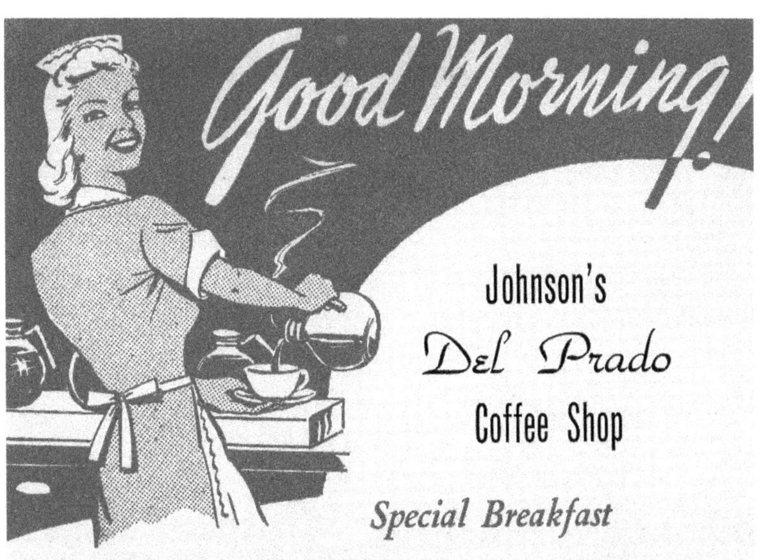

Ham, Sausage or Bacon, One Egg, Hashed Brown Potatoes and Toast 75c

FRUITS AND FRUIT JUICES

Orange Juice .20
Grapefruit Juice .20
Grapefruit, Half .20
Elberta Peach .30
Melon in Season .35
Berries in Season .35
Tomato Juice .20
Pineapple Juice .20
Stewed Prunes .20
Kadota Figs .30

CEREALS

Oat Meal
Puffed Rice
Cereal with Milk .30 with Cream .40
Shredded Wheat
Post Toasties
Pep
Corn Flakes
Grape Nut Flakes

TOAST AND ROLLS

Dry or Buttered Toast .15
Butterhorn, Snail .20
Milk Toast .30
Doughnut .10
Cream Toast .45
French Toast .60

WAFFLES AND HOT CAKES

Cream Waffle .40
Cream Waffle with Ham .90; Bacon or Sausage .80
Hot Cakes .40
Buckwheat .40; with Sausage, Ham or Bacon .90; with Fried Egg .65

EGGS AND OMELETTES

Two Eggs Boiled, Fried, Shirred, Scrambled or Poached on Toast .50
Plain Omelette .70
Jelly Omelette .75
Cheese Omelette .85
Minced Ham or Bacon Omelette .85
Ham and Eggs .95
Bacon and Eggs .85
Hamburger and Eggs .85
Sausage and Eggs .85

BREAKFAST SUGGESTIONS

Side Order Ham .50
Side Order Bacon or Sausage .40
Side Order Two Eggs .40
Calves Liver and Bacon 1.05
Small Breakfast Steak 1.95

BEVERAGES

Coffee .10
Tea, Pot .15 Cup .10
Refills .05
Chocolate, Pot .20

Minimum Service 15c Per Person

Johnson's Del Prado Coffee Shop was typical of coffee shops in the 1950s and 1960s. On Stockton Boulevard, the street is now part of "Little Saigon." *Sacramento Public Library.*

making business, or bought odd job lots to sell, so he took them up on the offer. Throughout summer, during winter vacations or "sick" days from school, we'd eat breakfast or lunch at Falor's Coffee Bar. Everything was made from scratch: handmade pastries, custards, scrambled eggs in cream, chicken and biscuits and mom's favorite, rhubarb pie. A fascinating collection of politicians, merchants and shoppers would hang out there. It was estimated Falor's served 1,500 customers a day. On top of the roof, the restaurant kept five thousand chickens to sell in the poultry shop downstairs. Lucky customers could pick out the one they wanted for that night's dinner.

Gas-tronomy

It's easier to be faithful to a restaurant than it is to a woman.
—Federico Fellini

Conventional wisdom holds that the automobile gave rise to roadhouses, roadside stands and country inns, but Sacramento had them all by 1850. Horse and carriage, stagecoaches, trains and then trolleys and streetcars took us farther and farther out (and back) of the central city. Oak Park's annexation and improved thoroughfares east, north and south let us get from place to place with relative ease. Towns once separated by hours of travel—Citrus Heights, Orangevale, Folsom, Carmichael, Elk Grove and Fair Oaks—now took half the time or less.

Those affluent enough to own automobiles enjoyed new freedom and choice, no longer tied to train or trolley schedules or forced to live, work and eat within a five-block radius (the distance most of us now will walk before using our car). Now, folks could live and eat wherever they wished and commute much more easily to school, club meetings or work.

Not surprisingly, new dining options sprouted up on the main roads already connecting us to far-flung communities. This vastly improved connectivity, coupled with more leisure time and a shorter workweek, drew us to the roads in record numbers for drives—around the country or cross-country. Improved roadways, highways, roadside hotels, motels and campgrounds made extended travel ever more comfortable and reasonable.

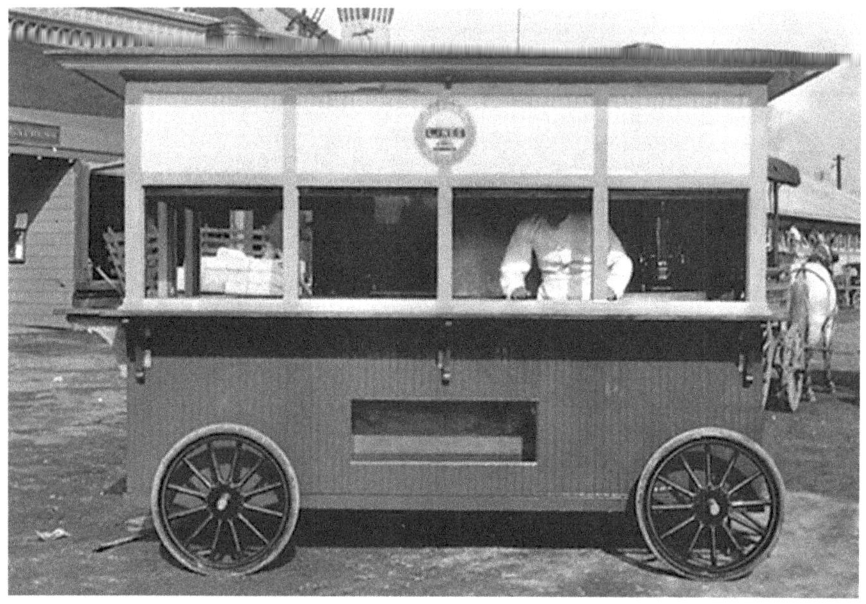

A mobile food cart met passing trains and sold food to travelers and local workers, the first "mobile-trucks." *California State Railroad Museum.*

Popular Mechanic and other publications ran articles in October 1922 about the Rodome, a contraction of road and home, supposedly under construction in Sacramento. The first of twenty all along the Pacific Coast, it was to offer full service for motoring tourists—car repair, motel, delicatessen, cafeteria, grocery store, laundry, play area and post office. The cost would be two dollars per night for one and four dollars for a family of up to six. The Sacramento architect E.C. Hemmings and a manager from the Travelers Hotel were hired, but it doesn't appear the project came to fruition.

Drive-ins started up in the mid-1920s, came of age in the 1930s and peaked during the 1950s. By the 1970s, they were mostly gone. With iconic architecture, flamboyant neon signs, quick service and ebullient servers, they were great places to stop for a quick bite. For travelers, they were reliable, consistent and inexpensive. In town, they provided a cocoon for those feeling (sometimes) anti-social or those who just plain wanted to stay in their jammies. Young men and women dropped by after cruising down K Street to swoon over cars or each other.

THE ROOT BEER KINGS

Mystery writer Walter Mosley was thirteen when he was first introduced to the X-Men during a Sacramento vacation. His folks' car had no air conditioning, so they stopped to cool off at an A&W Root Beer stand. In an August 2000 issue of *Vibe*, he said, "We sat under a festive umbrella at a metal table on a concrete floor. Flies swarmed, but the root beer came in a frosted glass mug, and there I met the paraplegic Charles Xavier and his well-trained mutants."

Root beer, made from syrups, took off in the late nineteenth century, along with other novelty foods. A unique blend of herbs, spices, barks and berries, it offered a refreshing new taste that was also believed to have medicinal benefits.

Already a favored drink in pharmacy soda shops and ice cream parlors, when a soda jerk impulsively decided to put in two scoops of vanilla ice cream, the first root beer float was born.

Roy W. Allen, a Midwesterner, roaming the country refurbishing and selling old hotels, met an Arizona chemist who'd perfected a recipe for a creamy, refreshing root beer. Convinced he could market the soft drink successfully, Allen paid $150 for the rights to manufacture and market the new syrup and opened a small walk-up stand in his adopted hometown of Lodi, California. On June 20, 1919, he sold his first root beer for a nickel.

Allen opened a second stand in nearby Sacramento. Buoyed by success and convinced the automobile was changing the way America ate out, he asked Frank Wright, an employee, to join him. Combining their initials, they became A&W Root Beer. In 1923, they opened a third Sacramento site, believed for many years to have been the first drive-in restaurant in America. Actually, Kirby's Pig Stand in Dallas, Texas, seems, more realistically, to own that claim. At the Sacramento stand, "tray boys" and "tray girls" took orders and carried the food back to customers who never had to leave their cars.

Eating in the car was novel, great for men on the go or on the road but also very convenient for families with small children. Envisioning a broad network of roadside stands, all carrying the A&W logo, Allen bought Wright out, trademarked the name and built the nation's first system of franchise roadside restaurants.

The franchises sold for a pittance (less than $100) and a pledge to purchase A&W's concentrate and dispensing equipment. Allen focused on small-town markets and owners who operated seasonally. Some stand owners added dime hot dogs and later hamburgers. In 1966, he sold the company, and real expansion began.

Doc's Place: The Root Beer King

"No one remembers where the first A&W Root Beer stand was, though it might have been off Alhambra and Stockton Boulevard near Stan's Drive In," Albert Breck says. "But, if you lived in East Sac, rode a bike or took the trolley, you knew that if you could rub two nickels together you could pay for a hot dog and root beer at Doc's Place. Of course, I could never figure out why either place called itself a drive-in because most of us walked up to the window to place an order. There was no inside dining, just an unpaved parking lot until after the war."

His wife, Martha, who grew up on Fifty-third and M Street, disagrees. "There were all kinds of cars! Doc's Place was on the old Highway 50, and cars and trucks would go barreling down the road and stop off on the way in or out of town. There weren't that many places around to eat or drink like there are now, with a fast food restaurant on every corner, so the marquee on top that read 'Doc's Place, The Root Beer King' was a real eye catcher."

Martha went to school with Doc's daughter Mildred Campbell and knew her brother Jimmy, who eventually became an owner of the business.

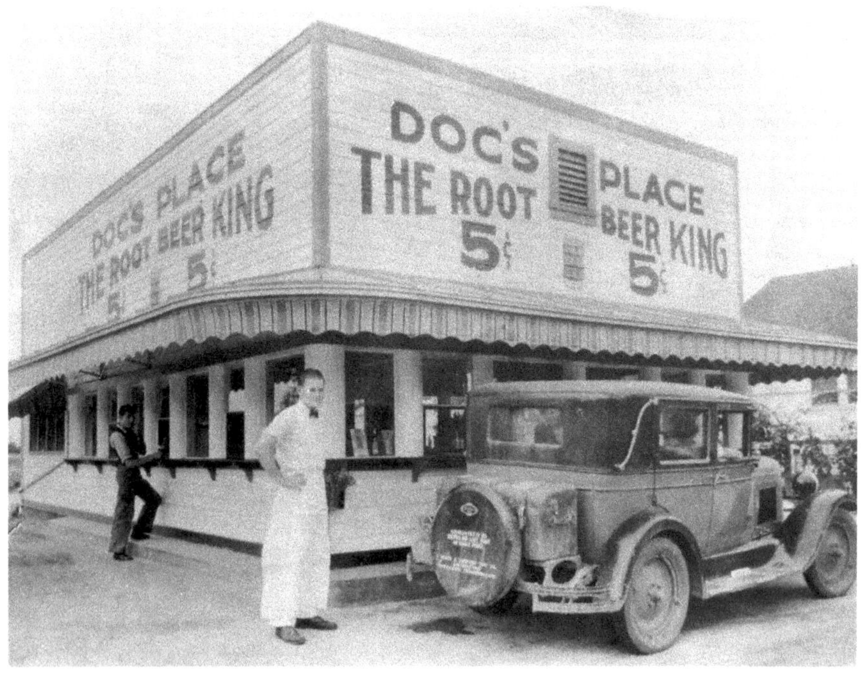

Doc's Place competed against big chains like A&W Root Beer. Fifteen cents covered a hot dog and frosty mug. *Albert Breck collection.*

Why was it called Doc's? "No one had medical insurance then, so if you had indigestion or a minor ache or pain you talked to the pharmacist or sought advice from anyone wearing a white coat. Doc Campbell always wore white. He lived next door so it didn't matter what time of day you came by, he'd be ready with sound advice. Root beer and other carbonated beverages were thought to have healing powers, then, too."

Jimmy Campbell closed the business in 1960. For a few brief months during the early '70s, a student from nearby Sac State opened up an Armenian restaurant with his grandmother offering lamb shish kebab, rice pilaf, and spanakopita. In 1976, the Sub Shack moved in, offering some of the region's best sandwiches, hamburgers and, we assume, root beer.

DRIVE-BY DINING

The term "drive-in" goes back to the post–World War I years when the automobile became the most important personal possession of most adult Americans. The drive-in was a wondrous place to eat. Carhops were most often women. They were hired for an obvious reason—they looked better in short skirts.

You could chow down at Karl's Drive-In, 3820 Broadway; L&M Drive-In, 501 Broadway; and Harvey's Self-Service Drive-In, 1211 Broadway. These were just the drive-ins on Broadway in the 1950s!

STAN'S DRIVE-IN

Stanley Burke came to Sacramento as a teenager. In 1933, he took a nest egg accumulated working odd jobs and purchased used restaurant equipment and an old food shack near the Libby McNeil cannery on Alhambra and Stockton Boulevard. He sold simple roadside fare—hamburgers, root beer, Coca-Cola and, now that Prohibition was over, beer.

He expanded the menu, claiming to create the first cheeseburger. He added more soda drinks and thick, creamy milkshakes that wouldn't spill if the glass turned over.

A man with vision, he anticipated America's fascination with girls, cars and car culture. Stan's all-female carhop staff was famous for working for

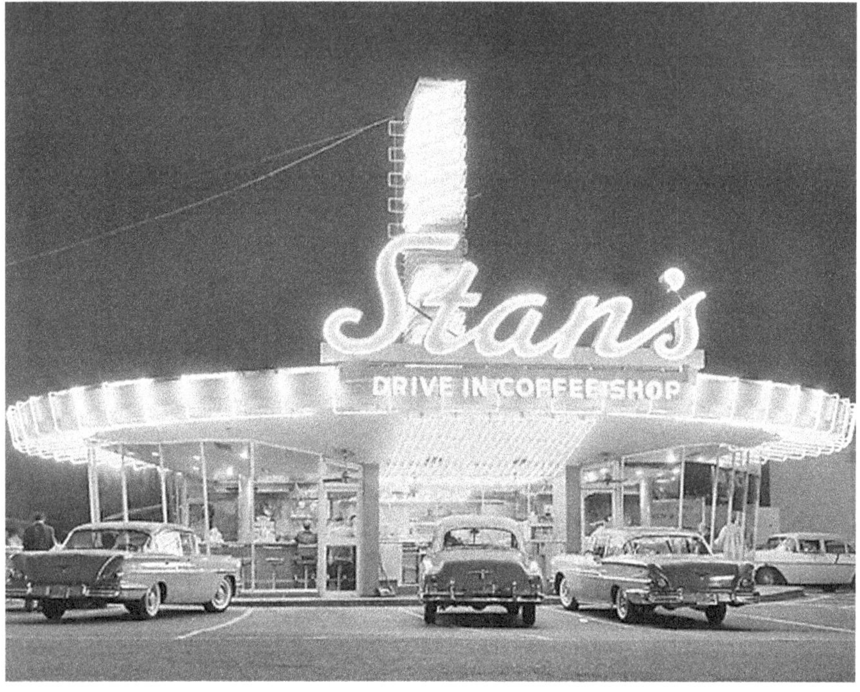

Stan's Drive-In, on Sixteenth and K Streets, featured "Legs," a sprightly female carhop, and curbside service. *Sacramento Public Library, Sacramento Room.*

free, knowing that the right amount of wit, fast service and flirtatiousness would lead to lavish tips. His favorite carhop was immortalized in neon, known to all as "Legs" on Stan's street-side marquees.

His first circular unit was built at Sixteenth and K Streets in 1941. Eventually, he owned six more in Sacramento and twenty-five up and down the state.

Stan's had a much more extensive menu than most drive-ins, including fried chicken, coleslaw and french fries, simple steaks and soups, plus a double burger with "everything." No need for special sauce. If you wanted ketchup, mustard and mayonnaise, you asked for it.

The desserts were oversized, from banana splits to sundaes and pies with fresh whipped cream. He had competitors. On Freeport Boulevard, Hart's Hamburgers was just across the parking lot. Shifting fashions and competition from chains, coupled with over-expansion, rising land values and poor management, eventually forced Stan's closure. None of his iconic drive-ins survived the wrecking ball. There is a Stan's in Osage, Iowa that has had non-stop carhop service since opening in 1954, but it's not related. Still, it's a nice homage.

Tiny's Drive-In used to have a neon sign, but county officials decided neon was too distracting and ordered its removal. Even without the sign, you couldn't miss this Fulton Avenue landmark. What made Tiny's stand out from all the rest, beyond the fact that it served a great bargain hamburger, was the mix of people in the parking lot or tiny dining room—slick-haired salesmen from nearby auto dealers, laborers, well-dressed secretaries and female executives and men in grey flannel suits sucking down root beer milkshakes.

Tiny's burger, described as massive, was only a fifth of a pound, thinner than most. It featured 18 percent fat ground sirloin, which was seasoned on the griddle and then placed on a toasted bun with diced onions, shredded lettuce and Thousand Island dressing.

TINY'S ROOT BEER SHAKE

A root beer shake used to be known as a Brown Cow in local soda fountains.

8 ounces of root beer
1 scoop of vanilla ice cream

Pour root beer into blender with ice cream and pulse until smooth.

ROADSIDE ATTRACTIONS

Highway 40, on the way to San Francisco, was the highway home of two of the most iconic and missed food halls of the era—the Milk Farm and the Nut Tree. Old Macdonald's Farm, off the Jackson Highway, was perfect for Sunday dinners or as a stop on the way to the Gold Country.

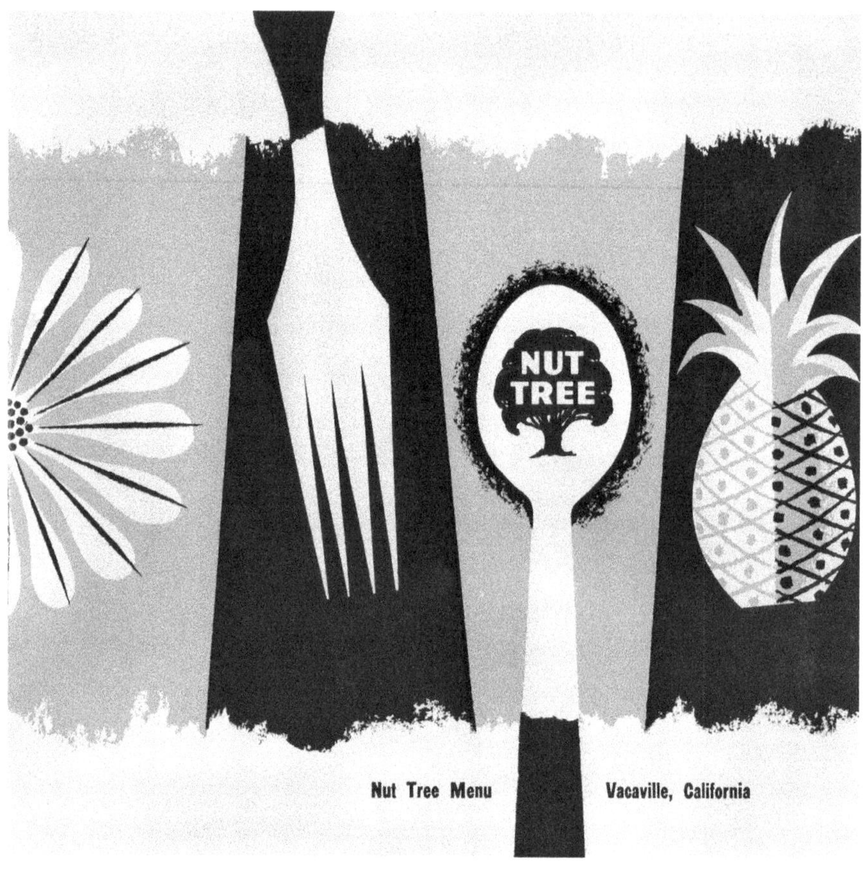

Motorists stopped by the Nut Tree along the Lincoln Highway long before it became the Knott's Berry Farm of the North. *Author's collection.*

Nut Tree

In 1921, under a spreading walnut tree, Helen and Ed "Bunny" Power started a small roadside fruit stand near their three-hundred-acre farm in Vacaville.

Thousands of cars passed by every day. The Powers saw the steady stream of cars as a steady stream of cash to augment their seasonal ranch income. They started small, serving folks who wanted a brief rest stop.

It grew into a mighty roadside institution, fueled by kids' desire to ride the miniature railroad, play in the toy shop, watch cockatoos fly overhead in a glass-enclosed aviary or watch planes take off and land at the air strip behind the restaurant. It wasn't a quick stop, but parents did stop—otherwise kids would pound them into submission from the back seat. And it was expensive.

When everyone else sold root beer for a nickel, Edwin purportedly sold his for a dime.

The Nut Tree was an early pioneer of California cuisine, serving fresh fruits and vegetable salads, vagabond sandwiches, Chinese chicken salad, chess pie and chocolate fudge cake. Waits of up to an hour and a half were not uncommon. The line would wind its way past a gift shop with Chinese trinkets double the price of those in San Francisco (the place you were most likely headed), designer cookies, pet rocks and expensive foodstuffs to take home.

Mavis Temple remembers it as the only place she could get her kids to eat oatmeal. "It had five grains and different kinds of fruits—papaya, banana, kiwi and strawberry slices, plus nuts and raisins. You could top it off with fresh cream or vanilla ice cream. They also had a great chicken curry that I still serve to this day."

Mavis, who is also an avid collector of Nut Tree collectibles, recalls the restaurant as a food pioneer. "They were the first to use a fruit garnish, make and sell their own miniature loaves of bread and offer ethnic food in the region."

Long before it closed in 1996, its allure had diminished. A family feud, declining revenue and changing tastes did the restaurant in. The main buildings were demolished in the fall of 2003.

NUT TREE POTATO SALAD

This salad was served alongside the Vagabond Sandwich Plate, which was actually a deconstructed sandwich of Ham, Turkey, and Cheese. Courtesy Mavis Temple.

4 pounds potatoes (about 12 medium) cooked in jackets
½ cup chopped parsley (reserve ¼ cup for garnish)
¼ cup chopped green pepper
½ cup chopped celery tops
¼ cup chopped mustard greens (optional)
¼ cup chopped green onions
½ cup chopped dill pickle
1 cup mayonnaise
¼ cup French dressing
Salt and pepper to taste
1 teaspoon dry mustard

Dice peeled potatoes. Mix ¼ cup of chopped parsley with the next 5 ingredients; take out about ½ cup of the mixture and add to rest of parsley; set aside. Toss remainder of chopped mixture with potatoes. Combine mayonnaise, French dressing and seasonings. Add to salad and toss to mix well. Pack into an 8- by 8- by 2-inch pan or shallow 2-quart baking dish. Sprinkle reserved parsley mixture over top. Chill. Lift out servings with a pancake turner. Garnish with sprigs of watercress or chopped celery tips.

THE MILK FARM

A 100-foot-high weathered sign, with a Holstein cow jumping over a crescent moon, is the only visible reminder of the Milk Farm outside Dixon. A family-friendly stopping point for travelers using U.S. Highway 40 between San Francisco and Lake Tahoe, it offered all the milk one could drink for five cents (including buttermilk), hearty chicken dinners and the best milkshakes in Northern California. A 1952 review from Duncan Hines said, "The Milk Farm, a roadside restaurant, began in business serving nothing but milk. Among their well-known dishes are buttermilk hot cakes, chicken pies, French fried prawns, steaks and hot corn bread. Also salads, apple dumplings and cream puffs."

Built by Karl Hess in 1928, it developed a strong local clientele, but a 1940 *Saturday Evening Post* feature about it boosted its popularity even more. Dixon, truly a cow town, acquired the nickname "Dairy Town." The Milk Farm was a nice place to stop, get out of the car, stretch your tired legs and backsides, use the much-needed bathrooms and eat.

It closed in 1986 after a storm caused extensive damage and the building was dismantled. It is stored somewhere, in the hopes that someone will want to rebuild it as a historic landmark.

"What most people don't remember is that there were two signs," Mavis Temple says. "There was the animated, neon sign you saw on the freeway and a slightly different neon sign with a cow jumping over a moon on the restaurant. That's lying out in a field going to rust."

Opposite, top: Restaurant collectibles are highly prized. This ashtray from the Milk Farm was given away…or stolen. *Author's collection.*

Opposite, bottom: The Milk Farm put the town of Dixon on the map. It was a popular destination for families out for a Sunday drive. *Author's collection.*

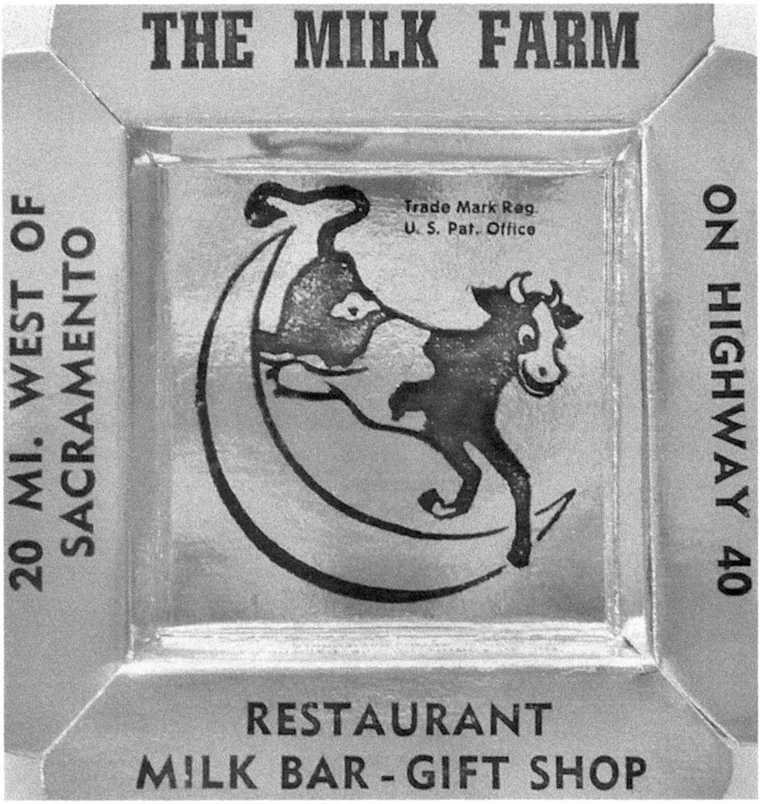

THE MILK FARM

20 MI. WEST OF SACRAMENTO

ON HIGHWAY 40

Trade Mark Reg.
U. S. Pat. Office

RESTAURANT
MILK BAR - GIFT SHOP

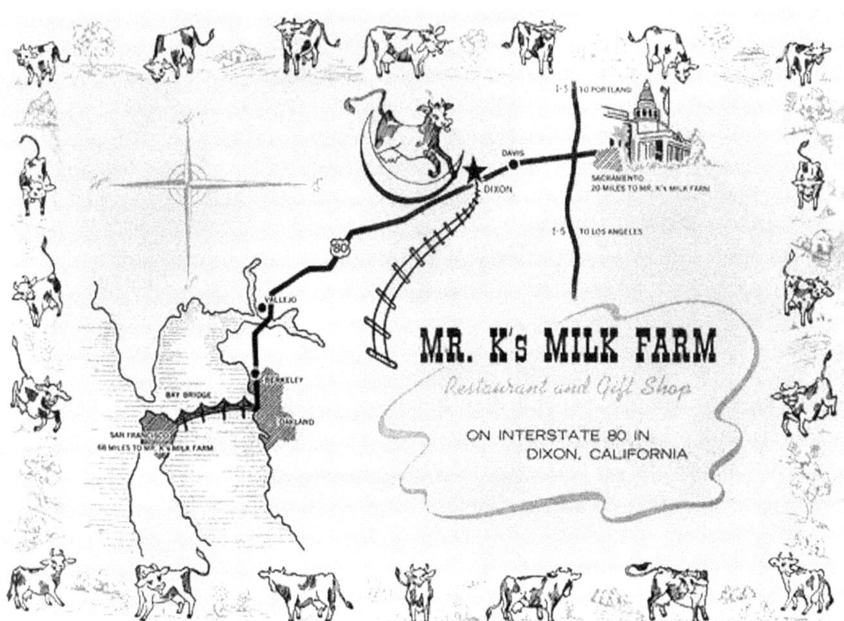

Mavis says that Milk Farm items are highly prized. She has an unrivaled collection of plates, matchbook covers, pie boxes, dairy bottles and placemats.

After a long drive from the Bay Area to Sacramento, Leo Dabaghian remembers, "It was a welcoming, comforting sign you were getting very close to home. It reminded me, as I'm sure it did others, of a happy carefree childhood. I couldn't pass by it without starting to sing..."

Hi diddle diddle,
The cat and the fiddle,
The cow jumped over the moon,
The little dog laughed to see such sport,
And, the dish ran away with the spoon.

APPLE DUMPLING

Courtesy of Jeannette Davis, a Milk Farm regular

Peel and core apples. Place on a portion of pie dough, then fill with cinnamon and sugar. Fold the dough over and bake until tender.

OLD MACDONALD'S FARM

Old Macdonald's Farm was a rambling farmhouse restaurant, way out in the country, off the old Jackson Highway. Its neon sign hosted a chef in a white toque chasing a chicken with a hatchet and the words "Chicken Dinner" superimposed on a big arrow that pointed down the road.

The farm was about a quarter of a mile farther down. The restaurant, housed in an old red barn, had multiple dining rooms and tables clothed in red gingham.

It served chicken dinners (from its own brood), biscuits, carrot salad and corn. If it had a more extensive menu, no one today remembers it.

What people do remember are the goats, ducks, lambs, donkeys, pheasants and wild turkeys that roamed free in the petting zoo and the peacocks fanning their feathers and preening for visitors.

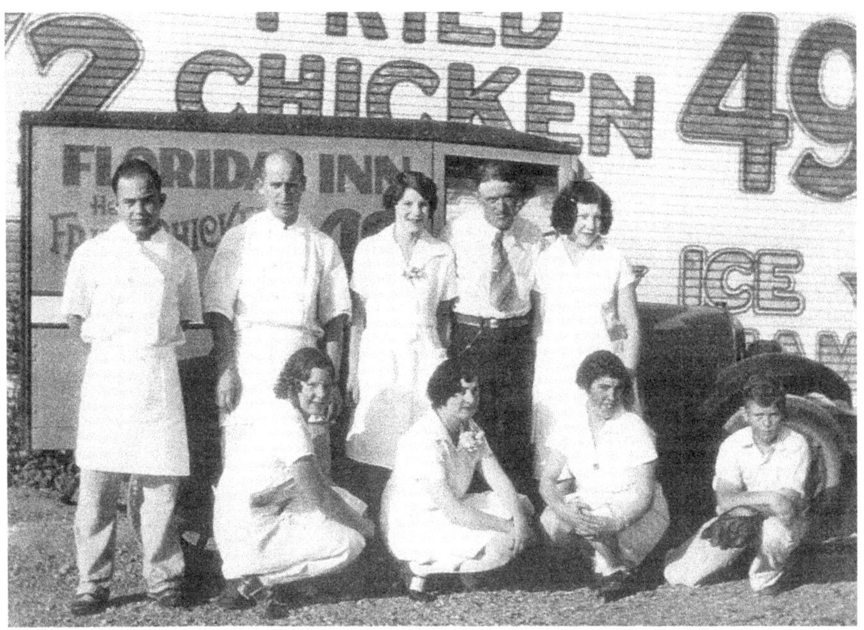

Sunday dinners meant a drive out into the country, or at least as far as Auburn Boulevard, Howe or Fulton. *Center for Sacramento History.*

Randy Grenz has fond memories of going to Old Macdonald's Farm in the 1960s. "They had absolutely fantastic chicken dinners. There was never any variability in the menu, corn and a little carrot salad and a great petting zoo I really loved. My mom always got mad at me because I always went out and petted the billy goat before I had dinner and I smelled like billy goat the rest of the evening."

Owners Pete and Palmera Velatagui, from Spain, passed away in the mid-1970s. The sign is still there, in sad decay. The Cordova Recreation and Park District, given the responsibility of salvaging it for posterity, is negotiating with a restorer to bring it back to its former glory.

Randy believes the farmhouse may still be there and that if you look in the windows, you can still see remnants of tables set, waiting for city guests to come for dinner.

SOUTHERN FRIED CHICKEN

Courtesy of Anna D. Joyce Roseville, Railway News, *August 1922*

Dress and carve a spring chicken dipped in beaten egg. Dredge in flour and fry in a pan with six slices of bacon till well browned. Serve hot with browned sweet potatoes.

You Want Fries with That...?

Anybody who doesn't think that the best hamburger place in the world is in his hometown is a sissy.
—*Calvin Trillin*

No white linen, steam-pressed tablecloths in these eating establishments. No fancy just-washed and hand-dried crystal glasses and fine china. No demitasse cups of coffee or tea. No maître de or wine steward. No nuthin' 'cept fast service by ever-hopping-to-it food servers and looked-back-upon memories of eating-joys, taste-pleasures and…loss…just loss.

The Sacramento food map had its landmarks and must-stop-at places wherever and whenever you ate out on the way to the Alhambra, Crest, Tower or Senator theaters or to some more distant final destination on pre-freeway streets and roads.

My favorite food memories usually involve hand-formed patties of ground beef, cooked on a griddle (charbroiled cookers were reserved for steak houses and hoity-toity food joints), or snap-when-you-bite-into-them hot dogs made with pure beef. They were served either on white grease-absorbing paper or small white chipped dishes or, most often, in small red plastic baskets, each one loaded with Laura Scudder's potato chips (produced at a Sacramento plant!). Or, better yet, freshly cut French-fried potatoes heavily doused with Heinz Tomato Ketchup (one of "57 Varieties") in real glass bottles.

The places where we ate these tasty treats of pure joy—along with homemade sandwiches, salads, soups, "Blue Plate Specials," apple or

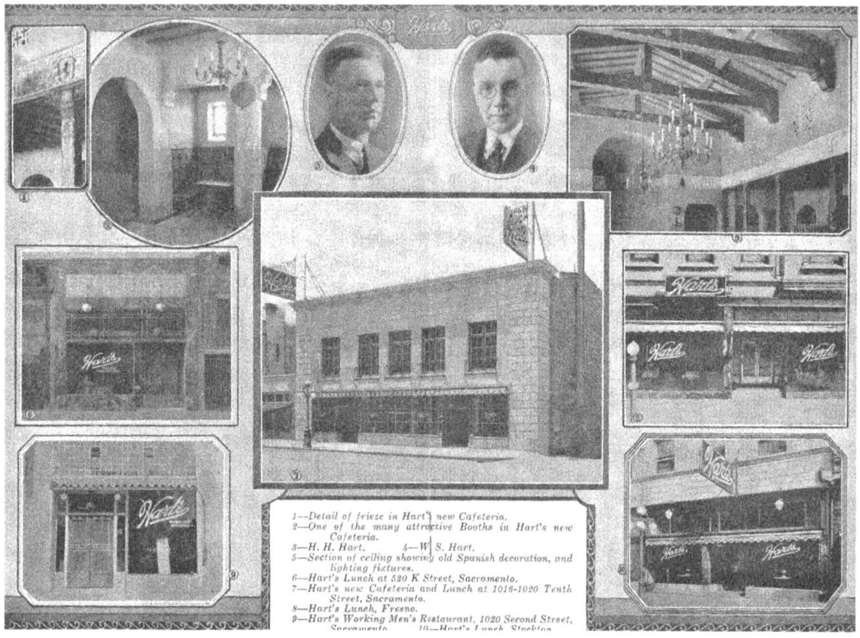

The Hart Brothers served three thousand people a day at Hart's Cafeteria and Hart's Lunch. *Sacramento Public Library, Sacramento Room.*

chocolate pie and vanilla, chocolate or strawberry ice cream—are gone: the lunch counters at S.H. Kress, W.T. Grant, Hart's Cafeteria, Lyon's, Sam's, the Milk Farm, Country Maid Creamery. Gone, too, are the specialized purveyors of burger and dog: Hart's Hamburgers, Stan's, Made-Rite, Harvey's, the original Jim-Denny's, Orange Julius, Frost-Top Root Beer, and oh so many other local burger and hot dog joints of our youth.

Also gone are the fats and lards of our childhoods. Our hearts and blood vessels may be better off now but not our taste buds. When these dastardly fats were removed from our pots, pans and deep fryers, the tastes of many foods were changed forever. Colonel Sanders's chicken and locally owned Jimboy's Tacos may be empires, but their flavors and textures are much different than when they were first concocted. This is especially true of the Colonel's eponymous creation—Colonel Sanders's "Kentucky-fried" pressure-cooked chicken. Gone are the chicken fat and other fats and oils required to create his "finger lickin' good" recipe. Anyone born after 1970 can't imagine the taste of his chicken and gravy. As for Jimboy's Tacos—no longer made with a large swipe of lard on each tortilla just before it is slapped on the grill—the motivation for the change

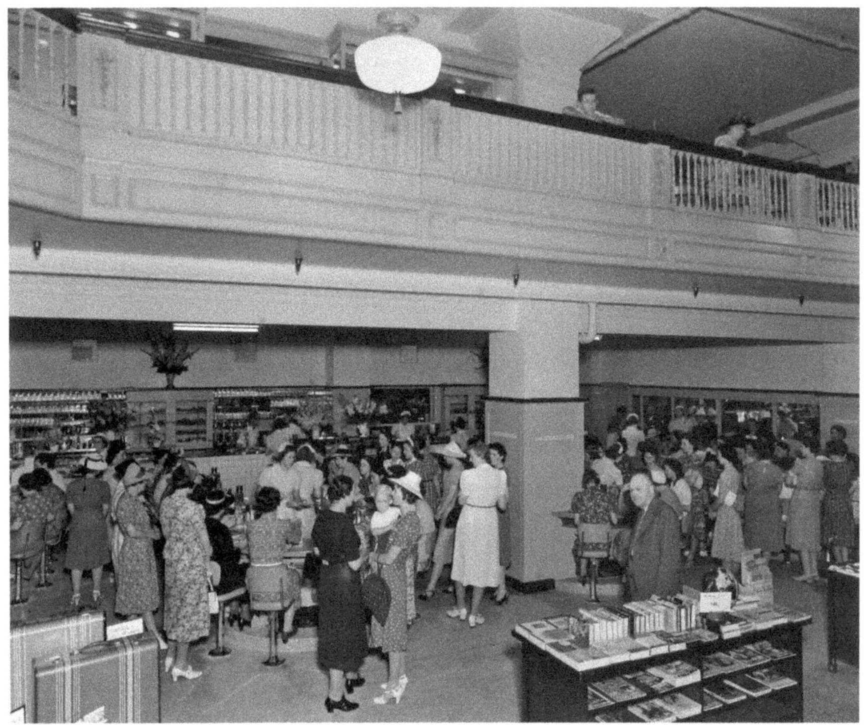

There were no reservations at department store counters. To assure a seat, you had to be ready to pounce. *Center for Sacramento History.*

in the company's slogan from "One Good Bite Deserves Another" to "Get Real. Get Fresh. Get Jimboy's!" cannot be questioned.

Department stores had lunch counters, dining rooms and a particular mindset: "Now that we've got them inside, don't let them escape into the great outdoors and into our competitors' stores." The tearooms at Hale's and others were filled with women and their daughters who came on weekends to enjoy their shopping experiences with style and elegance. Their dresses and gloves were in stark contrast to the "get 'em in and feed 'em" attitude down at the lunch counters. In those paragons of efficiency, the men were usually found taking their coffee and doughnuts before work or spending their half-hour lunch breaks with food that was fast to make but nothing to linger over.

S.H. Kress, in the middle of the block between Eighth and Ninth Streets, had it all! Inside, there was the shopper's paradise, with nearly everything a housewife or gent needed to make life more modern and civilized and for practically no money at all. Five and dime! The more well-to-do wouldn't be caught shopping inside a Kress store, but for the everyday working stiff and his bride (the workforce was still predominantly male), the Kress store was a sight for sore eyes and tight budgets. Downstairs was the toy department. I spent my youth in that place looking and touching the cap pistols and cowboy holster sets. Lash LaRue was my favorite cowboy back then. Lash wore a black outfit with a long bullwhip on his left side; this was the look for me.

Then there was the lunch counter, with all that it meant for a hungry kid back in the 1950s. I couldn't care less for the good things to eat—salads, soups, a three-square meal on a plate…egah! Give me a freshly steamed hot dog on a toasted piece of specially baked bread or roll with mustard, relish and onion. Now, that's heaven on a plate. The W.T. Grant store at the southwest corner of Eighth and K sold similar merchandise and had a similar lunch counter. But it was the joint behind the W.T. Grant store that had the tastes I still remember—Frost-Top Root Beer! Located in the parking lot between Grant's and the Original Mac's restaurant, Frost-Top was a shack no more than fifteen feet wide, with a door at each end. You stood at the counter (there were no stools or anything else to sit on) while the lone guy who worked there took your order and served you. No menu or chalkboard, either. Just hot dogs and root beer. The root beer came in ice-frosted glass mugs, just out of the white horizontal freezer. The hot dogs, made with beef, were bathed in a small water steamer behind the counter. They were the crown jewels of food; each one crisply snapped as you bit into it. As I got older and my taste buds matured, there were other places that came into my eating experiences but not my memory. Frost-Top was and is the one and only.

Mom was partial to Bob's, on H Street, just down from the Governor's Mansion. Once, she was sitting at the counter eating a burger and fries when two state police officers came in all in a panic. "What happened boys, did you lose him?" she quipped. The man next to her stood up, reached into his pocket for a dollar and said, "They just came in to get me." It was Governor Pat Brown, Jerry's dad, famous for eating out at local dives and crossing H Street in a robe and slippers to take in a swim at the Mansion Inn.

The Hickory Burger, the smoked and barbequed staple of the Hickory House at Thirteenth and J, was just one of the menu marvels that tempted BBQ fans, lured in by a smoky smell that could even overpower the big V-8's of the era. These "burgers" were piles of finely shredded and ground beef soaked in hickory-flavored sauce and piled high on a bun. These great

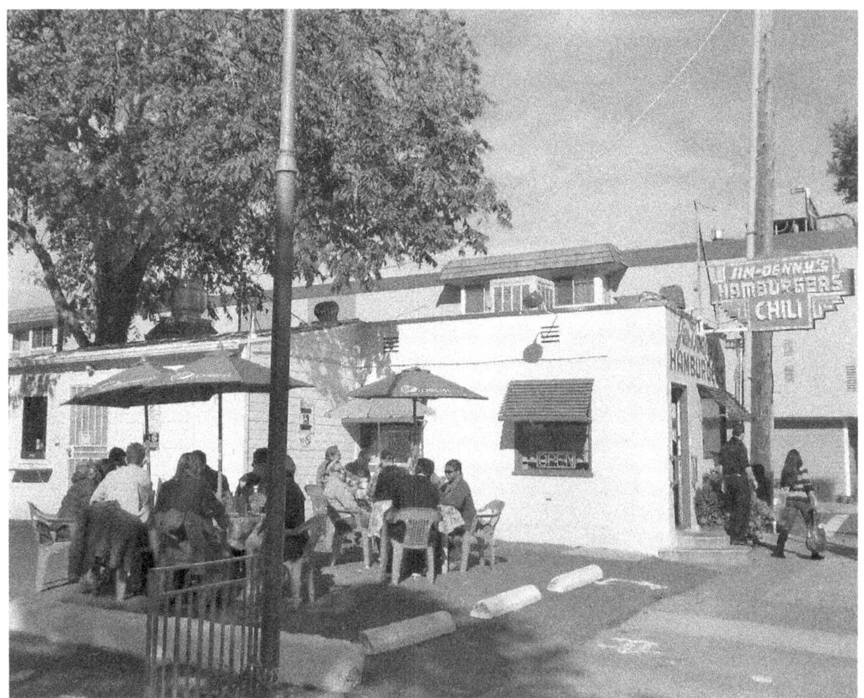

Jim Van Nort, of Jim-Denny's, was the burger man in Sacramento. People used to line up for Jim's signature burgers. *Author's collection.*

sandwiches were served with dill pickle chips on top, with onion and mustard too if you ordered them that way—which I did, of course. The Maid-Rite sandwich was constructed at 5006 J Street—the home of Hana Tsubaki Japanese restaurant for the past three decades. These were sort of highbred burgers. The beef was loosely steamed in a special cooker and then scooped into a pile and hand formed onto the bun, each one served with the ever-present mustard and pickle chips. Think Sloppy Joe without the sauce. The tastes were marvelous and different from the usual fare.

Jim-Denny's was another one of the undersized places that served burgers, dogs and typical diner chow. The small, white rounded stucco joint with about a dozen rounded stools is still there on Twelfth Street, north of J, and serves the same (but different tasting) food that it always served. But Harvey's Hamburgers was the place I miss the most—especially the original location on Broadway, at Riverside, right across from Edmonds Field, the home of the Pacific Coast League Sacramento Solons. That wondrous stadium, replaced by a GEMCO discount department store and now the home of

Target, was the place we could sneak into, through a hole in the back fence, and watch a great game of baseball and bring our burgers and fries, from Harvey's, of course. Burgers were only nineteen cents, matched by freshly cut French-fried potatoes. There was another reason Harvey's was a special place to eat—if you got a red star on your receipt, you could redeem it for a free meal. One of the waitresses would "palm" a receipt when a red star popped up on the cash register tape and slip it to Mom next time we came in, which was often!

The newest entrée into the burger wars was McDonald's, which first brought its golden arches to Sacramento near the corners of Fruitridge and Stockton Boulevards. In the mid-fifties, the "Golden Arches" could boast selling "more than twenty million burgers!" Priced even below Harvey's at only fifteen cents a sandwich, McDonald's quick service, fresh food and handmade fries soon became a regular stop for the burger-buying public. Alas, while McDonald's is now everywhere, the grilled burgers and freshly cut fries that helped it win the era's burger wars are long gone.

I spend a lot of time searching for new places with those old tastes. Once in a while I find one, and that's the time to celebrate. The Squeeze Inn at 5301 Power Inn Road dishes up a great and giant burger, served in those icons of the past: red plastic baskets. If you like cheese on your hamburger, then the Squeeze Inn is your place to go. They are magnificent structures, with the cheese oozing out of the bun and into the grill. Watching first-timers gaze at the marvel in front of them is a hoot. The Stagecoach Restaurant, at 4365 Florin Road, in South Sacramento, is still filled with the tastes of my youth. Its hamburger is still hand-formed!

If you want the look and tastes of the past, then why not play a little pool too? In the paragon of pool halls, the Jointed Cue at 2375 Fruitridge Boulevard, you will find a grease-covered grill and a counter with about ten stools. I don't know the physics, but somehow it has captured the old-fashioned tastes of a simple burger and fries. And it still uses red plastic baskets too!

The Secret of Great Hamburgers

The hamburger was the great American food discovery. Ground meat was the choice of the Mongol army, members of which used to put whole meat under their saddles and ride all day to "grind" it up and make it more tender.

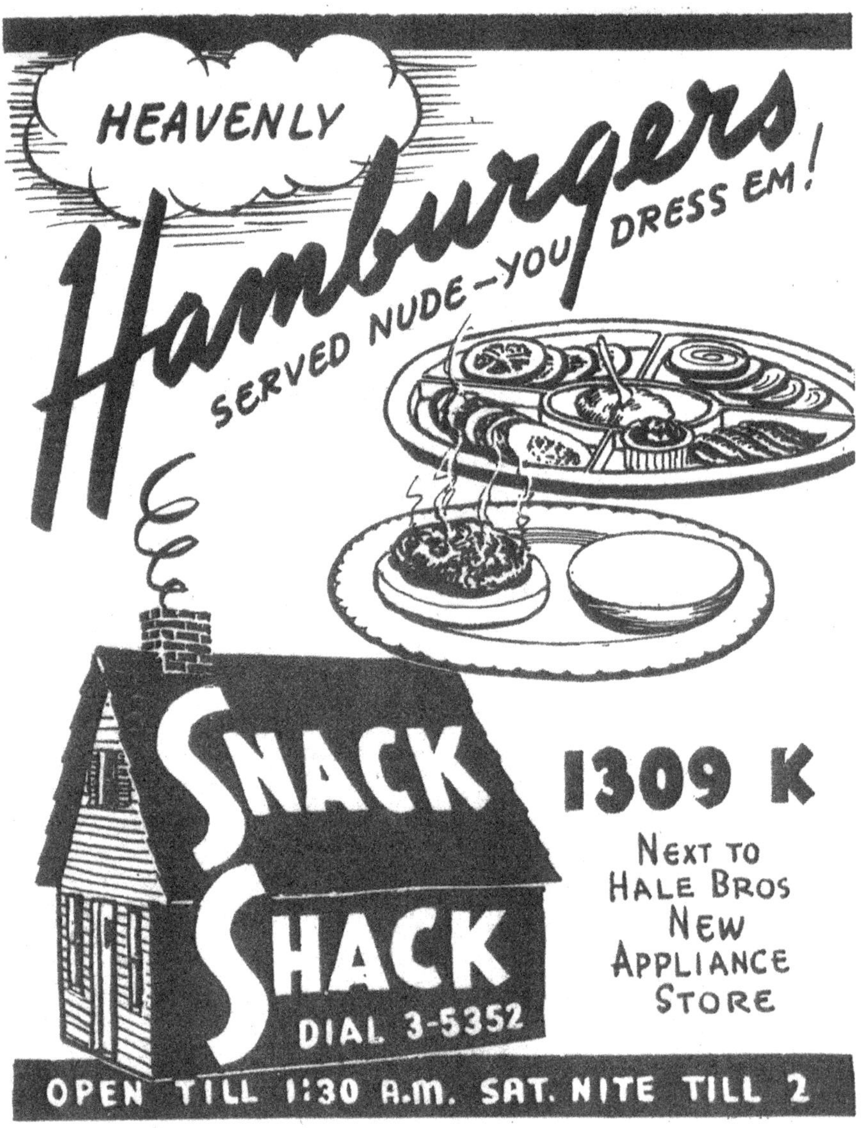

Hungry burger buyers made the Snack Shack a favorite. *Sacramento Public Library, Sacramento Room.*

Hamburg, Germany, is very important to the idea of ground meat as a food choice. Tah-dah, the name of the ground meat itself—HAMBURGer! The hamburger sandwich first gained national recognition when it appeared at the 1904 St. Louis World's Fair, but it doesn't get you any closer to the secret.

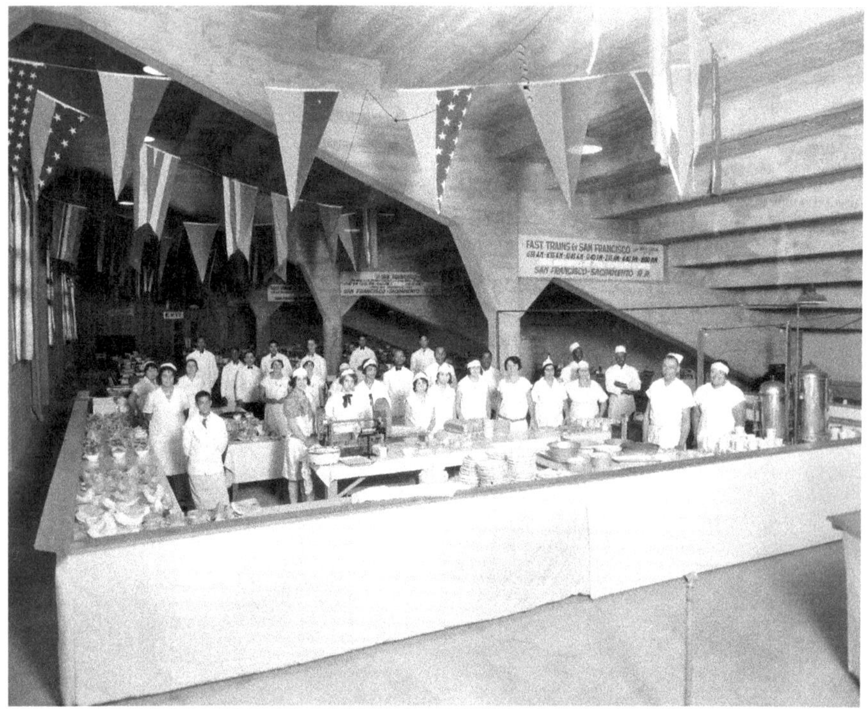

Dunlap's Cafeteria in the old state fairgrounds ran for forty-one years and introduced many to traditional southern cooking. Hamburgers were sold at the midway. *Center for Sacramento History.*

Nor do restaurant reviewers who rave about wonderful eight-dollar-and-up hamburgers they find all over this food-loving country. That's great, too, if you are looking for mushroom or blue cheese or caviar or Kobe beef burgers, but that's not what a hamburger is all about—putting on airs and dolling it up for the special people in the crowd.

The hamburger was first tasted in the midway, in dives and on the edges of communities, not the center. Working people ate hamburgers—working people with no time or money to eat a salad and then some form of meat and vegetable on a plate, with cloth napkins on their laps. The hamburger was eaten in "greasy spoons" or at America's county and state fairs, where food had to compete with balloons, side-shows and new products being sold by pitchmen with a "handy, dandy, never before seen" doo-dad that you just had to buy and take home.

That's where I first found flavor perfection: at the Sacramento State Fair during the early fifties. The fairground was located on Stockton Boulevard at Broadway and was the end-all and be-all to a youngster with a few cents in his pocket and a world of wonders in his eyes. Your family was along just to escort you to the next magnificent hall or display, explain what you were seeing and pay for all the food you were about to eat. The hamburger of memory and I first met at the edge of the midway, in a long trailer that was hauled from one fairground to another. There they were—cooking in a grease-filled and well-worn griddle alongside similarly bathed onions and red and green bell peppers. My father let me order one of these taste time bombs—without the pepper-onion mixture—and I first tasted what would become the journey of my life: to find the best-tasting hamburger in the world. A few years later, I added the onion and peppers.

Hamburger: The Recipe

First, pick the meat. This is the most important part of the recipe! Most restaurants go for the gusto in choosing low-fat, high-quality meat for their hamburger. This is just fine for gourmet eating but not for a great hamburger. Select hamburger meat that is about 20 percent fat. This gives both flavor and cooking oil to the process. Then, cook the meat in a cast iron pan; this gives the proper heat dispersal to the hamburger meat.

For eight to ten sandwiches, use approximately two pounds of good, freshly ground chuck. Hand form each patty to about six inches in diameter. Note: You may heat the pan at the same time you are preparing the meat to a point that a drop of water beads and floats on the hot metal (approximately 400 degrees). Do not season the meat at this point—you are making a hamburger, not a meatloaf!

As the hamburger cooks, add salt and pepper to taste. Cook the ground beef until it is the way you like the meat—this is a point I concede to you. Next, pick a nice firm bun (sesame seeds or not) and dill pickle chips, and a thick slice of tomato to top it off. Add condiments—mustard, mayonnaise and ketchup, if you want—put it all together and get ready to eat.

Now that you've got the burger, what do you serve with it? The standard hamburger side: French fries, of course.

MANOUSHAG HOVSEPIAN'S FRENCH FRIES

As told to grandson Tom Haseltine

Fill a deep-dish electric skillet to approximately 1½ inches from the top with solid Crisco oil. Heat to 450 degrees. Later you'll test the fries by putting one in, and if it turns brown too quickly, adjust the heat. (This recipe is from an old skillet that might just not be up to the task; 350 might be more appropriate.) Peel and cut Russet/Idaho potatoes into approximately ⅜"-long pieces. Rinse to release starch. Drain in colander, and dry with paper towel. Carefully place potatoes into hot oil to avoid splatter. Put as many in as you can (can overlap a bit) and stir continually to assure full cooking throughout. Depending on size, quantity and heat, it can take anywhere from eight minutes to fifteen or twenty. As they get really brown and crispy, remove with a strainer and place onto paper towels. Sprinkle seasoning salt or Mrs. Dash equivalent and/or garlic powder to taste. Repeat with second batch of potatoes as desired. Enjoy!

Political Watering Holes

By night Sacramento was a fraternity party writ large. Watering holes were plentiful. There was Bedell's just across the street from the Capitol, the bars at the Senator and Elk Club, Mirador Hotel, or Frank Fat's that doubled as a second office. After drinks and dinner women were the typical prey. Away from their wives and families, ensconced in a world of adolescent mascots, legislators made philandering a sport.
—California Rising: The Life and Times of Pat Brown, *by Ethan Rarick*

In a March 10, 2005 article in the *Los Angeles Times*, George Skelton described the political "watering hole circuit" from the 1960s to the 1980s. "We'd start perhaps at Posey's, with its huge horseshoe bar on the south side of the Capitol, or maybe David's Brass Rail, a hole-in-the-wall on the north side frequented by Governor Jerry Brown. Then we'd hit respectable Ellis in a new office building, head to Fats for dinner and wind up getting blotto at the grungy Torch Club half a block away, playing an oldies jukebox."

That was the reporter's circuit. Bill Bagley, vice-president of the California Republican Assembly in the 1950s told *Sacramento Bee* reporter Bob Sylva that he took a different route. "The routine (back then) was to go to Ellis' for drinks, Fat's for dinner, and, around 10 p.m. go to the Torch Club or drive over to the El Mirador Hotel. Some legislators, in order to conserve gas, were known to drive through Capitol Park. It's reputed that I've even done that."

Ken Saunders, a former lobbyist, spent time at Fat's but has the fondest memories of the El Mirador Hotel, with its view of the Capitol from the fourteenth floor. "It was one of the few places where you could relax after

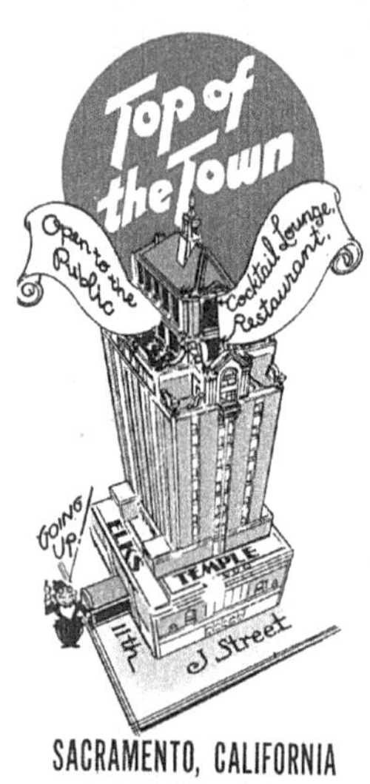

The view of California's Capital City from a vantage point high atop the city's tallest building, plus the atmosphere of ease and comfort, makes this the spot to visit in Northern California.

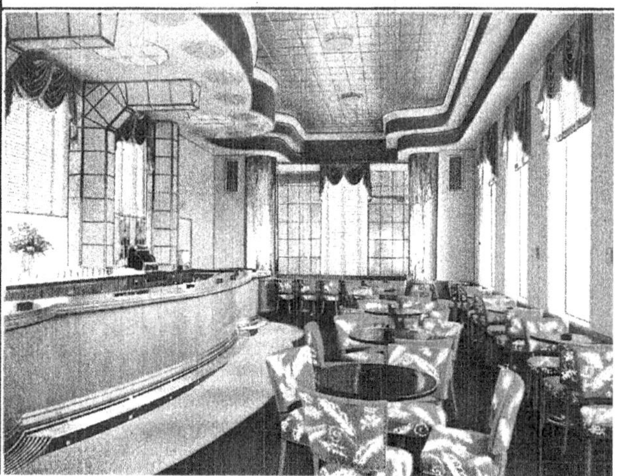

The Top of the Town, on the fourteenth floor of the Elks Building, had the best view in town. It was a popular meeting place for Capitol types. *Sacramento Public Library.*

a brutal day at work, order a drink, a great dinner and dance with a female staffer or secretary, or if you weren't feeling amorous, with your wife."

Regardless of which route a lobbyist, reporter or legislator took, sometime during the night, they all crossed paths.

Rose King, the student journalist who broke the story that Ronald Reagan didn't pay taxes (after he told the world "taxes should hurt"), remembers Governor Jerry Brown coming into David's at 10:00 p.m. and ordering a pizza, delivered from nearby, because David often didn't even offer peanuts. Others referred to David's as the place nearest the Capitol for those on a strictly liquid diet.

Capitol Lunch Clubs

Posey's Cottage had a motto: "A Restaurant You'll Always Remember… Serving Food You'll Never Forget."

Most people remember the action in the bar, the mysterious derby hat hanging off the sign out front, and a locked room where politicians and lobbyists met every Tuesday for lunch, and the Prime Rib and Hangtown Fry Governor Reagan thought the best around.

Founded in the early 1950s by Indiana native Richard T. Posey, Posey's Cottage closed in the early 1990s but left its iconic neon sign and slightly tilted derby hat. The beloved restaurant was a victim, owner Dick Posey said, of redevelopment. Too much dust from new government building construction drove people away. In reality the place had lived past its pull date and well past Proposition 9, which ended the almost seventy-five-year spree of lobbyists picking up the tab.

Posey's Cottage housed the "California Derby Club," one of the most enduring of the legislature's lunch clubs, where members from both sides of the aisle could socialize, drink and eat politics. Of course, lobbyists paid for everything. Author James Richardson described the clubs and their atmosphere in his book *Willie Brown, A Biography.*

> *The clubs operated out of the public eye. Their colorful names, such as "Caboose Club" and "Derby Club," evoked colorful origins. The Caboose Club was composed of legislators who had been old railroaders before they were elected. The Derby was a collection of legislators and lobbyists who wore English bowlers while eating and carousing. Assembly Speaker Jesse Unruh ran his own feast, called the "Tuesday Club," meeting for breakfast on Tuesdays at the same time as the Derby. Another club, more of a drinking clique, was called "Moose Milk" after a concoction served up at all hours at a nearby hotel.*

POSEY'S HANGTOWN FRY

12 medium-sized shucked oysters
3 tablespoons all-purpose flour
½ teaspoon salt
Dash pepper
1 beaten egg
2 tablespoons butter
6 eggs
⅓ cup milk
¼ teaspoon salt
6 strips of bacon, sliced into ½ inch pieces

Pat oysters dry with paper towel. Combine flour, salt and the pepper. Dip oysters into egg mixture and then flour mixture. Melt the butter or margarine in a 10-inch skillet over medium heat. Cook oysters in butter till edges curl, about 2 minutes on each side. Remove. Cook bacon. Remove most of grease. Beat the 6 eggs with the milk and salt. Pour into skillet with oysters. As egg mixture begins to set on bottom and sides, add bacon, then lift and fold over. Continue cooking and folding for 4 to 5 minutes or until egg is cooked throughout. Remove from heat. Makes 3 or 4 servings.

Bedell's

In 1939, Edwin Bedell opened his signature restaurant at 1117 Eleventh Street. By the fifties, it had joined Frank Fat's, the Senator Hotel, Posey's Cottage and the El Mirador Hotel as a premier gathering place and watering hole for the political elite in the Capital City. Bedell's was packed three deep at lunch and dinner by Capitol staffers, lobbyists, politicians and tourists all hungry for access to unadulterated, raw power.

Bedell, no stranger to Sacramento hospitality, grew up at the Hotel Clunie, owned by his stepfather. He enjoyed the business, the ebb and flow of meeting new people, and in the twenties began managing it, though not yet twenty himself. He opened the Clunie Coffee Shop—the first, he claimed, in Sacramento.

By 1936, he had his own advertising agency and was making $6,000 a year. In 1938, his stepfather sold him part ownership of the Clunie. A year later, he opened Bedell's, a combination cocktail lounge and fine dining restaurant, offering superior food and ambiance, top-notch service and capable and discreet bartenders, making it a powerful draw for political notables and Hollywood celebrities. During twenty-two years of operation, it has been said more legislation and careers were made at Bedell's than across the street in the Capitol, but then again, they say that about the other watering holes, too.

Wedge of Iceberg Lettuce with Buttermilk Blue Cheese Dressing

3 ounces crumbled blue cheese, plus some reserved to crumble whole
1 cup buttermilk
½ cup mayo
1 clove minced garlic
2 tablespoons fresh minced parsley, 1 tablespoon for top

1 tablespoon white wine vinegar
1 iceberg lettuce head, quartered
Salt and pepper to taste

Crumble blue cheese. Mix with rest of ingredients. Whisk until blended. Put one wedge per plate and pour ¼ of dressing on each one. Sprinkle parsley on top. Salt and pepper to taste. Good with Thousand Island dressing, too.

FRANK FAT'S

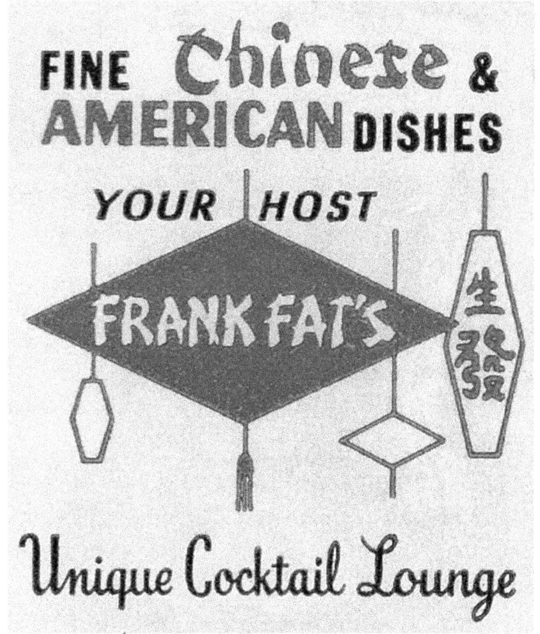

Frank Fat's specialties were pepper steak, banana cream pie and access to the Capitol's power elite. *Center for Sacramento History.*

Frank Fat immigrated to the United States from Canton, China, at age fifteen. Early on, he washed dishes at the Sutter Club and waited tables at the Hong King Lum, his uncle's Chinese restaurant. By 1939, using money saved by his wife and augmented by a benefactor's loan, he bought a run-down building, once a speakeasy on L Street. He and his growing family toiled, from lunch and long into the night. They even made home deliveries.

Former lobbyist Ken Saunders has said, "Frank had a natural understanding of people and what made them tick. He had a rare ability to remember everyone by his or her first name and treat them the same way, no matter their stature. It was (and is) a place where you met over drinks and hammered out deals that had almost ended in fisticuffs earlier in the day."

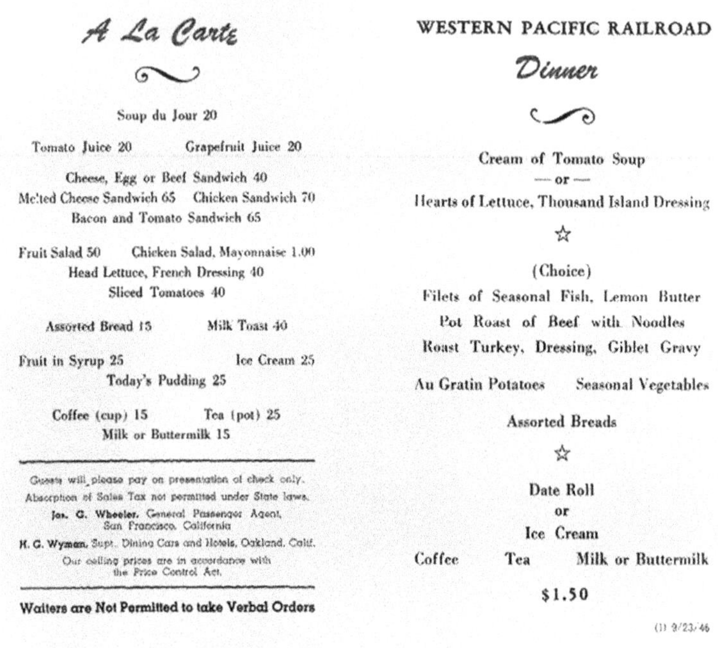

A La Carte

Soup du Jour 20

Tomato Juice 20 Grapefruit Juice 20

Cheese, Egg or Beef Sandwich 40

Melted Cheese Sandwich 65 Chicken Sandwich 70

Bacon and Tomato Sandwich 65

Fruit Salad 50 Chicken Salad, Mayonnaise 1.00

Head Lettuce, French Dressing 40

Sliced Tomatoes 40

Assorted Bread 15 Milk Toast 40

Fruit in Syrup 25 Ice Cream 25

Today's Pudding 25

Coffee (cup) 15 Tea (pot) 25

Milk or Buttermilk 15

Guests will please pay on presentation of check only.
Absorption of Sales Tax not permitted under State laws.
Jos. G. Wheeler, General Passenger Agent, San Francisco, California
H. G. Wyman, Supt. Dining Cars and Hotels, Oakland, Calif.
Our ceiling prices are in accordance with the Price Control Act.

Waiters are Not Permitted to take Verbal Orders

WESTERN PACIFIC RAILROAD

Dinner

Cream of Tomato Soup

— or —

Hearts of Lettuce, Thousand Island Dressing

☆

(Choice)

Filets of Seasonal Fish, Lemon Butter

Pot Roast of Beef with Noodles

Roast Turkey, Dressing, Giblet Gravy

Au Gratin Potatoes Seasonal Vegetables

Assorted Breads

☆

Date Roll

or

Ice Cream

Coffee Tea Milk or Buttermilk

$1.50

(1) 9/23/46

Legislators would commute to their home counties on the train or meet lobbyists out of view of prying journalists' eyes. *Sacramento Public Library, Sacramento Room.*

Fat's was expensive, but no one cared; a lobbyist or an expense account paid for it anyhow. Proposition 9 severely curtailed lobbying, but Fat's weathered the ten-dollar lobbying limit.

It was not only politicians who wheeled and dealed. Seasoned veterans of the Sacramento Corps of Engineers recall sitting down to a "mild libation" to hammer out politely that which didn't always lend itself to sober discussion.

Frank Fat died in 1997, but his children have preserved the fine traditions of Fat's Family of Restaurants, which now includes the original, Fat City Bar & Café in Old Sacramento and facilities in Roseville and Folsom.

Senator Hotel

The Senator Hotel, overlooking Capitol Park at Twelfth and L Streets, was famous for good food and intimate dining. Even its coffee shop served choice corn-fed steaks, chops and prime rib at moderate prices. In bygone days, Ken Saunders said, "Lobbyists would rent suites of rooms to offer as inducements for a vote. It offered steaks, prime rib, scotch and attractive women, who didn't need a monetary inducement to spend the evening."

The heart of the business and shopping district, it was *the* hotel for many years. It hosted Charles Lindbergh after his famous solo flight crossing the Atlantic and numerous Hollywood glitterati, and it was one of the few hotels and restaurants that didn't discriminate against minorities; Ella Fitzgerald, Duke Ellington and Pearl Bailey occasionally stayed there when performing in Sacramento. Eugene "Pineapple" Jackson of the "Our Gang" comedies remembered being able to order ice cream any time of the day or night.

ANTONINA'S

Antonina's, a very classy restaurant in the Heilbron Mansion on Seventh and O Streets, offered white tablecloth service, a wine steward and fairly expensive meals. Named after Antonina Dickiara, matron of the family that operated the Capital Tamale Café, it made a sophisticated addition to Sacramento's eating scene when it debuted in the mid-1950s.

The food was sublime, even if the menu (by today's norms) sounds less than gourmet: Tenderloin of Beef En Brochette, Roast Chicken Antonina with Wild Rice and Broiled Lamb Chops with a manchette, a frilly white paper cuff.

Dolores Costella recalled, "It was an intimate place Sacramento's leaders felt comfortable in. Just two blocks from the hustle and bustle of the Capitol, it was a discreet place to meet. If a politico wanted to stay clear of prying eyes, he could take his 'lady friend' upstairs for a quiet tête-à-tête on the second floor."

She also remembered it as a place mothers and daughters enjoyed with friends before heading off to the nearby Crocker Art Gallery or while shopping. "We'd wear white gloves, a little cocked hat, our Sunday best, and order an opulent meal, with salad, soup, an entrée and occasionally a little 'tipple' to keep the heart going."

Nathaniel Goodell, who also built the Governor's Mansion and Pioneer Hall, designed the four-story, Italianate-style mansion in a neighborhood of resplendent homes. During redevelopment, most were razed to make way for office buildings. Fortunately, Antonina's eluded the wrecking ball. The house was built for August Heilbron, whose wife would order plain soup cups direct from Havilland and then hand paint them to sell in their grocery store or at private soirees. Regrettably, Antonina couldn't serve from Mrs. H's vintage ware but did offer fine, flavorful soup in fine, delicate china bowls, which sported a handle on each side. A lady could delicately bring the bowl to her lips without spilling a drop.

Roast Chicken Antonina
Courtesy of Dolores Costella

1 roasting chicken, preferably free range, cut in half lengthwise
½ stick butter, softened
4 Idaho potatoes, sliced
1 large onion, sliced ¼ inch thick
Spice blend of garlic powder, onion salt, paprika and white pepper to taste
Sprinkle of olive oil

Ask the butcher to cut chicken in half for you down the backbone, if you can't do it yourself. Pat dry. Let it come to room temperature. Lift the skin away from the breast and spread butter gently underneath. Lay the chickens on a bed of sliced potatoes and onions. Sprinkle seasoning blend and oil over chicken and potatoes. Preheat oven to 450 degrees and cook for about seventeen minutes per pound. Remove from oven. Let rest for twenty minutes before serving. Serve on top of the potatoes and onions. Antonina didn't serve this with garlic, but add whole garlic cloves too. Serves two to four.

Epithet for the Sacramento Hotel

The revolving door has gently turned behind the last department guest, the crisp white linens will no longer billow to the hands of chambermaids, the once bustling lobby is stilled with only the echoes of a glorious past remaining.
—Joseph Allan Beek

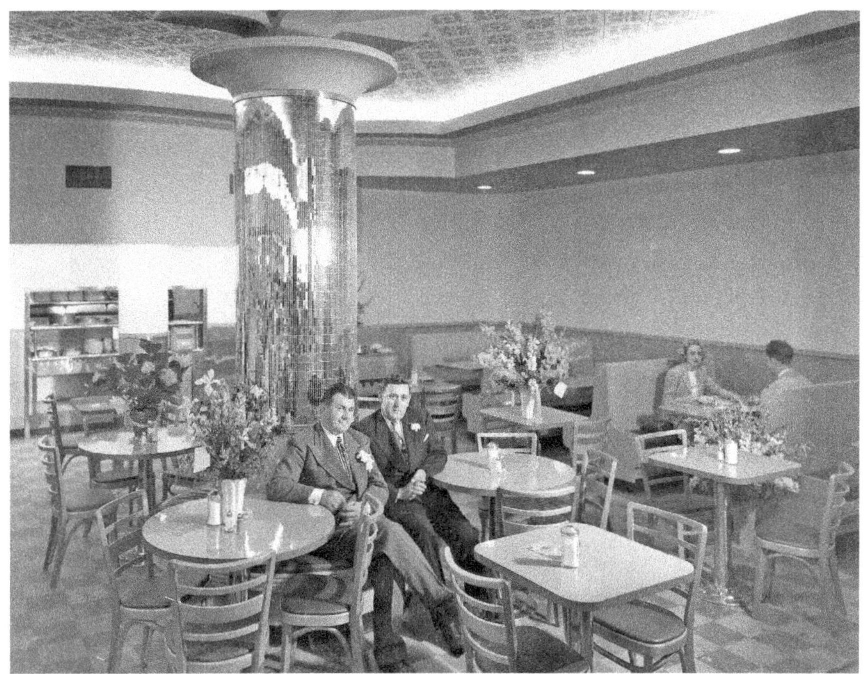

George Johnson's many restaurants were also a popular place for Sacramento's state workers and legislative staff to go with their families. *Sacramento Public Library, Sacramento Room.*

Many believed political decisions, though announced at the Capitol, were decided at the Sacramento Hotel at Tenth Street.

Joseph Allan Beek, the longest-serving secretary of the Senate in California history, lived in the Sacramento Hotel when the legislature was in session. In an article he penned for the *Sacramento Union* on April 29, 1956, he refers to it as "the center of political intrigue, fine cuisine, comfortable guest rooms and a favorite of distinguished visitors."

> *It was through the hotel's warmly lighted lobby that Governor Hiram Johnson and the great William Jennings Bryan made their way, arm in arm to dinner in the great dining room where the elite of Sacramento took their meals. This event occurred in 1913.*
>
> *The Sacramento Hotel dining room, when the century was in its teens and during the 20's, was an impressive place with its staff of uniformed waiters, its orchestra stationed on a dais on the south side of the room, its list of all the things good to eat and its impressive prices. A good dinner cost a whole dollar.*

Young fellows like Earl Warren couldn't afford to eat there. He was not yet chief justice of the United States. He was in 1919 a clerk of the assembly judiciary committee and got only $6 a day.

Joseph Hauser was the maître d'hôtel. For years he reigned over his domain, the Walnut Room, like a benevolent dictator but loved by staff. To be in the Walnut Room when this artist perfectionist officiates at the making of crepe suzette or a cherry jubilee was never to be forgotten experience.

His approach was that of a Svengali performing some fabled illusion, flanked by comely attendants in the person of waitresses on either side of the gleaming copper chafing dish. With the ceiling lights turned off the blue glow of burning alcohol lent an eerie effect.

As the master made each move you overheard quick, hushed orders to his assistant, "now, now a little brandy—no, no not too much...Now the cherries, quickly, please...There the plates, the plates, hurry, hurry"...and so on until the bountiful masterpiece was complete.

CHERRIES JUBILEE

This dish is best in season and with fresh-pitted cherries, not the canned cherries used by so many home cooks. Recipe is from Aldo's Restaurant.

¼ cup fresh squeezed orange juice
¼ cup brown sugar
2 tablespoons Grand Marnier or kirsch
½ pound fresh pitted cherries
½ teaspoon real vanilla extract
1 pint vanilla ice cream
1 tablespoon orange zest from the orange

Heat a sauté pan (copper is best), add orange juice and brown sugar and cook until sugar dissolves. Add the cherries and vanilla, and sauté for about four minutes. Remove pan from heat and add the liquor. Return to heat and ignite with a long-handled lighter, being careful to not singe your eyebrows. Place vanilla ice cream in nice crystal dishes and baste the cherry sauce on top. Dust with the zest and serve. Makes two servings.

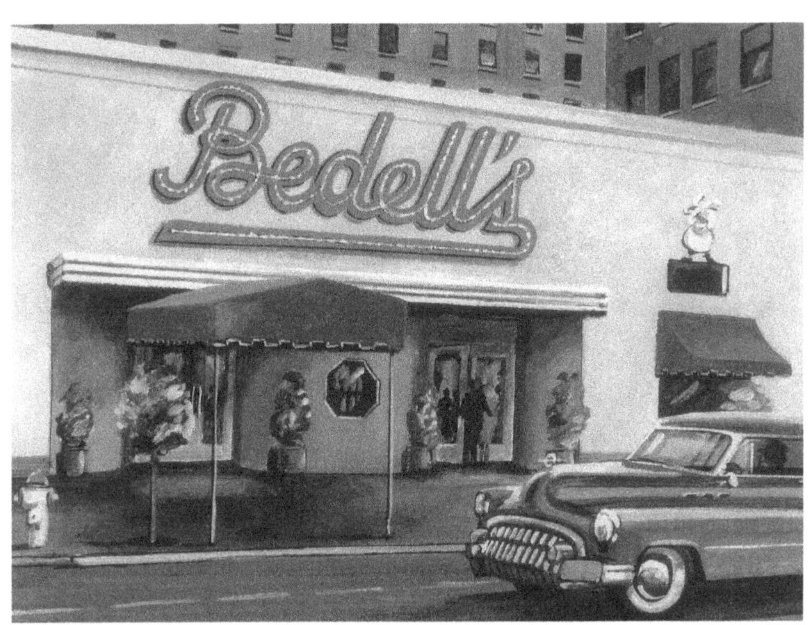
Bedell's

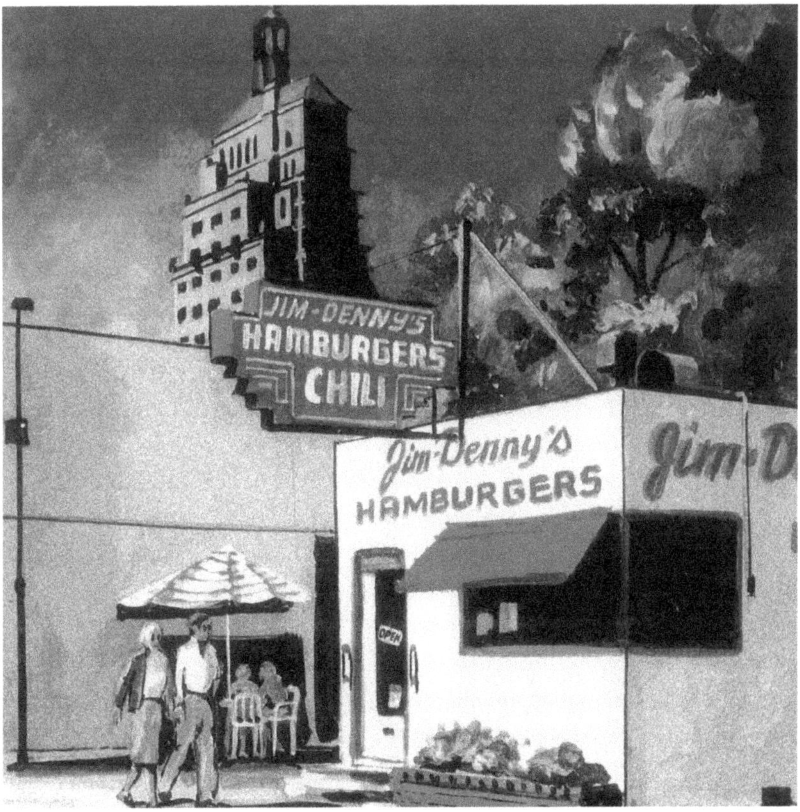

JIM-DENNY'S
HAMBURGERS
CHILI
Jim-Denny's
HAMBURGERS
OPEN

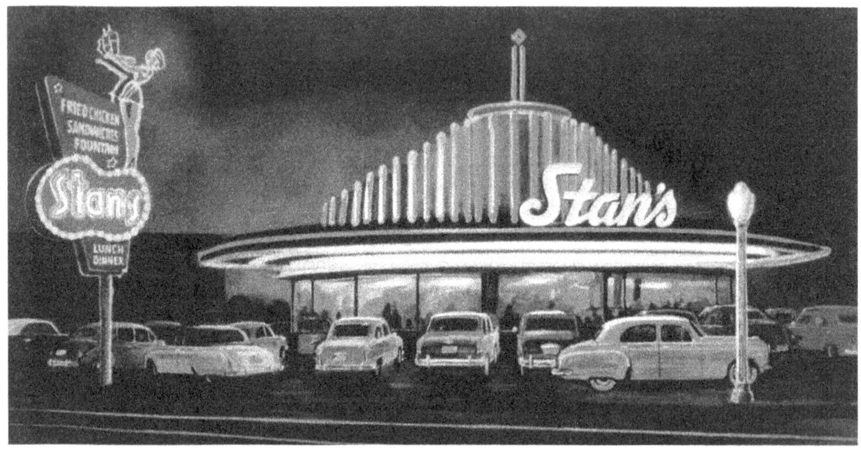

Stan's Drive-In was known for iconic architecture and beautiful carhops. *Bob Miller.*

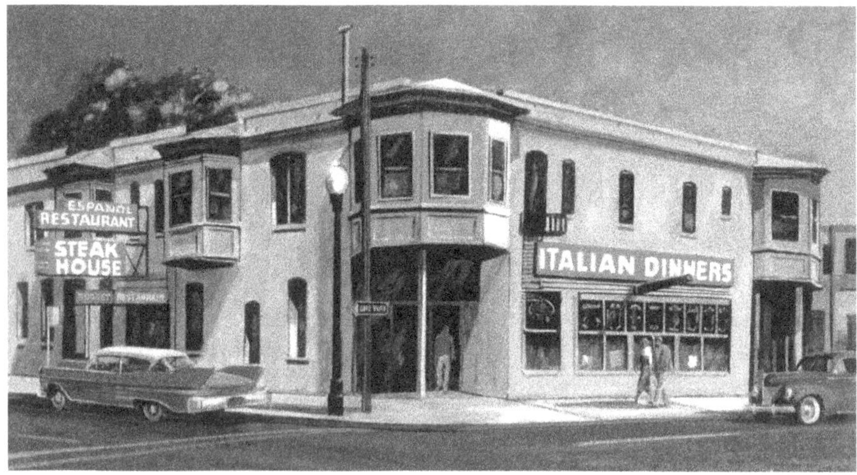

The original Espanol was a boardinghouse for sheepherders who would hire out to local farmers. The Luigi family added Italian fare. *Bob Miller.*

Previous page, top: Bedell's, two blocks from the Capitol, rivaled the Rosemount Grill with the size of its menu. *Bob Miller.*

Previous page, bottom: Jim-Denny's, open since the 1930's, still serves burgers and more inside this small stucco loaf of a building. *Bob Miller.*

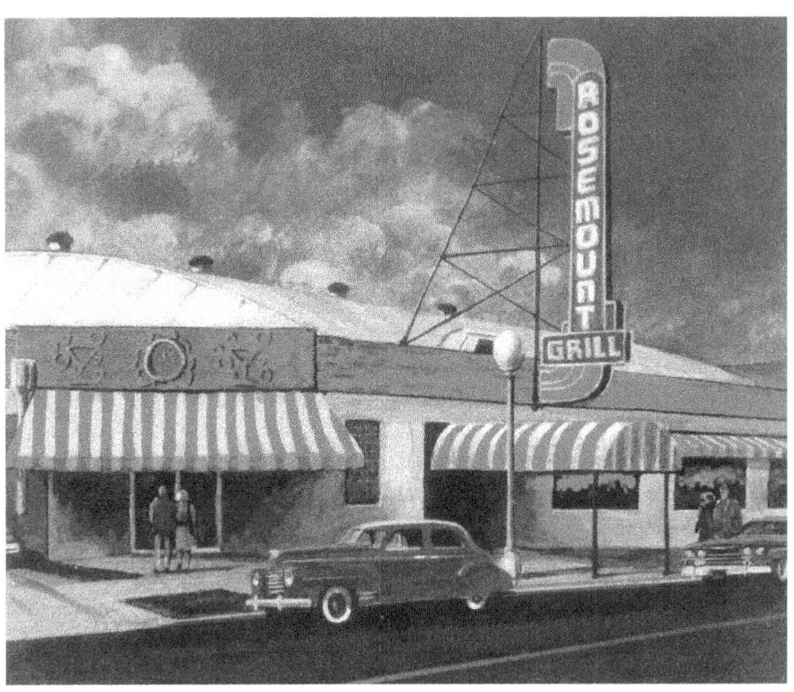

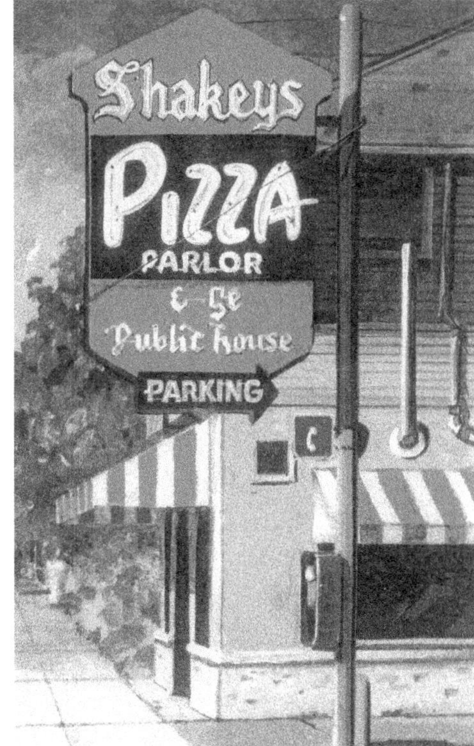

Above: "The Rosemount Grill's menu took longer to read than the *Sacramento Union* newspaper." *Bob Miller.*

Right: Shakey's Pizza Parlor chain started on the corner of J and Fifty-seventh Streets, near Sacramento State College. *Bob Miller.*

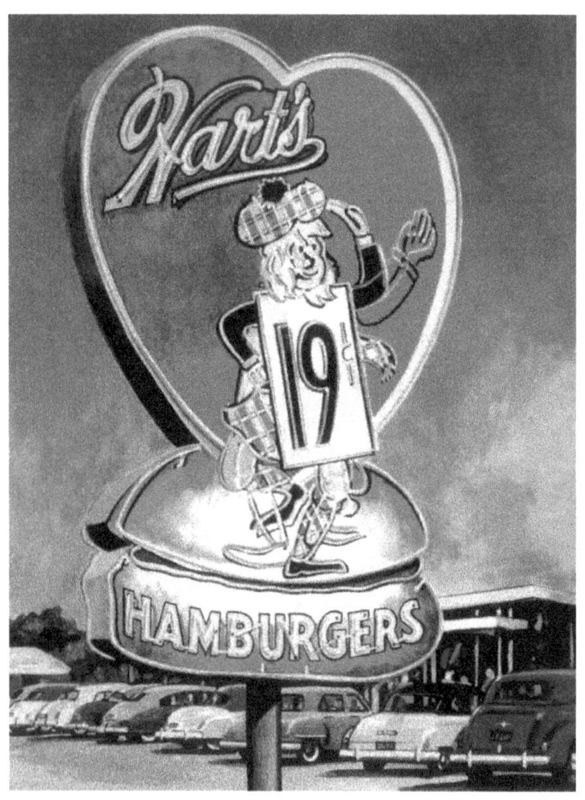

Hart's Hamburgers started a bidding war with Stan's Drive-In just across the parking lot. McDonald's won. *Bob Miller.*

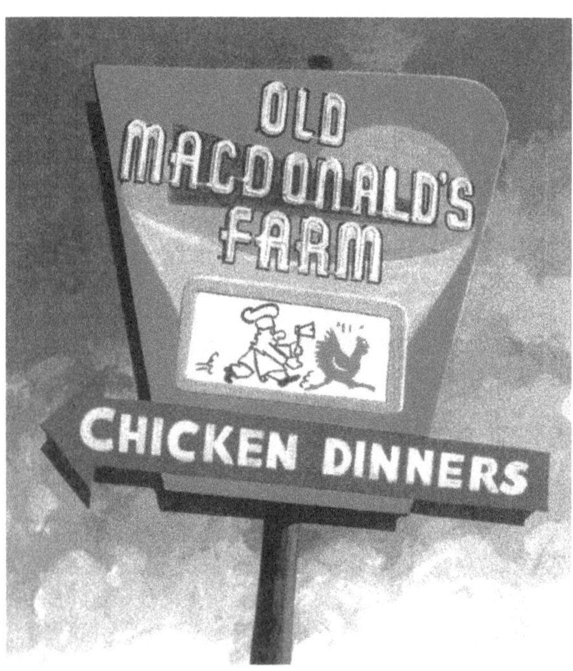

Old Macdonald's Farm had a petting zoo for kids, who hoped what they were petting wouldn't be on the menu. *Bob Miller.*

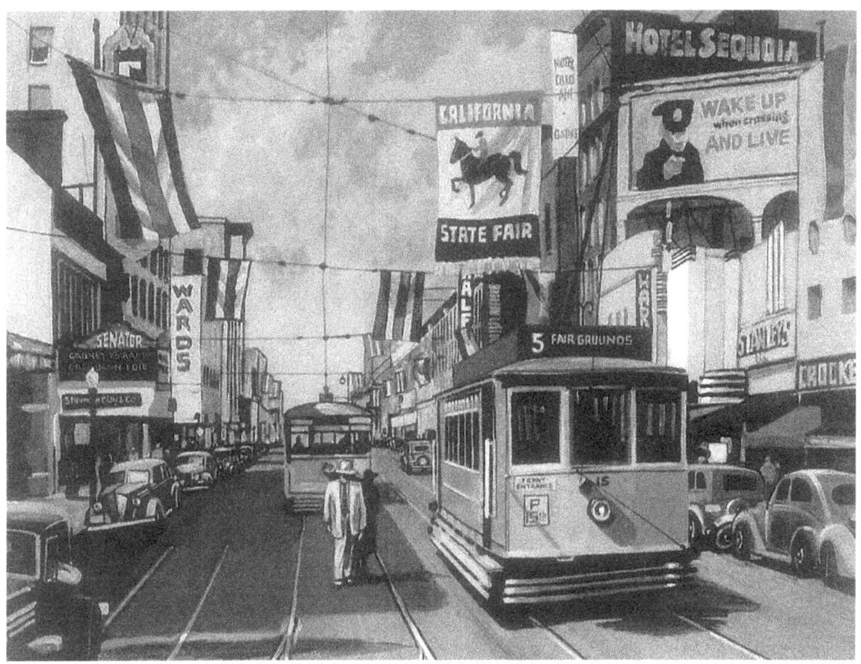

Special trolleys ran from downtown to the California State Fair on Stockton Boulevard and Broadway every summer. *Bob Miller.*

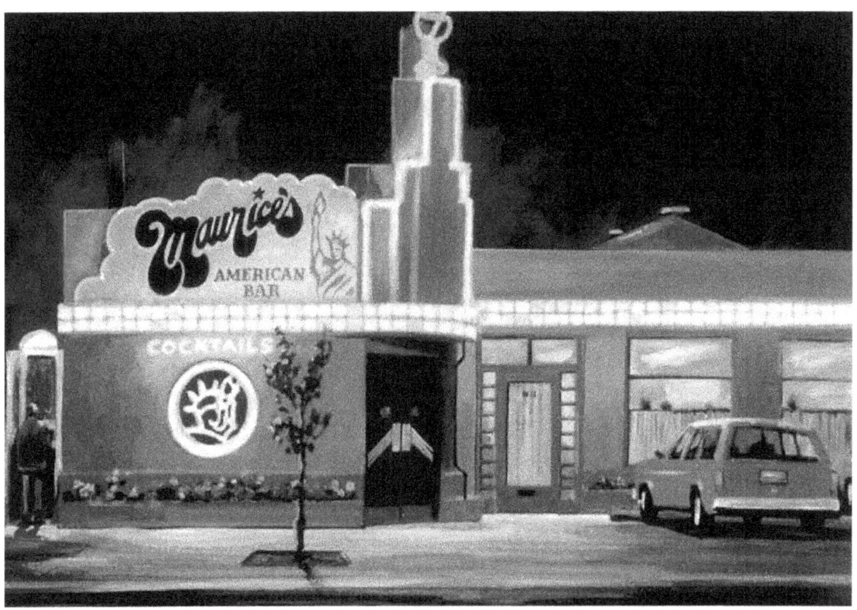

Maurice's American Bar was the hangout for Capitol staff and hip jazz types. It was equally successful as Melarkey's Place. *Bob Miller.*

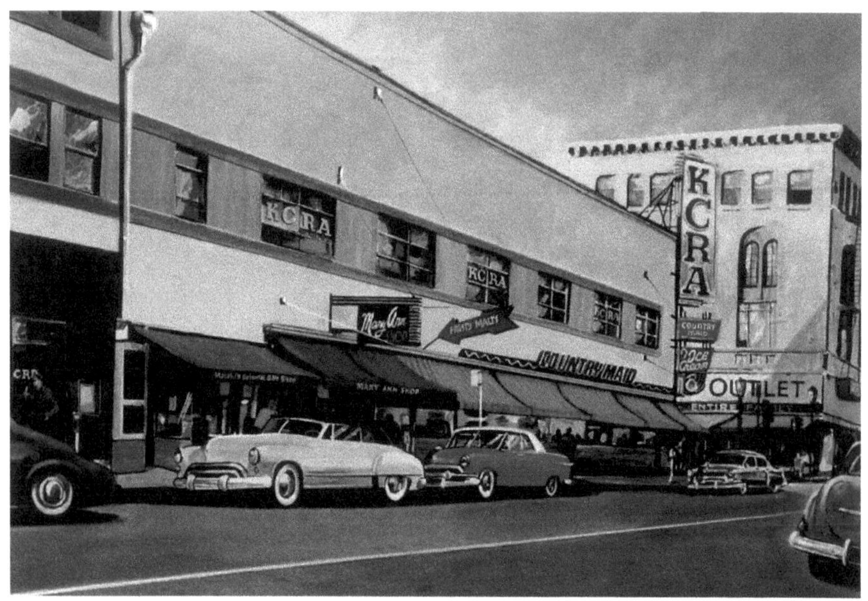

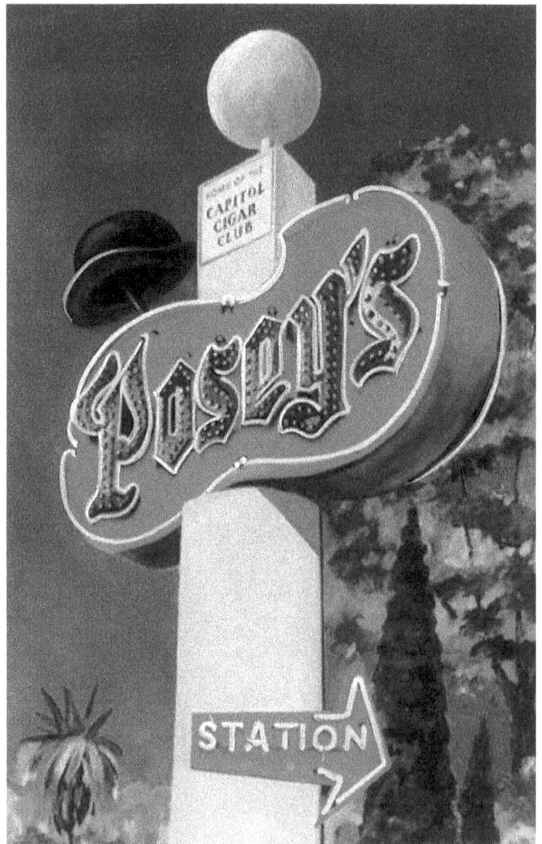

Above: Country Maid was open for breakfast, lunch, dinner and after-movie ice cream sodas. *Bob Miller.*

Left: Posey's Cottage, home to the Derby Club. Ronald Reagan, when governor, ordered the Hangtown Fry. *Bob Miller.*

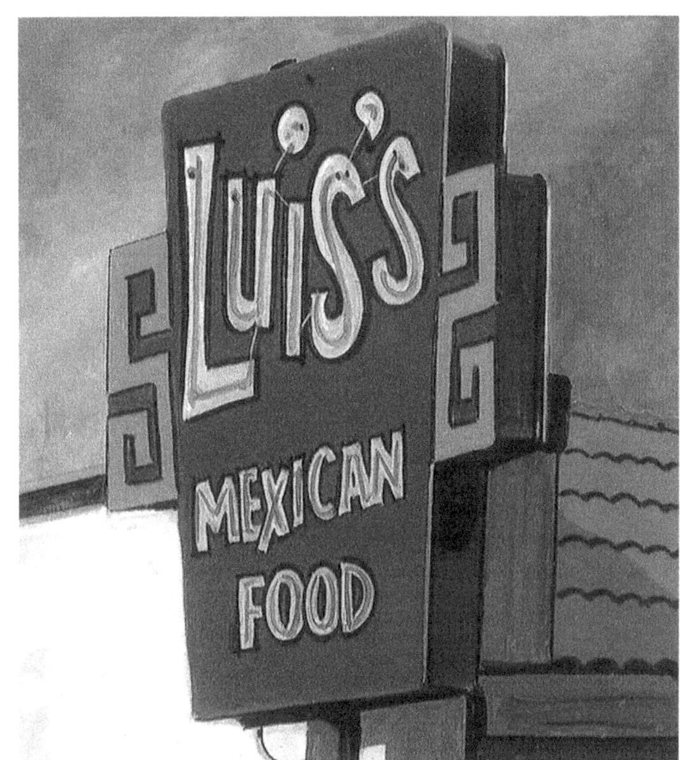

Luis Leyya mounted photos of himself and visiting celebrities on nearly every inch of the walls of his restaurant, Luis's. *Bob Miller.*

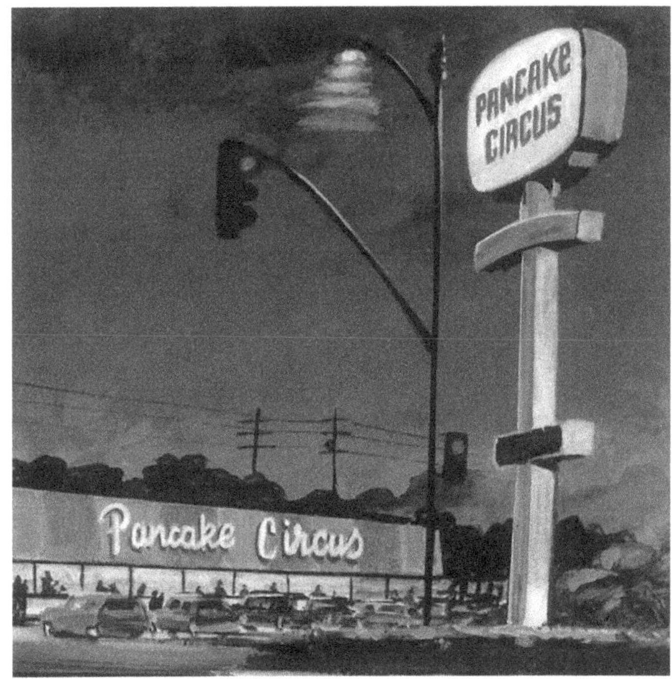

Pancake Circus is a popular breakfast and lunch place. Regulars have been coming here for fifty years. *Bob Miller.*

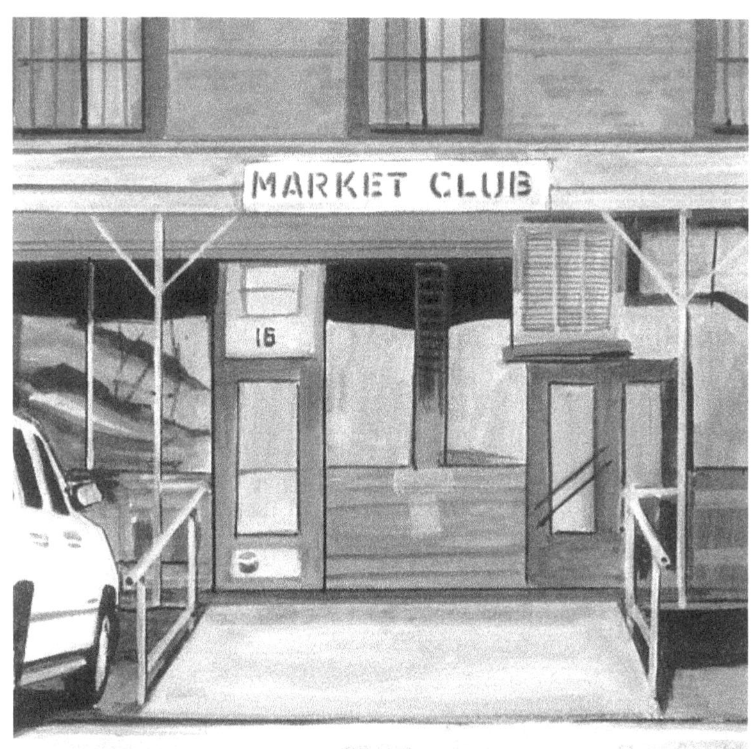

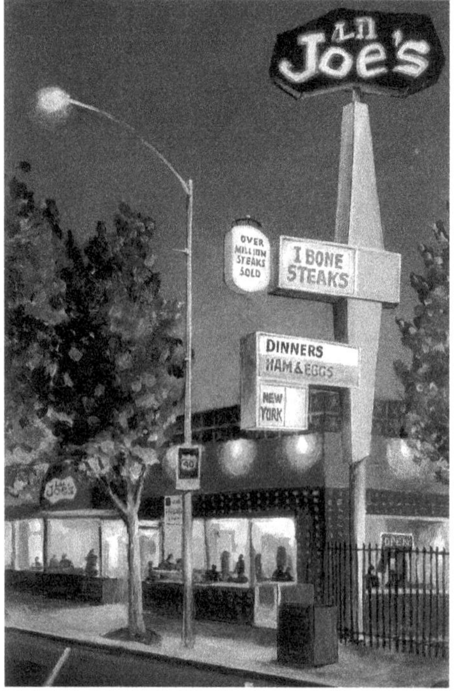

Above: The Market Club started in 1933. Owners Jim and Mona Sakata kept the original menu, developed in the '50s. *Bob Miller.*

Left: Lil Joe's made its reputation on $1.39 steaks. The price is higher, but this neighborhood institution still draws large crowds. *Bob Miller.*

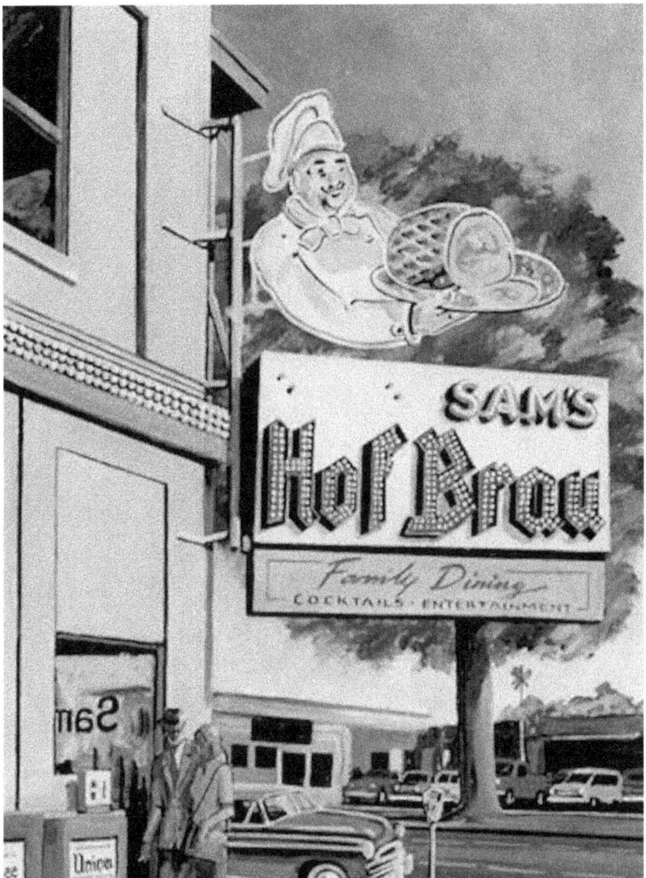

Right: Sam's Hof Brau on Watt Avenue and El Camino still serves thick pastrami, corned beef, turkey or prime rib sandwiches, dipped in au jus. *Bob Miller.*

Below: Robert's Fish Grotto served rainbow trout and fresh salmon from local rivers in season. *Bob Miller.*

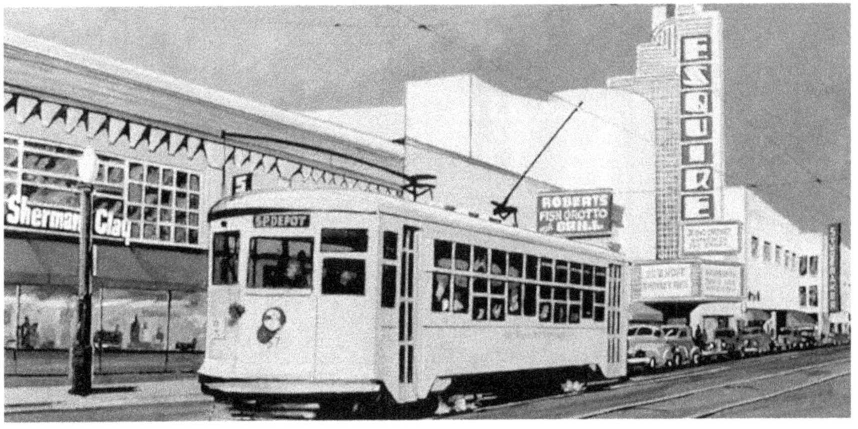

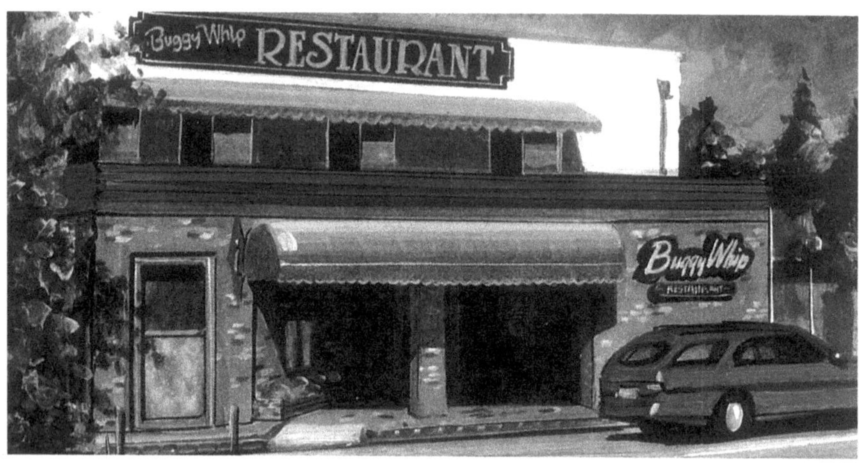

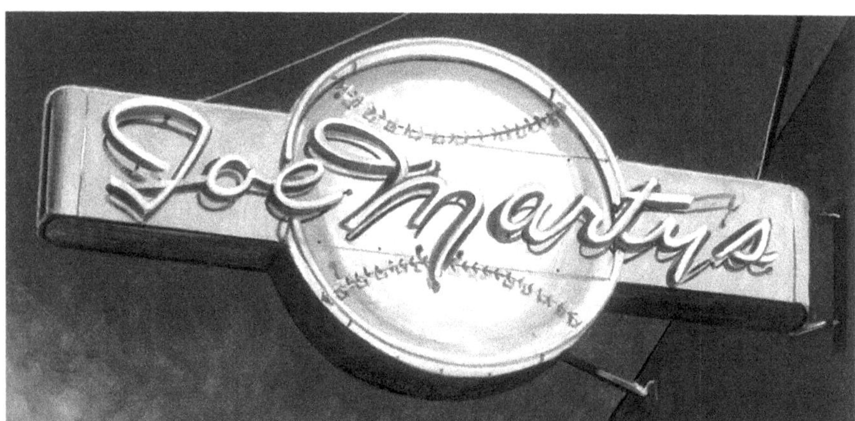

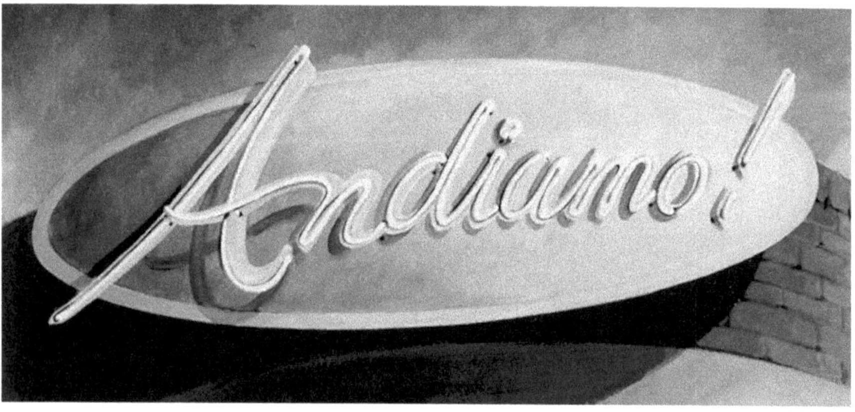

Top: The Buggy Whip was a mainstay of Fulton Avenue's "Restaurant Row." *Bob Miller*; *Middle*: Joe Marty's El Chico introduced Sacramento to pizza. Broasted chicken, served up alongside sports memorabilia, was a specialty. *Bob Miller*; *Bottom*: Andiamo took over the Rosemount Grill. It too is gone, but the Mikacich family still operates the Limelight. *Bob Miller.*

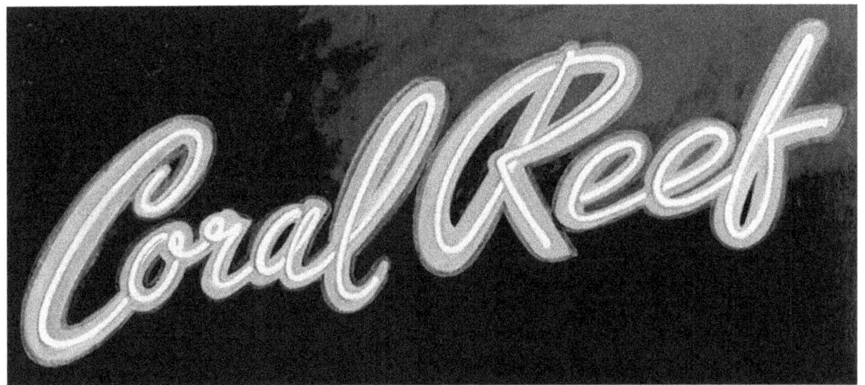

"The Reef" was everyone's favorite place for drinks, great service and lampshades you could etch your sweetheart's name on. *Bob Miller.*

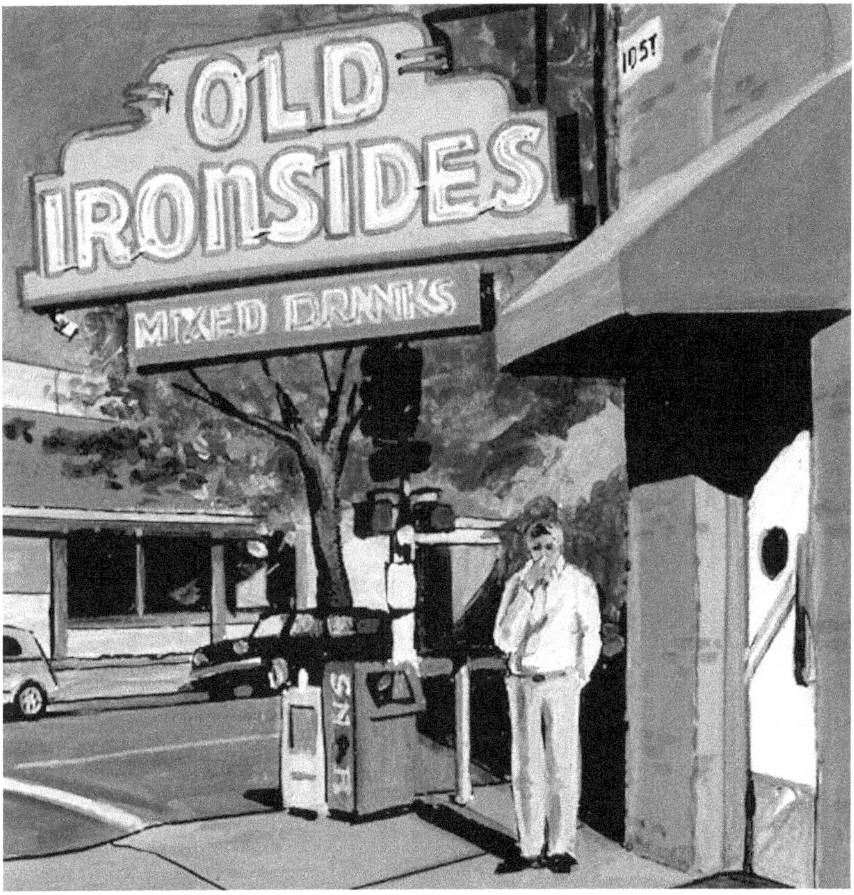

Old Ironsides, the first legal bar to open after Prohibition, still serves lunches. It's a great place to go to connect with the past. *Bob Miller.*

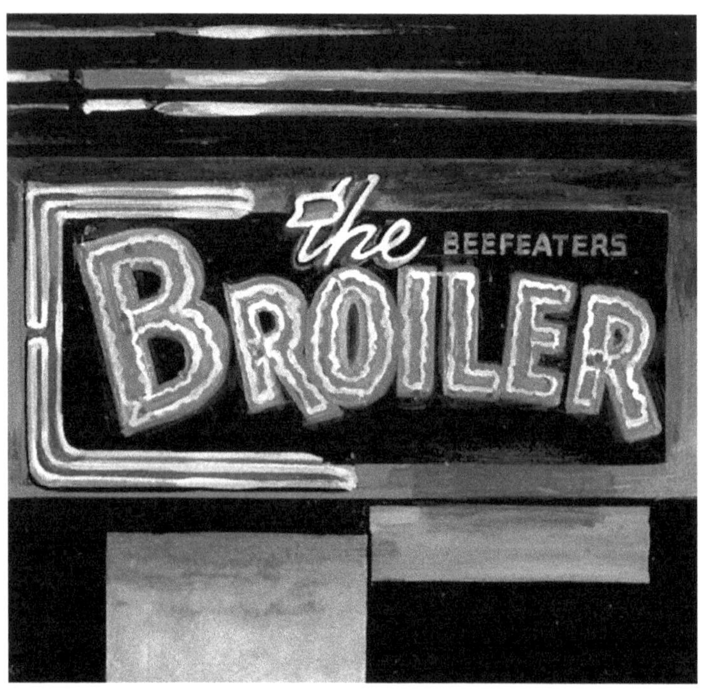

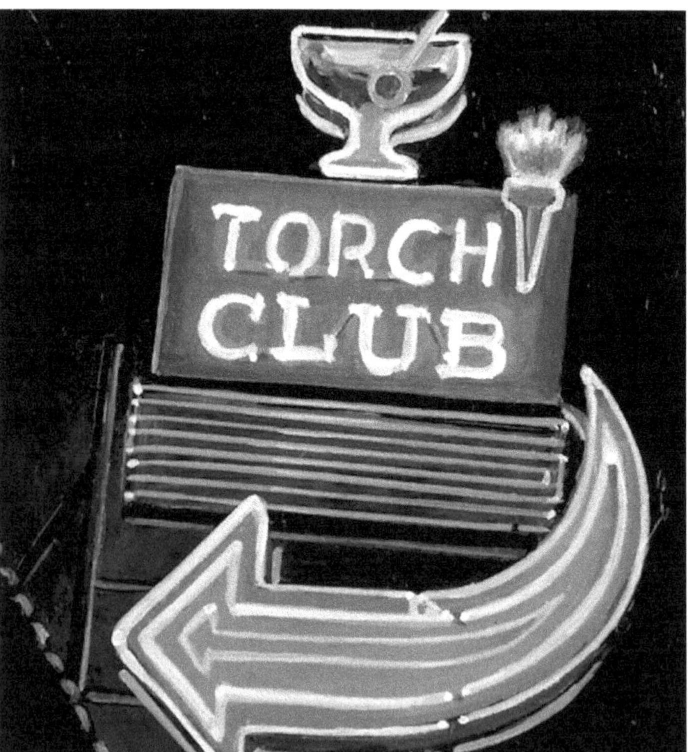

Left, top: The Broiler is one of the great steakhouses and the last of an era. *Bob Miller.*

Left, bottom: This popular spot warrants its own book. The stories we could tell about B.J. the D.J., B.T. Collins and the Capitol crowd! *Bob Miller.*

Opposite, top: Sim's Diner served "soulful" food: grits, greens, chicken, ham, macaroni and cheese and bread pudding. *Bob Miller.*

Opposite, bottom: The SooHoo brothers still operate Chinois City Café. The Ming Tree, Chinois East/West and other SooHoo eateries are gone. *Bob Miller.*

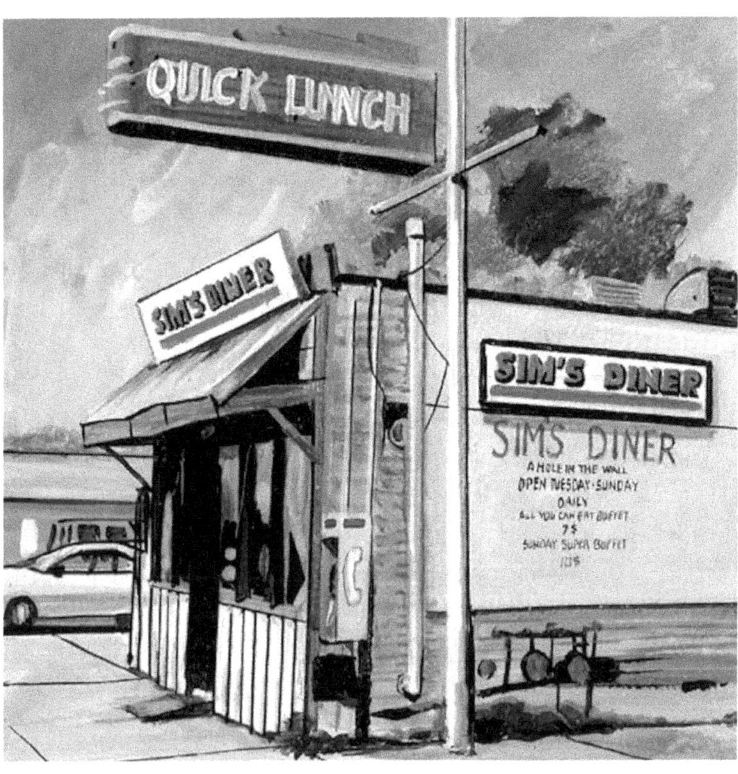
QUICK LUNNCH
SIM'S DINER
SIM'S DINER
SIMS DINER
A HOLE IN THE WALL
OPEN TUESDAY-SUNDAY
DAILY
ALL YOU CAN EAT BUFFET
7$
SUNDAY SUPER BUFFET

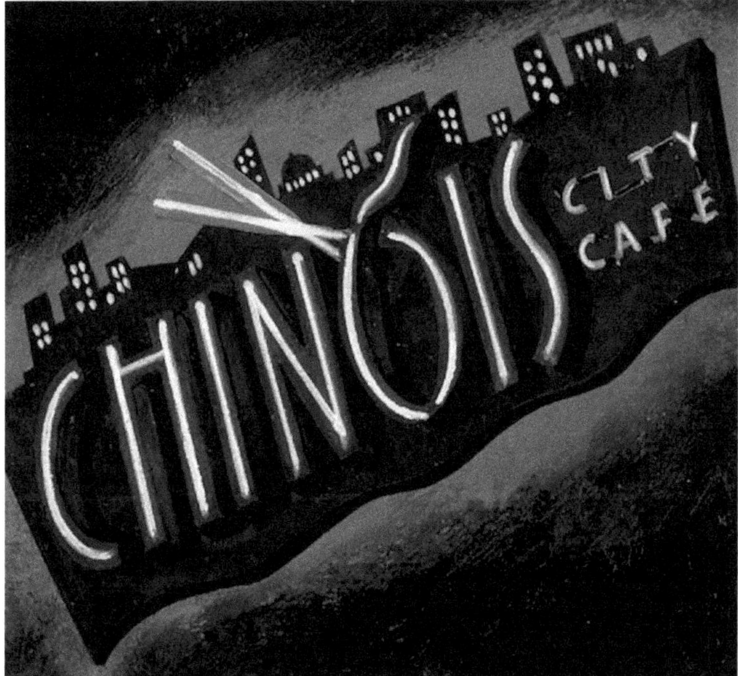
CHINOIS
CITY
CAFE

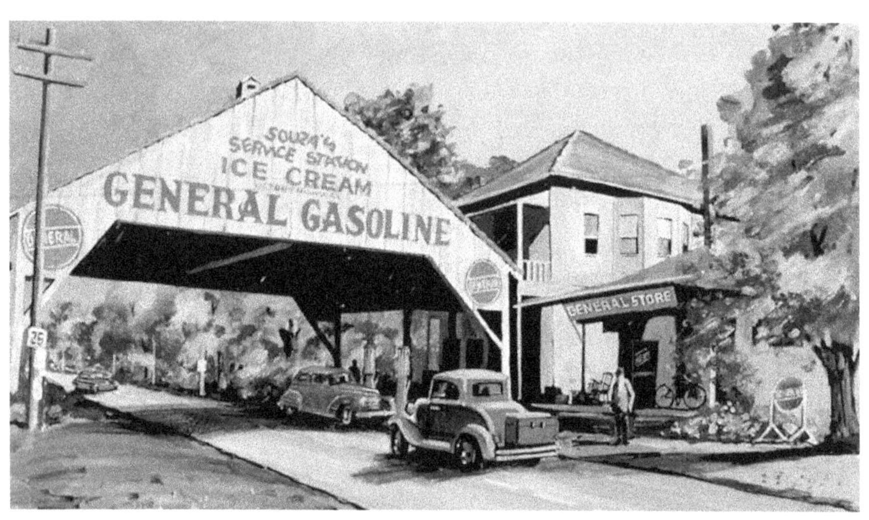
SOUZA'S
SERVICE STATION
ICE CREAM
GENERAL GASOLINE
GENERAL
GENERAL STORE
25

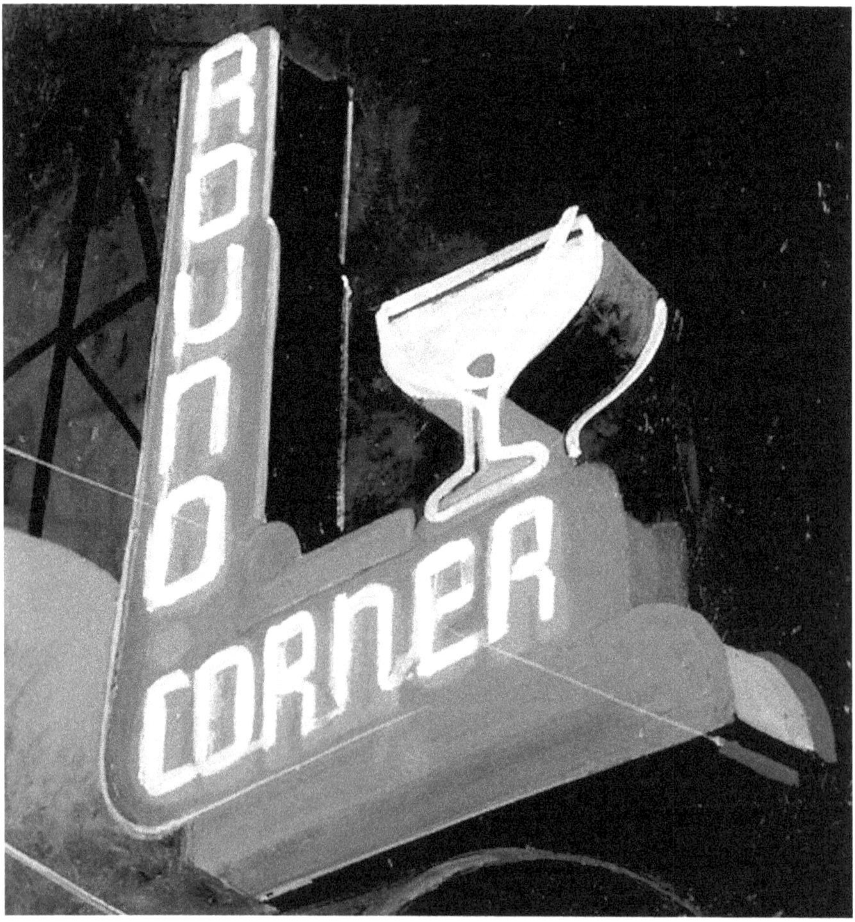

ROUND
CORNER

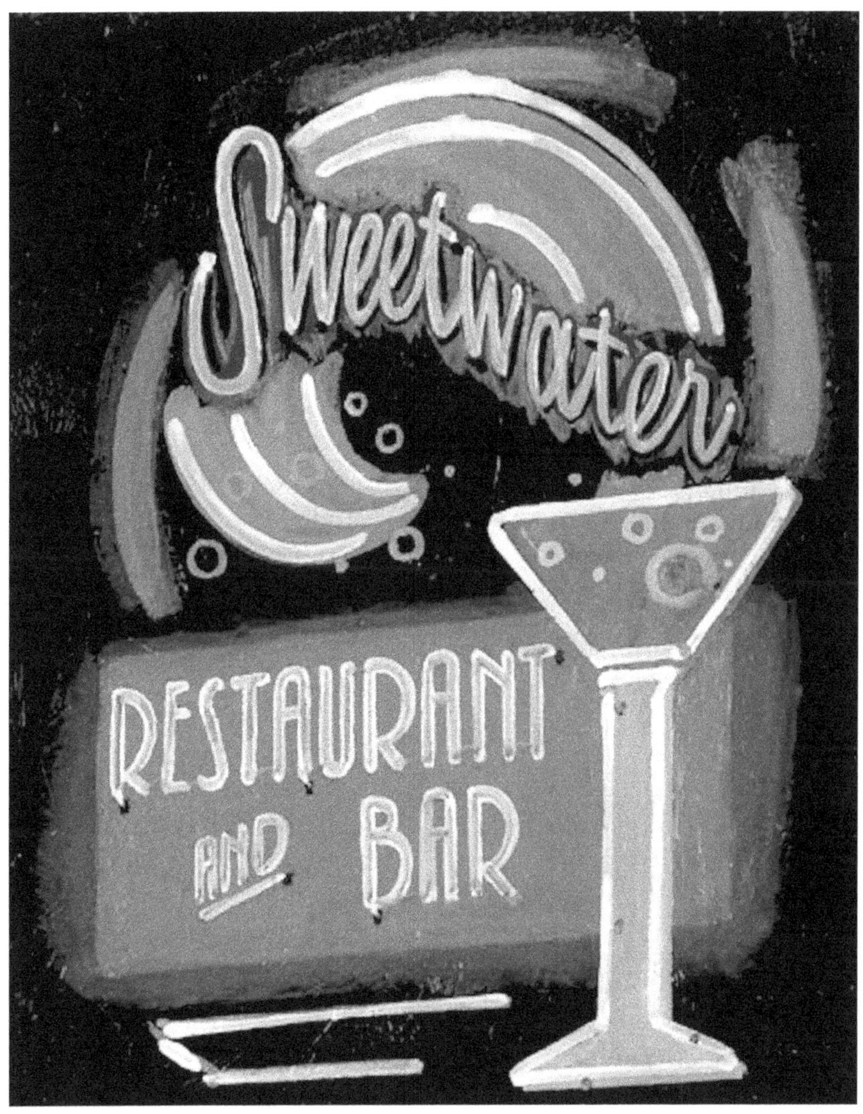

Sweetwater Restaurant and Bar took over Shakey's old place on J Street and was an immediate hit. It moved to Midtown and closed shortly after. *Bob Miller.*

Previous, top: On the old levee road, toward the Delta, Souza's, now gone, straddled the road. It sold gas, ice cream and other confections. *Bob Miller.*

Previous, bottom: The Round Corner is an old bar in Poverty Ridge. Its kitchen serves up sublime vegetarian fare. *Bob Miller.*

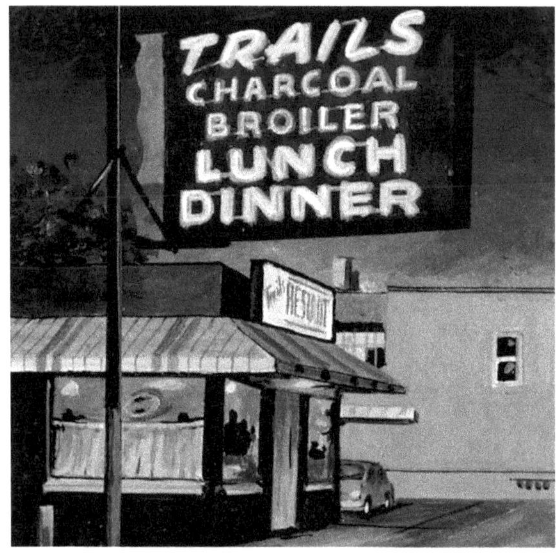

Trails was owned by Hollywood actress Esther Williams and her husband. It's still there, serving the same grub it has for fifty-plus years. *Bob Miller.*

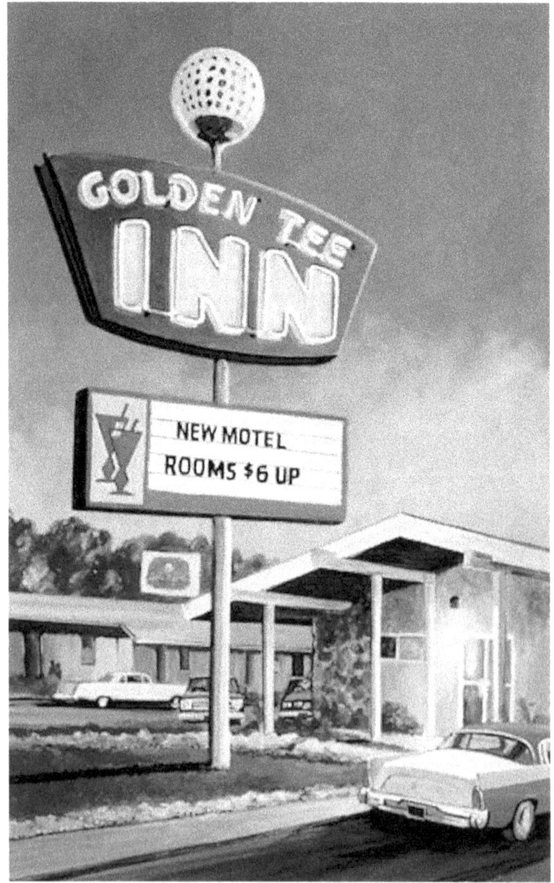

Golden Tee was right off the freeway opposite a golf course. Unprepossessing from the roadway, it was one of Sacramento's fine dining establishments. *Bob Miller.*

It's All American Food

If your mother cooks Italian food, why should you go to a restaurant?
—Martin Scorsese

Cecil B. DeMille's *The Greatest Show On Earth*, the big motion picture in 1952, won a cartload of Oscars, including Best Motion Picture, and spawned many imitators. Just about every circus-related name turned up on restaurant signs, as well as on decorations, outside and inside. Stop in at Pancake Circus, 2101 Broadway, and see all the paintings, doo-dads and décor. Similar signs and motifs were proclaimed at the Carousel, Arden Fair's Food Circus, the Big Top and others.

Similarly, *Bonanza*, *Rawhide*, *Wagon Train*, *Roy Rogers* and other television series and/or movies of the time, gave us the Buckboard, Trails, Chuck Wagon, Sam's Ranch Wagon, Sam's Rancho Villa, Hickory House, Ponderosa and so forth, evoking the Old West. They served MEAT (steak and ribs) in large portions, grilled, with all the trimmings.

World War II's Pacific Theater conjured up South Seas–related dining halls. Tiki Village, Zombie Hut, Bob's Tiki and, the most beloved, Maleville's Coral Reef. Oddly, none of them offered Hawaii's favorite food, SPAM. What they did serve were the era's signature drinks, complete with little Japanese paper umbrellas.

World War II's European Theater introduced GIs to pizza. Joe Marty's El Chico on Broadway introduced it to us, followed closely by Luigi's Pizza on Stockton Boulevard. In 1954, Sherwood "Shakey" Johnson opened the

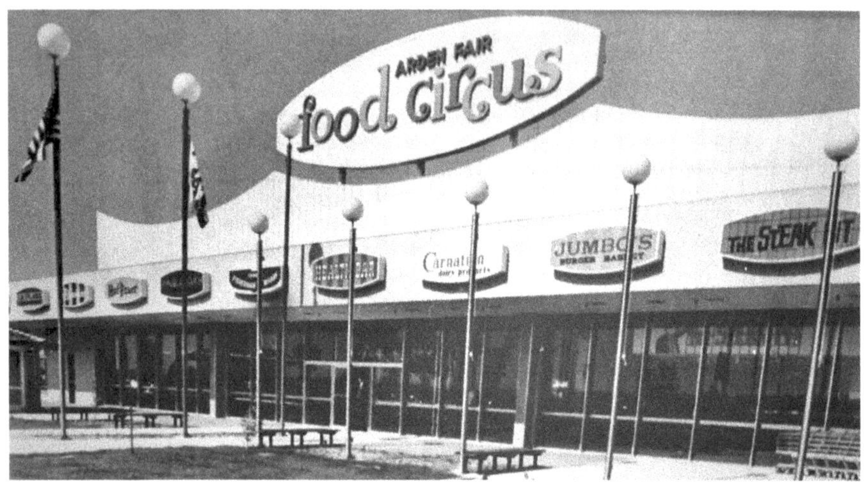

Food Circus, at Arden Fair, was a dining Shangri-La where many tastes could be satisfied in a single visit. *Author's collection.*

first Shakey's Ye Public House on Fifty-seventh and J Street, the beginning of America's first pizza chain franchise.

Many Sacramento restaurants sported animal themes: the Ram, Hereford House, Palomino Room and, much later, the Monkey Bar. Especially during the '50s, Sacramento had its share of Atomic, Rocket, Sonic, Jet and Aviator eateries, many started in the 1950s when kids in elementary school were instructed to "duck and cover."

Some restaurants were eponymous, named for the owners: Americo's, Luis's, Chez Paul, Mario's Italian Cellar and Zeke's, to name a few. In the Delta, three are still open—Tony, Guisti's and Al the Wop's.

Southern-themed and black restaurants also flourished, from fine dining establishments like Dunlap's Dining Room to more folksy places like the Plantation, Sim's Diner, Danny's Bar-b-que and dozens of neighborhood joints serving ribs, chicken and home cooking.

Ethnic restaurants—Chinese, Mexican, Armenian, Japanese, Korean, Greek, Middle Eastern, Italian, Indian, German, Filipino and lots of others—were often named for locale or type of food served. Casablanca, the House of Shish Kebab and Fuji Sukiyaki immediately identified the ethnic origin of the restaurant.

Collectively, they represent American cuisine, because (except for a few indigenous foods that grew naturally in California) our people and foodways almost all immigrated here from somewhere else. Greek Americans, in

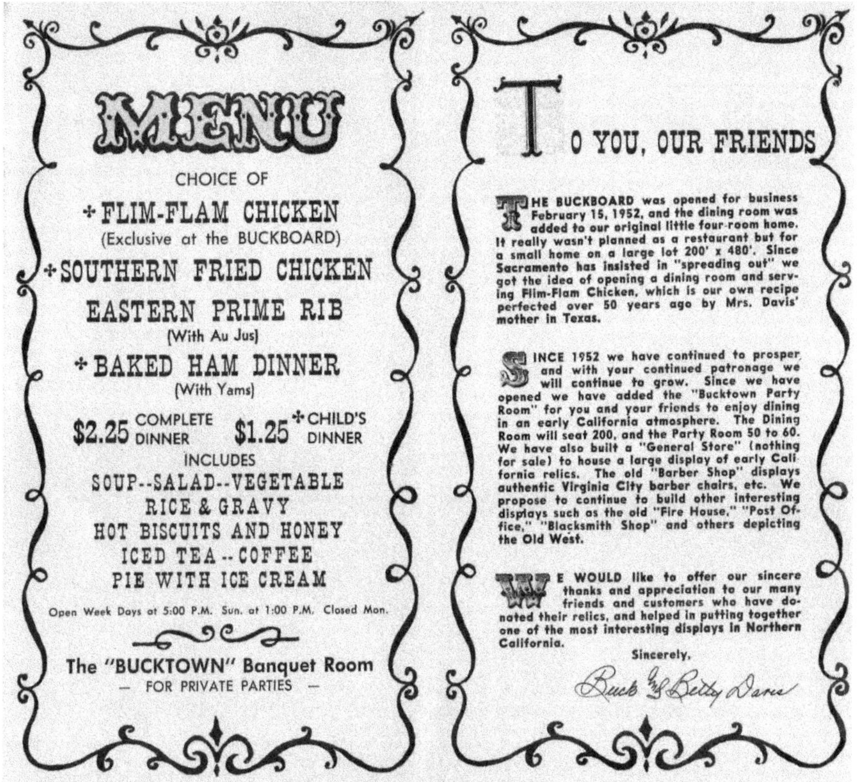

MENU

CHOICE OF

✣ FLIM-FLAM CHICKEN

(Exclusive at the BUCKBOARD)

✣ SOUTHERN FRIED CHICKEN

EASTERN PRIME RIB

(With Au Jus)

✣ BAKED HAM DINNER

(With Yams)

$2.25 COMPLETE DINNER $1.25 ✣ CHILD'S DINNER

INCLUDES

SOUP--SALAD--VEGETABLE

RICE & GRAVY

HOT BISCUITS AND HONEY

ICED TEA -- COFFEE

PIE WITH ICE CREAM

Open Week Days at 5:00 P.M. Sun. at 1:00 P.M. Closed Mon.

The "BUCKTOWN" Banquet Room

— FOR PRIVATE PARTIES —

TO YOU, OUR FRIENDS

THE BUCKBOARD was opened for business February 15, 1952, and the dining room was added to our original little four-room home. It really wasn't planned as a restaurant but for a small home on a large lot 200' x 480'. Since Sacramento has insisted in "spreading out" we got the idea of opening a dining room and serving Flim-Flam Chicken, which is our own recipe perfected over 50 years ago by Mrs. Davis' mother in Texas.

SINCE 1952 we have continued to prosper, and with your continued patronage we will continue to grow. Since we have opened we have added the "Bucktown Party Room" for you and your friends to enjoy dining in an early California atmosphere. The Dining Room will seat 200, and the Party Room 50 to 60. We have also built a "General Store" (nothing for sale) to house a large display of early California relics. The old "Barber Shop" displays authentic Virginia City barber chairs, etc. We propose to continue to build other interesting displays such as the old "Fire House," "Post Office," "Blacksmith Shop" and others depicting the Old West.

WE WOULD like to offer our sincere thanks and appreciation to our many friends and customers who have donated their relics, and helped in putting together one of the most interesting displays in Northern California.

Sincerely,

Buck & Betty Davis

The Western theme didn't always mean steak; the Buckboard also prepared fried chicken. *Center for Sacramento History.*

particular, often open restaurants with "American food" representing our melting pot culture. George and Eppie Johnson are Greek American, but their restaurants—Johnson's Del Prado, Eight Pillars Coffee Shop, the Cordova Lodge and Eppie's—served up a little bit of everything from German burgers and hot dogs to Italian pastas and on to English steaks and Yorkshire pudding. Americans originally from Yugoslavia and Croatia ran the Rosemount Grill. Capitol Tamale Café's Italian American owners treasured their African American staff.

Mexico, especially, gave many dishes to all the people of the West, including Sacramento. Before the California Republic became a state of the Union, Mexico encompassed the land, culture and people west of the Rockies. Over the last 150 years, from Sutter's Fort in 1839 to Lalo's on Twenty-fourth Street today, Mexican-type restaurants have enriched the Sacramento region.

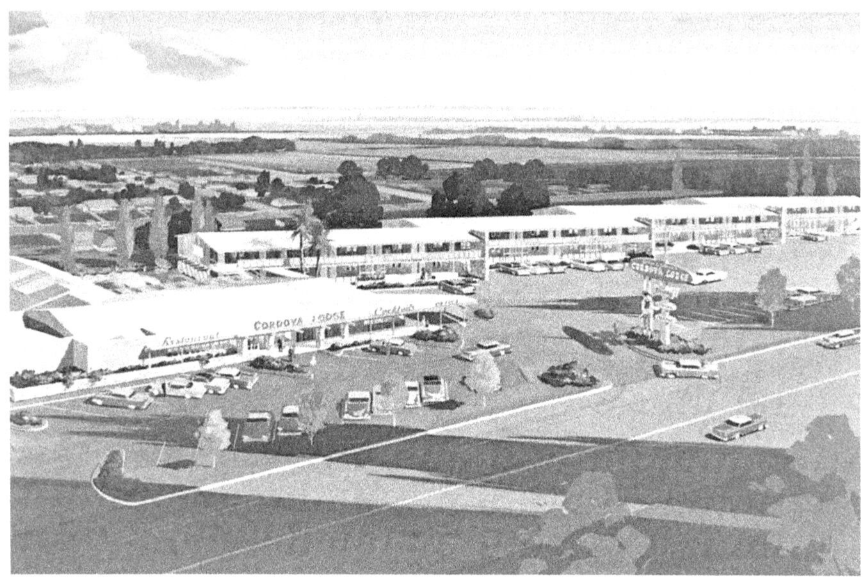

Cordova Lodge was owned by George Johnson, who also owned the Del Prado and other popular eateries—more than forty-five in his lifetime. *Sacramento Public Library.*

War in Southeast Asia during the 1960s and 1970s brought an influx of Vietnamese, Thai and Cambodian immigrants to the Sacramento Valley. Just like everyone else who came in the past, they began by opening restaurants, a quick way to assimilate into the United States. Little Saigon, along the eastern portion of Stockton Boulevard, reverberates with tastes of these distant homelands.

Strangely, the only ethnicity without restaurant memorialization here is that of the Native Americans. Go figure.

The Most Diverse City in the World

From its inception in 1849, Sacramento has retained its status as one of the most diverse cities in the world. During the gold rush, over 25 percent of new arrivals came from outside American borders. Many of them found work in the food, alcohol and beer industries quickly arising to fill a need in the rapidly growing city. They brought with them very different customs, traditions, tastes and ways of living, some that affect the way we eat today.

Immigrants, longing for the taste of home, tended to cling to the foods they knew. Restaurants, cafés and saloons chose names that would attract those from their hometowns, home states or home countries. In this tradition, Connecticut, New York, French Hotel, Saloon Louisiana and New Orleans flourished.

There was one cuisine, however, popular with people from all cultures and walks of life. Asian immigrants from Kwangtung Province near the Pearl River added a savory cooking style other new arrivals found appealing. Chop suey houses served rice and hot brewed tea, as well as stir-fried and steamed dishes. "However much Caucasian miners feared, ridiculed and discriminated against the Chinese, they loved their food," notes Joseph Conlin, author of *Bacon, Beans, and Galantines.*

Though only a handful of Chinese had settled in Sacramento at the start of the gold rush, by 1852, they accounted for 10 percent of the population. They took on the hardest, most menial labor, working on the railroad and in mines, dams, fields and restaurants. The first Chinese restaurants were small, cramped places, with not much more than a pot, water and fire. They catered to their own compatriots, utilizing fresh vegetables, dried roots and fish they imported from home and using every part of the animal. Later, they saw an opportunity to nourish the rest of Sacramento society, which was largely male and all thumbs when it came to feeding themselves.

Chinese restaurants were plentiful by the start of the 1860s. A small party—including an elected county judge, a physician, a West Point military man and two *Sacramento Bee* reporters—was invited to a Chinese New Years dinner in 1861. They met their hosts Ah Teen and Oy Tye, two prominent merchants at the Ye Chin restaurant on I Street. They asked for stationery to record the twenty-six courses they were offered, including such delicacies as birds nest with hard-boiled eggs; and Quichi, a complex dish of fishes' gills, fishes' tails, fishes' bones and Chinese parsley, jellied and mixed. A different champagne was offered with each course—Mumm, Sillery and Heidesick.

On January 3, 1861, the *Sacramento Bee* wrote, "The table was set up with cloth, knives, forks, plates, spoons and napkins, very much like ordinary tables, with celery in glasses and salt in cellars, but there was no bread or butter or potatoes or chopsticks to be seen."

Not everyone thought Chinese food was potentially palatable, however. The *Daily Union* of July 21, 1882, reported:

> *Returning to our train we passed through that part of the city known as the Chinese settlement, where we saw a number of Celestials picking up the*

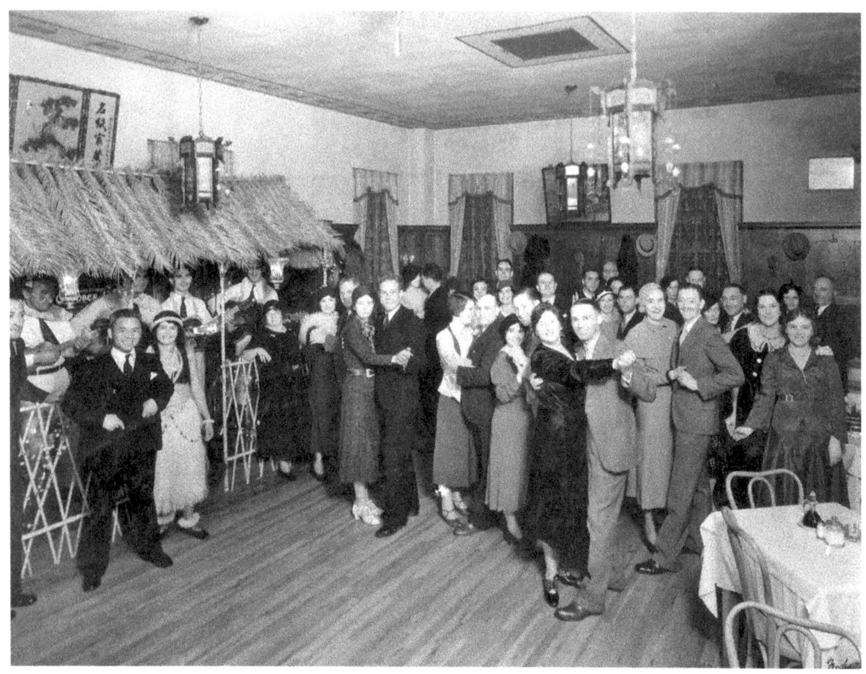

Hong King Lum was open for almost one hundred years. Frank Fat got his start here. *Sacramento Public Library, Sacramento Room.*

> *great filthy black beetles that were crawling upon the ground under the arc lights. Upon inquiry we were informed that these were to be used in making some kind of soup. A shiver came over us at the idea of such a thing and had our suppers not been well anchored it is not difficult to tell what the result would have been.*

The Sun Sun Café, the Asia and New Tientsin Café all offered American and Chinese food. The Hong King Lum stood at the crossroads of a once thriving Chinatown, at Third and I Streets. It closed in 2004. Had it lasted a few more years, it would have celebrated its 100th anniversary. Hong King Lum could host banquets for up to one thousand people for family weddings and special occasions.

Mar Fong's, at Sixteenth and Broadway, opened at 10:00 p.m. and stayed open until about 10:00 the next morning to serve the night crowd.

Ding How Café was on the corner of Twenty-eighth and Broadway. Norm Sayler lived nearby. "The neat thing about that place was the big tall Chinaman that was in there. I would go in, and he would say, 'Norman want

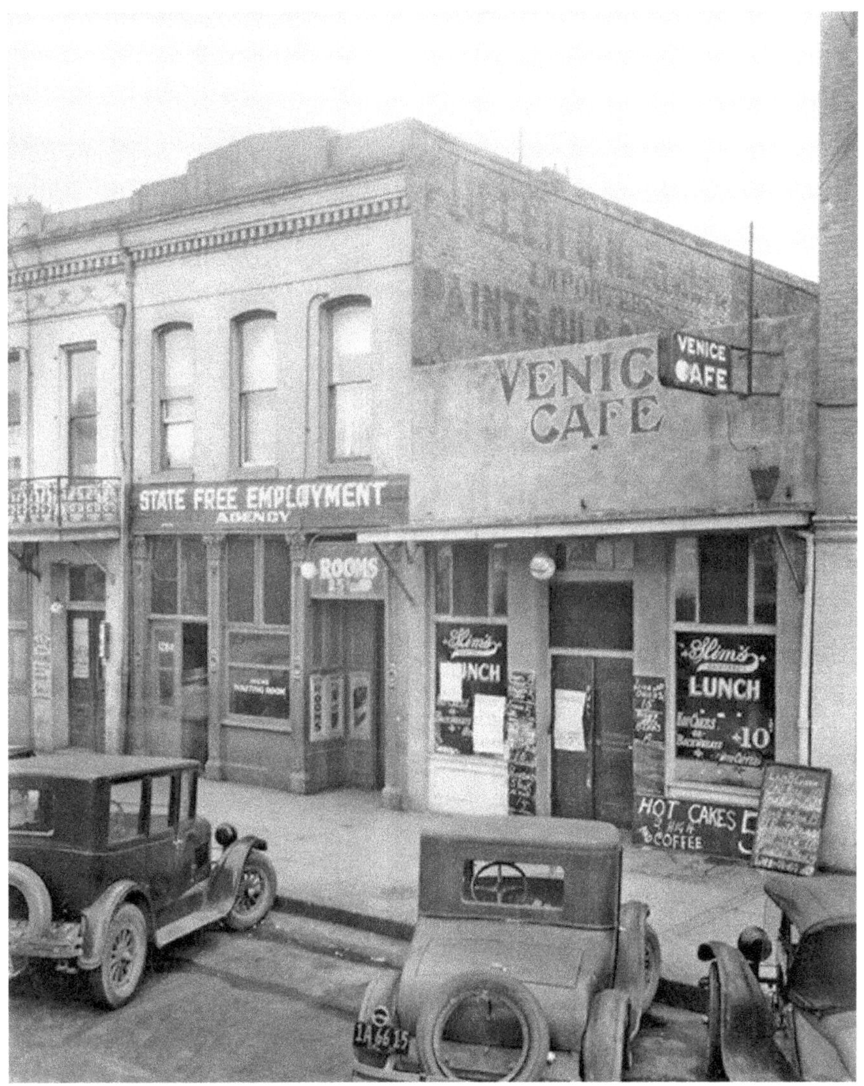

The once active Embarcadero was littered with small lunchrooms and job halls that provided labor to farmers, canneries and industry. *Center for Sacramento History.*

pan-fried noodles with lots of ketchup.'" Harry Burns used to eat at Ding How at least once a week and loved almost everything on offer, except for the Chicken Egg Drop Soup. "They'd boil a pot of water and the chicken would skate across the top, trying not to get wet, as the egg dropped."

Wakano Ura Chop Suey, the schizophrenic eatery with a Japanese name and a Chinese cook, lasted for many years on the West End, as well as at its location on Tenth Street, where it, and many other Japanese restaurants, moved when displaced by redevelopment.

It wasn't the only Japanese-owned restaurant serving chop suey. Sacramento actor Noriyuki "Pat" Morita ran Arnold's Diner on television's *Happy Days* for many seasons. His cooking and comedy career started at his father's restaurant, Ariake Chop Suey Palace. It was located on Fourth Street between M and N Streets. It was a real family affair. His aunts and cousins served the food. Known simply as "Nori," he would entertain at banquets for up to three hundred customers. He once described the enterprise to the *Los Angeles Times* as "a Japanese family running a Chinese restaurant in a black neighborhood with a clientele of blacks, Filipinos and everybody else who didn't fit in any of the other neighborhoods."

Hong Kong Café

Hong Kong Café opened at 320 L Street not long after World War II, with partners Suey Ming Ng, Fong Choy, Low Hop Joe and Wong Wah Hook. Redevelopment in the 1950s and 1960s would destroy their West End neighborhood. The Hong Kong Café moved in 1962 to 501 Broadway. It

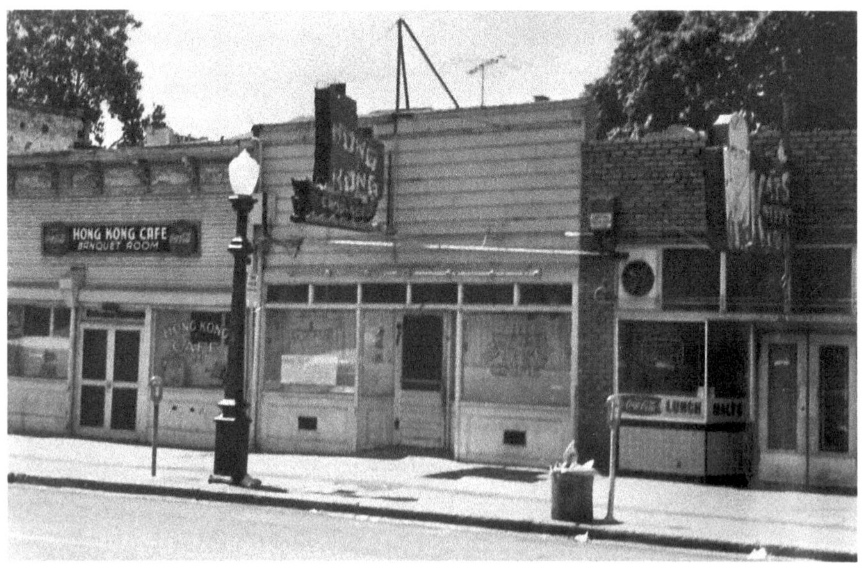

Hong Kong Café offered some of the most authentic Chinese food in Sacramento. *Sacramento Public Library, Sacramento Room.*

offered an à la carte and a set menu that included chicken with egg drop soup, egg foo young, pork chow mein, sweet and sour chicken and fried rice. One family meal came with thick battered shrimp to dip in hot mustard sauce, barbeque pork, fried won ton with a sweet red sauce and foil-wrapped chicken. Once in a while, the waiters would encourage trying something new, like bitter melon with beef, boiled chicken with ginger, green onion and salt dipping sauce and Chinese long beans or short beans, whatever was available in season, or written in Chinese for native speakers.

After the lunch rush, the cooks prepared a family meal or sat in the dining room and made won ton, the blur of their hands so fast your eyes could barely adjust to the action before they were on to the next one.

Leo Dabaghian ate there often. "I enjoyed it for its simple peasant food. They didn't have shark fin's soup and deer tendon, shrimp with walnut sauce and other more aristocratic dishes. No fish tanks with fresh catfish, mussels or oysters. Just incredibly substantial, tasty, satisfying and affordable, real working-class food. Frankly, I've never tasted better barbeque pork anywhere."

Gai Lan (Chinese Broccoli)

Courtesy Joy Gee

10 ounces Chinese broccoli (gai lan)
1 teaspoon salt
1 slice ginger (about ½-inch thick)
Sauce:
3 tablespoons chicken broth or water
2 tablespoons oyster sauce
1 tablespoon Chinese rice wine or dry sherry
½ teaspoon sugar

Wash the broccoli. Cut off any wooden ends, and either keep whole or cut into bite-sized pieces (about 2 inches long). In a large saucepan, add just enough water to cover the broccoli. Add the salt and ginger. Bring to a boil. While waiting, prepare the sauce. Combine the chicken broth or water, oyster sauce, white wine or dry sherry and sugar. Bring to a boil in a small saucepan. Turn the heat down and keep warm while blanching the broccoli. Add the Chinese broccoli to the boiling water. Blanch until the stalks are tender but crisp (3–4 minutes). Drain. Pour the sauce over the broccoli. Toss. Alternatively, you can stir-fry the blanched stalks and sauce. Serve immediately. Serves four.

Fried Won Ton

1 green onion, sliced
1 slice ginger
½ pound ground pork
1 tablespoon soy sauce
1 teaspoon sesame oil
1 egg, lightly beaten
Oil for deep-frying
48 won ton wrappers, or as needed
Water

Mince the ginger. Combine the ground pork with the soy sauce, sesame oil, and green onion. Add the lightly beaten egg. Heat the oil to 375 degrees. Lay a wonton wrapper in front of you. Place a teaspoon of the filling in the middle. Fold up the wonton in a triangle and twist the ends toward each other. Deep-fry the wontons in batches until they are golden brown, turning to make sure they brown evenly. Drain on paper towels. Serve with sweet and sour sauce.

REFLECTIONS ON FUJI SUKIYAKI

By Scott Burns

Before the 1880s, there were few Japanese in Sacramento, as the Japanese government did not allow labor immigration until 1884, when our two governments reached an agreement on quotas. Sacramento's first Japanese boardinghouse, the Tamagawa Inn, opened in 1891, offering possibly the first Japanese food in a public establishment. By 1920, 5,800 Japanese residents lived throughout the county, the second-largest in the state, living in the West End or the towns of Florin, Perkins, Mayhew or Sutterville. On the eve of World War II, Japantown centered in the vicinity of Fourth and M Streets, and it supported a commercial hub of nearly five hundred Japanese-owned businesses; a neighborhood of family homes and boardinghouses; and Buddhist, Methodist, Baptist and Tenrikyo churches. One of the landmarks was the Buddhist Church of

Sacramento, founded in 1899, at 1221 Third Street—the second-oldest Jodo Shinshu Buddhist Temple in the United States. The church quickly outgrew its capacity and moved to 410 O Street the next year, where it remained until 1958. That is when it and Japanese businesses that had reopened after their owners returned from internment faced the second diaspora of Sacramento's downtown redevelopment project. The church moved to its present site at 2401 Riverside Boulevard. The church's annual Japanese Food and Cultural Bazaar, entering its sixty-sixth year at the time of this writing, introduced many Sacramentans to their first tastes of teriyaki, tempura and sushi or sashimi.

But if you wanted to try Sukiyaki, Bata-Yaki, Shabu-Shabu or other traditional Japanese dishes, you had to leave the festival and walk down the alley to Fuji Sukiyaki, located at 2422 Thirteenth Street, the building now occupied by Iron Steaks.

Most people knew it simply as Fuji, but Fuji Sukiyaki was the name and its signature dish. For the uninitiated who have never had a Japanese meal that wasn't served grilled, barbequed or raw, Sukiyaki consists of thinly sliced meat, usually beef but sometimes pork or chicken, that is slowly cooked with vegetables in a broth of soy sauce, sugar and mirin. It is served in a shallow iron or steel pan and traditionally accompanied by a beaten raw egg used for dipping. Bata-Yaki and Shabu-Shabu are first cousins. For Bata-Yaki, just add a heart-healthy ⅓ cup of butter to the broth and stir-fry instead of simmer. (Don't cook away the broth!)

Some menu-challenged diners mistakenly called for Butter-Yaki. Fuji didn't object; it was clear what you wanted. Shabu-Shabu was similar in composition, but the meat and vegetables were brought fresh to your table with a pot of seasoned broth and dipping sauces. You could cook your own meal at your own pace. (The name Shabu-Shabu is an onomatopœia, derived from the sound made when the ingredients are swished around in the cooking pot.)

That was another reason for going to Fuji: the pace. It was leisurely. That may be because many of Fuji's hostesses and waitresses wore traditional kimonos and geta (wooden sandals). The kimonos were elegant; the geta failed every OSHA regulation on the books. (That's OSHA as in Occupational Health and Safety Administration, not OSHI as in Oshitashi—a cold spinach appetizer you could order on the side.) It's hard to rush customers in and out when your staff is setting the slow example by serving them with baby-steps.

Many of the customers were regulars and had their own assigned waitresses. Chiziko was so attuned to my dining habits that she not only knew what I wanted depending upon the night of the week or the occasion but also whom I was supposed to be with. One time she refused to serve me because I dared show up with a woman who she knew was not my partner at the time. I got back to Chiziko's good graces when my partner explained to her on our next visit that it was ok for to me have "lady-friends" as long as the meal was all we shared.

With the advent of the great sushi/sashimi boom in the 1980s, Fuji remodeled to a much larger two-story structure and added a bar, an upstairs special event room and three sushi chefs. (Premiere Sacramento chef Buu "Billy" Ngo, now owner of the Kru Japanese Cuisine at 2516 J Street, got his start as a Fuji busboy and later a sushi apprentice.) You could still order the classics, but the more contemporary grilled and raw dishes that now dominate Sacramento's Japanese cuisine became the focus and Fuji had stiff competition from the newer and trendier establishments.

Fuji closed in 2004 or 2005. Its three soupy specialties are still served in some of Sacramento's remaining Japanese restaurants but typically as a nod to tradition and not as the pride of the menu. (An exception is the venerable Nagato Sukiyaki, now Sacramento's oldest Japanese restaurant, at 2820 Marconi Avenue.) Alan Honda's Megami Bento-Ya, at 1010 Tenth Street, still serves Bata-Yaki, but it is rarely ordered as customers flock instead to the more familiar grilled items and sushi/sashimi. Two relative newcomers have recently reintroduced Shabu-Shabu to Sacramento cuisine—Heat Shabu Baru, 2416 Eighteenth Street, and Shabu Japanese Fondue, 1730 16th Street. Fuji traditionalists probably cringe at hearing the dish described as a "fondue", but if marketing can bring this traditional tasty treat back to Sacramento, who are we to argue?

SHABU SHABU
Courtesy of Elaine Nakamoto

1 head Napa Cabbage, in bite-size pieces
2 leeks, cut in 2-inch diagonal pieces

8 shitake mushrooms
2 carrots cut into 2-inch diagonal pieces
Konbu (seaweed)
8 cups of water
1 pound rib eye steak, sliced thin
Ponzu or sesame sauce

Cut the vegetables into bite-size pieces. Boil the water and put Konbu into the pot. Attractively assemble the meat on a tray. Assemble the vegetables on a separate tray. If you have a Shabu Shabu pot, add the broth. Everyone can then add their own vegetables and beef and cook to their liking. Dip cooked beef into a ponzu or sesame sauce. Good ones are available in Asian markets, or there are excellent recipes on the Internet.

DUNLAP'S DINING ROOM AND THE ZANZIBAR

The history of African Americans in Sacramento begins like it does for many others who came when gold was discovered in the foothills of the Sierra Nevada.

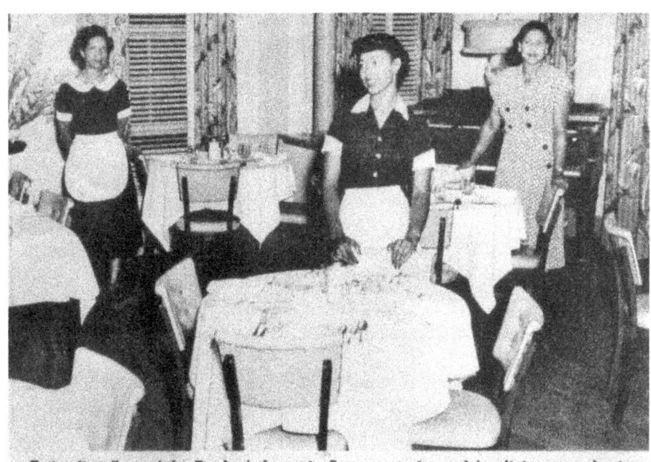

Entire first floor of the Dunlap's home in Sacramento is used for dining room busines
The Dunlap's daughter, right, is dining room hostess. She also supervises help an
manages business. Dining room has normal seating capacity of eighty-five. Has equi
ment to serve five hundred.

DUNLAP'S DINING ROOM SERVES EXCLUSIVE CLIENTEL IN SACRAMENTO

Dunlap's Dining Room was open for thirty-eight years. Owned by a prominent African American family, it catered to a white clientele. *Center for Sacramento History.*

Some came on their own as freemen. Others, enslaved, accompanied their white owners. Whether slave or free, their motivation remained the same, according to historian Clarence Caesar. In a documentary hosted on KVIE, he said, "Like others who made their way here, African Americans had the idea or the inspiration to get rich quick, to be able to find enough gold to do what they wanted to do economically, financially, and socially, which in many cases meant becoming rich enough, if you were a slave for instance, to buy your freedom or the freedom of relatives or if you were a freeman to be able to have enough of a stake in your society to be able to purchase property back east."

Many found jobs as porters, cooks or waiters in local hotels. In 1853, there were 338 black residents and 51 of them were listed as cooks. The St. George was particularly open to hiring blacks, as was the Orleans. They also found jobs in boardinghouses that catered to blacks.

In the first decades of the twentieth century, the African American population remained small. "While they usually found steady work in blue-collar jobs, a significant number of African Americans opened their own businesses catering to a diverse clientele. There were simply not enough black customers to keep them afloat," said Caesar. "It wasn't until the war when McClellan Air Force Base, Mather Air Force Base, Beale and all the local military facilities in and around northern California attracted large numbers of African Americans that the population swelled," he continued.

Among the best-known spots was Dunlap's. The Dunlap family had been a part of Sacramento since the 1850s, when Isaiah Dunlap came for the gold and stayed. George Dunlap, Isaiah's son, was born in Sacramento in February 1884.

He built a house in Oak Park in 1907, as a wedding gift to his wife, Annie Louise, when the property nearby was still mostly strawberry fields. After the birth of their first daughter, Audrey, in 1908 and second child, Doris, in 1912, the house was expanded to eight rooms. George was successful, and they could afford the improvements. He had worked his way up to chef on Southern Pacific's dining cars.

He began a private catering venture and operated restaurants in downtown Sacramento. Mrs. Dunlap worked with him, catering out of their home.

In 1917, he contracted to operate Dunlap's Cafeteria at the California State Fair every summer. In 1919, he got the contract for the food concession stand for the Sacramento Northern Short Line, which merged with Western Pacific Railroad in 1927.

The Depression changed everything. Western Pacific gave notice that Dunlap's food service contract might not be renewed. Annie Louise suggested they open a "tea room" in their house, inspired by travels in the South with George. Annie Louise's vision and culinary talent combined with his food service experience provided the perfect combination. On March 29, 1930, they served their first meal.

Dunlap's Dining Room quickly became a Sacramento landmark, famed for its fine food, gracious hospitality and homey atmosphere. It attracted the capital's movers and shakers, where politicians like Governor Earl Warren could relax and enjoy a good home-cooked meal.

There was no printed menu. George and Annie Louise provided three options: chicken, fried or smothered; baked ham, served with candied yams; and T-bone steak, served with a pin-wheel fried potato. A fritter or a dish of green vegetables was served on the side.

Audrey served as hostess, and Doris and two cousins, Margaret and Alberta Butler, waitressed. If they needed extra hands, they hired neighborhood kids.

For young women like Maria Postman, "it was like being invited to eat in someone's home. The kind of place that taught you the social graces, how to handle a fork, sit up straight, keep your napkin on your lap and delicately wipe crumbs from your lips."

Dunlap's Dining Room served a white clientele, while Dunlap's Cafeteria, at the California State Fair, served all comers.

Maria's husband, Mike, who worked summers at the state fair, remembers, "Dunlap's Cafeteria was the only place that blacks and whites could sit side by side to enjoy the Dunlaps' incredible food. In those days, whites wouldn't frequent a place with a mostly black clientele, at least [not] one that didn't offer music."

Caesar concurs. "Blacks didn't feel comfortable eating at Dunlap's—in fact, George Dunlap actively discouraged blacks from eating there. He'd allow them to use the banquet room for special occasions when the Dining Room wasn't open."

After thirty-eight successful years in operation, the Dunlaps discontinued serving meals in 1968. The house sat empty for almost twenty years. The property was placed on the National Register of Historic Places in 1992. Audrey decided to donate the house and its contents to the city. In 1995, the Sacramento History Museum in Old Sacramento opened an exhibit that re-created the small, homey restaurant. Visitors can still view the original rose dining room, chairs, place settings and even the registration book—a tribute to the Dunlap family's contribution to Sacramento's restaurant history.

Club Zanzibar

William Burg wrote in his book, *Sacramento's K Street, Where Our City Was Born*, "In the 20's Jazz was wild and disobedient music, considered to be responsible for the downfall of American morals. In the 1950's Jazz was the one place that people of all color could come together to enjoy a camaraderie not possible elsewhere."

Club Zanzibar, located at 530 M Street, was one of many Sacramento jazz clubs located in the old West End in the 1940s and 1950s. Owned by William C. "Nits" Jackson and Isaac and Louise Anderson, during the almost-decade it was open, it boasted one of Sacramento's first interracial clienteles, fine dining, fried chicken and other southern fare and quality entertainment. Louis Armstrong and Dizzy Gillespie were known to participate in informal Sunday afternoon jam sessions at the club with local musicians, a widespread practice among jazz musicians of the period. The area attracted other big names in jazz and blues. Billie Holiday, Cab Calloway and Duke Ellington played in clubs nearby.

Club Zanzibar closed in 1949 after state liquor control officials revoked the club's liquor license amid rumors of prostitution. Many African Americans

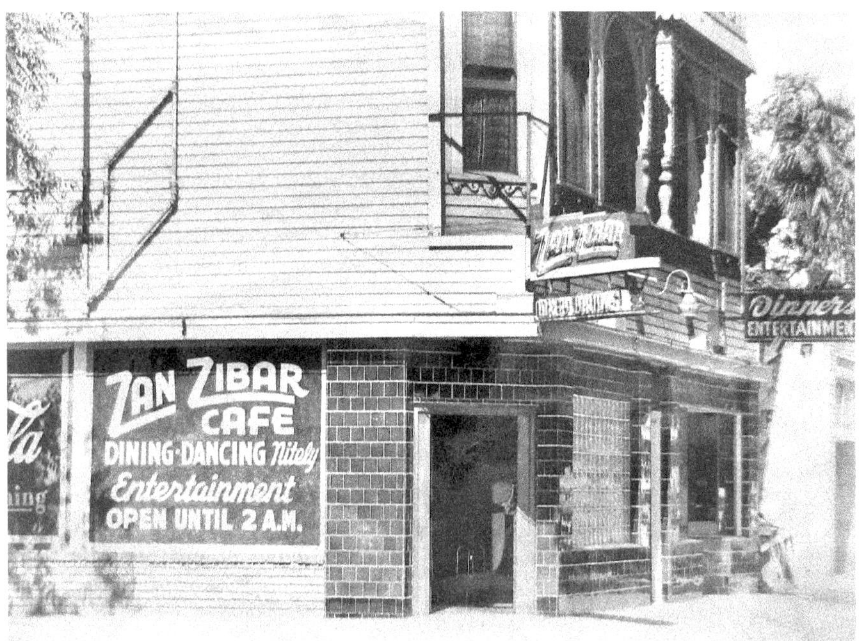

The Zanzibar Night Club offered integrated eating, dining and dancing. *Author's collection.*

who lived in the area at the time disputed the allegations. "Despite its controversial demise," Clarence Caesar says, "the social and cultural impact of the Club Zanzibar remains an intriguing story within the larger cultural and ethnic history of Sacramento."

HOME-STYLE FRIED CHICKEN
Courtesy of Rose Burns

2½-to 3-pound frying chicken, cut into pieces
Crisco (enough to have the chicken pieces completely submerged in it)
½ cup flour
Blended seasonings including garlic powder, onion powder, paprika, salt and pepper
Salt and freshly ground black pepper to taste

Wash the chicken thoroughly and pat the pieces dry with paper towels. Heat the Crisco to 350 F in a heavy cast-iron skillet. Place remaining ingredients in a brown paper bag and shake to mix well. Then, add the chicken pieces a few at a time and shake to ensure that each piece is well coated with the mix. Place the chicken pieces in the skillet and fry, uncovered, for 8 minutes, turning as the chicken browns. Check for doneness by pricking the chicken with a fork. The juices should run clear with no trace of blood. Remove and drain on paper towels. Serve hot, warm, or room temperature.

THE MEXICAN INFLUENCE

Ernesto Galarza, author of *Barrio Boy*, moved to Sacramento in 1910. He describes the population near the boardinghouse he lived in as a mix of ethnicities that included Mexican, Japanese, Chinese, African American, Filipino and Indian. Food connected them in ways that nothing else could. Although Mexican food was always a popular street food, Mexican restaurants were not part of the mainstream until the mid-fifties. Socorro Zuniga, a Sacramento artist, explains: "We didn't eat out in restaurants. We

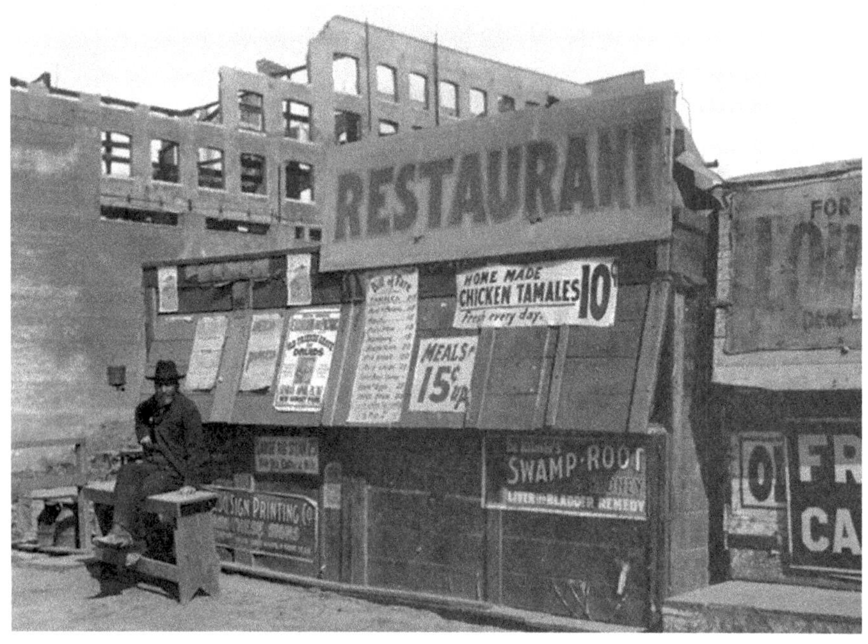

Tamale vendors sold their wares on Sacramento's streets long before they were popularized at the 1893 World's Columbian Exhibition. *Author's collection.*

didn't have to. Our mothers were great cooks. Besides, they tore down all of our restaurants when they leveled skid row in the West End."

At the end of the nineteenth century, there was one item that crossed cultures, and that was tamales.

John Sutter enjoyed tamales when he visited Monterey. His cooks served a dish to visitors at Hock Farm, possibly a precursor to tamale pie. By the 1880s, tamale vendors, mostly men, plied their wares to workers on the night shift or revelers coming home from a night of drinking at the corner tavern.

The tamale business was not entirely a Hispanic pursuit. Portuguese, English and German surnames surface in newspaper articles and police blotter reports. Some children as young as eight or nine were caught selling tamales, and the adults were reprimanded for flouting existing child labor laws.

On April 9, 1887, the *Pacific Rural Press* gave an account of the history of the tamale, how they were sold and how they were to be eaten. We've abridged it, slightly.

> *Most Americans like the tamale from the start. When properly made it is a most satisfying dish for a midnight lunch. The tamales, all hot and*

steaming, are placed in baskets, covered up with cloths and napkins, to retain the heat, and peddled about the streets like hot corn. The peddler, generally a Mexican, carries with him a few plates and knives and forks. His customer seats himself wherever he can find a place to sit down; on a chair in a saloon, or on a box or the edge of the sidewalk out of doors, a napkin is spread on his knees, the plate and knife and fork placed thereon, and the table is set. The Mexican then cuts one end of the cornshuck envelope and taking hold of the other shakes the tamale out upon the customer's plate. He then patiently stands by until the tamale is devoured, when he "clears up the table," packs his dishes into his basket, hangs the basket upon his arm, and strides away with a cry of "Ta ma-a-l-e!" that rings for blocks thereafter.

On April 29, 1890, the *Sacramento Daily Union* posted a story from a horseracing reporter, in Sacramento to cover the California State Fair.

One peculiarly deep-rooted Sacramento habit is tamale peddling. Without tamales Sacramento apparently would be lost. "No sooner do the shades of night cast their dusky mantles over the bosky streets," as either Lord Byron or Bill Nye remarks, then, armed with a pail filled with sections of cold deceased hens stuffed with sand, garlic and sand, a misty lantern, chiefly serviceable to make the darkness darker, a large percentage of the lesser Castilian property-owners of Sacramento, shuffle around the streets (and the less frequented they are the more the tamale fiends seem to like it), and snuffle in husky growls "tamal," "tamalees," "tamalyes," "tomla," "taml" and such other changes on the original word as their fancy dictates.

This is kept up until fully daybreak, when the tamale army reluctantly goes home to manufacture a new load for the next night. Although even in the recollection of the oldest inhabitant no one has ever been seen to buy tamales, the business seems to have such a fascination that once engaged in it only the grave can break it up. It is, however, suggested that the tamale-habit victims are paid not to howl out in certain portions of the city, and in this manner are rapidly making fortunes.

The *Sacramento Daily Union* also reported on the first "canned" tamales in January 1898. W.D. Stalker sent a friend in New York two cans of Sacramento tamales, as he wanted it to be known that "the tamale is capable of being canned, just like other fruit." The friend requested another one hundred pounds put up in cans to be sent to Florida for the enjoyment of friends yachting.

There were many humorous episodes reported in newspapers, but none so egregious as the close call of a man who chose death rather than eat them. The *Daily Union* headline of February 13, 1906, blared: "WOULD RATHER DIE THAN EAT TAMALES. Blacksmith Refuses to Let Mexican Force Meal Down His Throat."

By 1896, the tamale had gone mainstream and was sold in restaurants designated for that purpose. The Tortola Café and Capitola Tamales offered "chicken Spanish, beans Spanish, and other Spanish dishes." The Capitola, at Ninth and L Streets, boasted of an experienced Spanish cook, whose "frijoles, enchiladas, chili con carne, tortillas as well as tamales and chicken Spanish, all nutritious and healthfully stimulating," would be served day and night.

The Capitol Tamale Café was the favorite of state lawmakers and other political figures. On April 17, 1917, on the day the United States entered World War I, Ciro Ferrera and his son-in-law O.F. Barbaria opened a tamale house on Eighth Street between K and L Streets. Both men had been employed in tamale cafes, and they thought they could improve the product. They thought other Mexican food was too hot for the average customer and decided to tone it down. They allegedly sold the recipe for their sauce to Hormel, which used it in the company's canned mini-tamales. It remained a popular restaurant for decades before a fire, possibly arson, closed it down.

Sorry, We're Closed

What keeps me motivated is not the food itself but all the bonds and memories the food represents.
—Michael Chiarello

Employment was at an all-time high. Hope soared, and money flowed. By the mid-1950s, most families could afford a television, a trip to a downtown movie house and an occasional visit to a neighborhood eatery. By the 1960s, Mom went back to work, Julia Child popularized food television and we put a man on the moon and moved out to the suburbs. Still, most people rarely ate out for dinner.

However, the Coral Reef, Aldo's, Ken's Red Barn, Buggy Whip, Scheidel's Bavaria, Chuck Wagon, Wulff's, Palomino Room, Golden Tee, Ram, Rosemount Grill and a handful of others brought in droves for special occasions.

Samuel Nolan, in an article in *Gourmet* in 1952 wrote, "We remember certain restaurants not because of the food, or the taste, or the ambience of the room, or convenience, or any of the 20 reasons people list for choosing a place to eat. We remember the places we have a strong emotional tie to, where we had our first date, proposed to our wife, or experienced our first taste of something exotic. We celebrate the moment, not the place, but the place and moment are intertwined forever."

Aldo's

Aldo's, in Town and Country Village, an elegant dining establishment, served haute cuisine, vintage wines and classical music to a loyal following.

Almost any given night, it was *the* place for romantic interludes, celebrating business deals over fine wine and brandy or breaking into an impromptu aria around Mario Ferrari's grand piano. It was where most Sacramentans of a certain generation were introduced to fine dining.

Aldo's was owned by longtime restaurant pioneers Italian-born Aldo Bovero and Paris-trained chef Paul Coulat. After apprenticing in his native Nesteier, France, Coulat fled into the Pyrenees when World War II turned Europe upside down. He continued his culinary education by working in

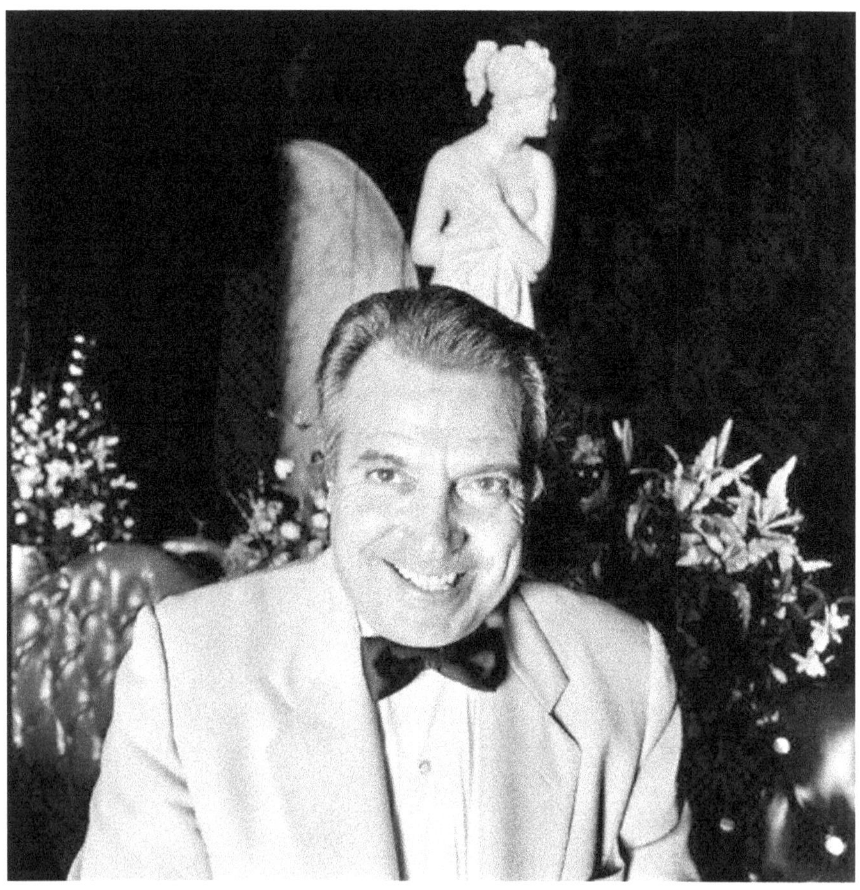

Aldo Bovero was the maître d' and the face of his restaurant, though Paul Coulat, the chef, should receive more of the credit. *Center for Sacramento History.*

hotel kitchens in France, New York and San Francisco. Aldo's parents ran a small restaurant in Turin. At thirteen, he quit school and, soon after, his parents' small restaurant to begin apprenticing in hotels, eventually finding his way to Sacramento.

Maryann Burk Carver, a cocktail waitress and hostess, in her memoir, *What It Used to Be Like: A Portrait of My Marriage to Raymond Carver*, shares some of her experiences at Aldo's.

"They operated two dining establishments in one building, prior to opening Aldo's. The Pine Cone served unexceptional American fare while the Flambé Room had truly gourmet, French-inspired cuisine. The two couldn't wait to get out of their contract for the Pine Cone and concentrate on perfecting classic, intimate dining."

Aldo, ever the consummate showman, prepared flambé dishes, steak Diane, crepes Suzette, cherries jubilee and other specialties.

They understood the risk they took by moving so far away from the city center into an area that was farmland just a few years earlier. Nevertheless, they created an elegant place with a menu rich with silky sauces, escargot, Tournedos de Rossini, Lobster Thermidor and flambés.

Aldo, urbane and genteel, escorted guests to their table, freshly set each day with cut flowers. His quiet but firm hand silently directed formally attired waiters to provide fresh silver for each course and brush off table crumbs using a sterling silver brush and crumb tray.

Waiter Pete Vereschzagin would roll a flambé cart tableside, brandishing copper skillets and the ingredients for linguine à la vongole, medallions of veal au champagne, crepes aux framboises and other specialties de maison, all ignited in a flurry of wine and fire.

After twenty years of backbreaking work and hot kitchens, Paul Coulat, eager to satisfy his appetite for hunting and fishing, retired. Coulat's successor, Tom Forsea, lightened the cuisine, adding more fish and lighter pastas. A few years later, Pete Vereschzagin left to purchase Jim Ford's hamburger business.

In 1999, Aldo sold the business to chef John Jacobs and signed on at the Sutter Club. Jacobs couldn't make a go of it and closed shortly afterward.

Myron Owen was a busboy at Aldo's in the late '60s. He watched in the summer of 2012 when they bulldozed the restaurant, which had experienced a number of incarnations but none as endearing or unforgettable as the original.

"Aldo's was the last of them," he sighed. "Where can you go today where the waiter wears a tuxedo and they send you home if you aren't wearing a tie?"

L'Escalopine De Veau Au Champagne

8 thinly sliced veal pieces (3 ounces each)
Salt and white pepper
¼ stick of butter
1 minced shallot
8 ounces sliced mushrooms
½ cup dry white wine (chardonnay)
1 cup heavy cream, warmed
Fresh parsley, finely chopped
2 tomatoes cut in half and broiled
2 dozen Parisienne potatoes, roasted
12 asparagus spears, cooked and cut in half

Place veal between waxed paper. Pound veal slices with the smooth side of a meat tenderizer. Season with salt and pepper. Dust with flour. Sauté in butter two minutes on each side. Remove. Place on a serving platter to keep warm. Add shallot and mushroom to pan for a minute. Add wine and deglaze the plan over high heat. Add warmed cream, let simmer for 5 minutes. Remove. Place veal escalopes on the serving platter. Lap with the reserved sauce and sprinkle with parsley. Lay on top of asparagus spears. Garnish with broiled tomatoes and roasted potatoes.

The Ram

The Ram, steeped in tradition, was a popular spot for the lunch crowd and the after-work drinking crowd and was still romantic enough for a date. When Richard Hart opened in 1957, everyone thought he was crazy. He was—crazy like a fox, anticipating the growing population shift away from downtown and out to the suburbs.

The dinner menu was eclectic, served with a tureen of soup, a salad and sheepherder bread. Entrees might include a Basque goulash, prime rib, Petrale sole and a smattering of pasta dishes. Duck hunters could bring in their catches, and the cooking staff would clean, gut and cook them. A few hunters couldn't stand to eat the animal they killed, so if timing was right, other patrons could share in their bounty.

In the 1970s, Hart sold out, and a little while later, Dick Love took over. He maintained quality and also offered escargot, oysters and seafood cocktails to accompany a martini.

"The Ram offered my boyfriend and I champagne with dinner, when we were sixteen," Gail Robbin reminisced. "My boyfriend was in a tux. I was wearing a long evening dress, so it should have been obvious we weren't twenty-one. When the waiter took our order, he asked if we wanted a drink. We looked at each other and thought, 'Why not!' Halfway through dinner my mother came in and began taking photos. I was so embarrassed I started to cry. The waiter came over and asked if something was wrong. I told him my mother had ruined my junior prom dinner. He looked at me and said, 'I guess the next drinks are on the house!'"

Rosemount Grill

Time stood still at the Rosemount Grill. From one decade to the next, it looked and felt the same—wooden booths with white curtains for privacy, a hook for a gentleman to hang his hat, fresh linens, polished silverware, waitresses in black and white uniforms and a menu that reflected the past.

Peter Valerio, George Lucich and Joe Ostoja opened a lunchroom in 1915 at Ninth Street and Annex Lunch, down the street. They developed a menu reflective of the time, serving milk toast, tongue, Boiled Beef Spanish, steak, hearty soups, chops, oysters and a full bar. It attracted crowds of businessmen at lunch, ladies shopping and couples and families for dinner and after the theater.

In 1945, the proprietors moved to 3145 Folsom Boulevard, and their patrons moved with them. John Neumann ate at the original, the Folsom location and Andiamo, which took over the spot when the Rosemount Grill closed. He remembered:

> *It was Sacramento's signature restaurant. Everyone ate there, as much for tradition as for food. Often four generations would eat together. The menu went on for pages! Red Jello for dessert, tapioca pudding, Hangtown Fry, pot roast, meatloaf, fresh turkey with mashed potatoes and gravy, a corned beef sandwich. Felt like tea? It came with a sterling silver pot. They'd add*

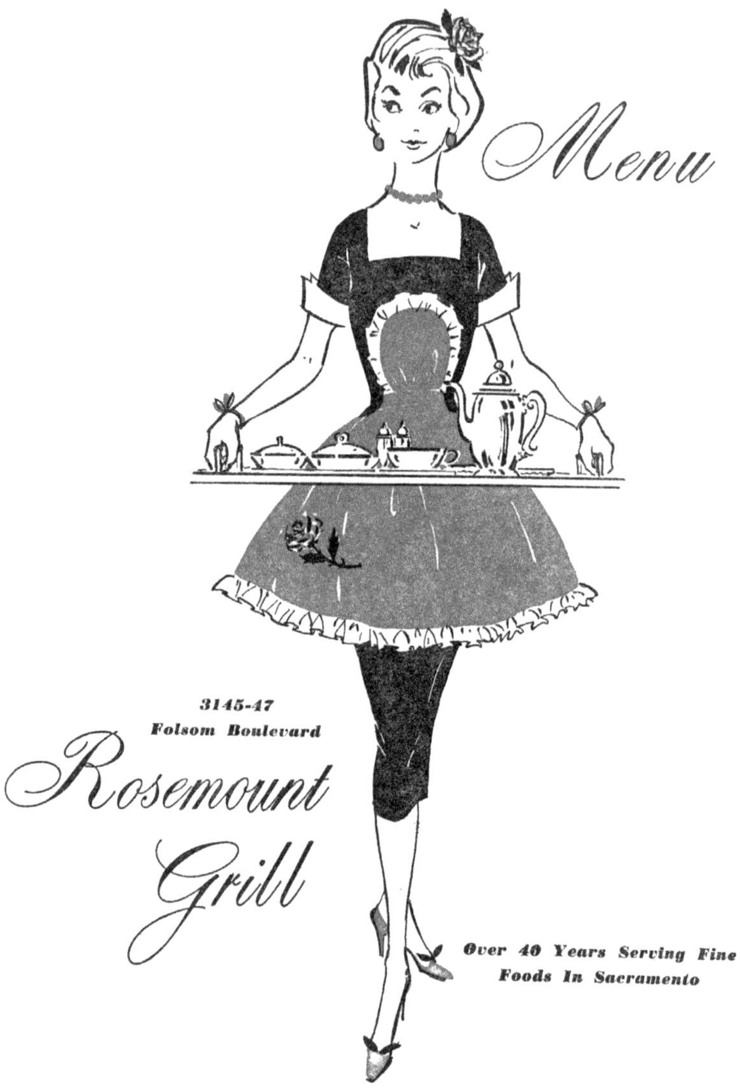

The Rosemount Grill lasted seventy-five years. For those who thought it never changed, this menu proves it did…just a little. *Sacramento Public Library.*

> *items but never eliminate any, so old folks would come and order the same thing they had as children. Every bite was a memory.*

Neumann also explains why he thinks it closed down so suddenly. "Pete Valerio had passed, and his daughter, I think, tried to take over. Problem was, Pete's best customers had died before him. People saw the place as quaint. Patronage had plummeted. The menu was behind the times. There were hundreds of options for where to spend your money eating out, and it was old school. I guess it was just time for school to let out."

TURKEY RICE SOUP

2 tablespoons olive oil
½ onion, finely chopped
1 large carrot, grated
2 ribs celery, chopped
4 cups turkey broth
¼ teaspoon dried thyme
1 bay leaf
½ cup white rice
2 cups leftover turkey, chopped
Salt and pepper, to taste

In a medium soup pot, heat oil over medium heat. Add onion, carrot and celery and cook until onions become soft and translucent. Add turkey broth, thyme, bay leaf, rice and turkey. Bring to a boil and simmer for ½ hour to 1 hour until the rice is cooked through. Season to taste with salt and pepper.

BUGGY WHIP

The Buggy Whip was always a sure bet. An old-school steak house when it opened at the end of the Eisenhower administration, it took on the swagger of the Mad Men and Rat Pack era but, unlike its patrons, never seemed to grow older.

Old friends—and we do mean *old* friends—would meet once a week for lunch. It was the place for Valentine's dinner, family reunions or company banquets.

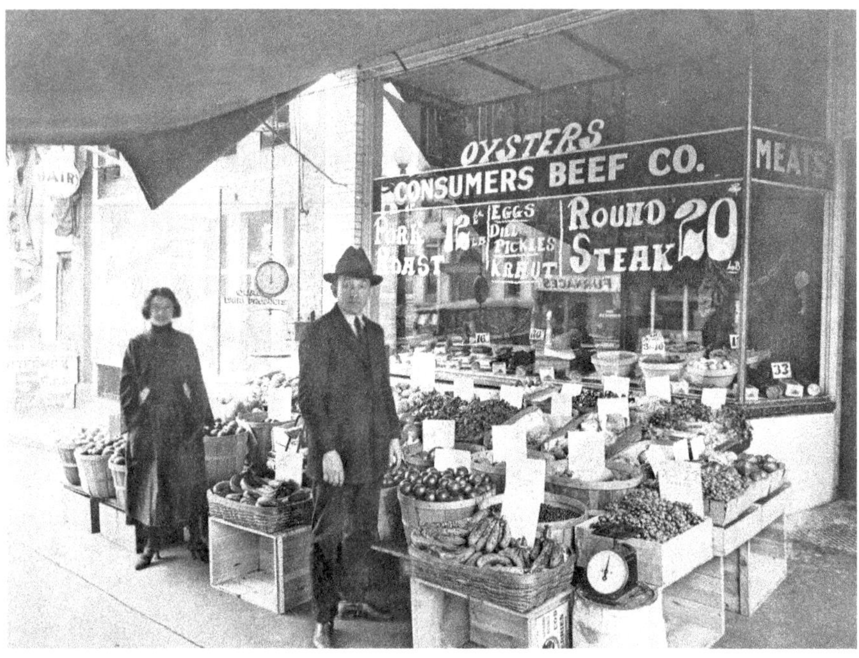

Grocery stores sold oysters in the shell, take-out chowders and stews and supplied local restaurants including the Annex, another Peter Valerio restaurant. *Author's collection.*

John Hull used to frequent the place when Aaron LeSieur had owned a French restaurant at the same location. "I think he knew that type of cooking was coming to an end. He predicted a direct reproach of Rosemount Grill–style dining with its page upon page of food selections. He knew the only way to survive was to close the old place and create something new, so he added some investors with the idea of opening a classic steakhouse."

One investor was Joe "Torchy" Torchia, a well-known gambler and horse race bookie who, at twenty-nine, wanted to go legit. He jumped in feet first, taking on some of the day-to-day management. The partners couldn't agree on a name. Joe suggested the Buggy Whip, based on the crop jockeys used to spur horses to run faster in harness races.

Tony Tripodi, Joe's half-brother, tells the story in his book *Requiem for Torchy: The Life of a Gambler*:

> *To increase patronage Joe came up with a gimmick. For $5 he offered a special steak dinner with champagne for 2. He made deals with a butcher & the owner of a liquor store to get steaks and champagne at reduced prices. Huge crowds of people came to the restaurant...looking for a bargain.*

They got what they wanted but had to wait for an hour or more to be served. Naturally they ordered drinks at the bar and profits soared.

To assure customer loyalty, he would invite his favorites for Saturday morning breakfasts of crabmeat and eggs and a quick card game before opening for lunch.

There were rumors that he always "flashed a large wad of cash," but when customers opened up the January 19, 1970 *Sacramento Bee* newspaper they were shocked to read that Joseph J. "Joe" Torchia, forty-one, had been shot to death in a brutal robbery and murder.

His death didn't seem to hurt business. It flourished for another forty years. The place was always packed, the wait staff and hostesses pleasant and the meals top-notch—dry-aged steaks and prime rib. Either because of a need for upgrading or disputes with the union or with the IRS, co-owner Larry LeSieur put up a sign on the door that read, "Remodeling: Closed for repairs. Thank You."

It never reopened.

"THE REEF"

Maleville's Coral Reef served Cantonese and American dishes with a side dish of Polynesia. Paper-wrapped chicken, pineapple spareribs, pressed duck with nuts, shrimp-topped salad, pupu platters, pineapple and bananas and, most say, the best bartenders. In survey after survey, the Coral Reef is Sacramento's most revered lost restaurant.

We asked Tom Tolley, a bartender at "the Reef," as most people refer to it, to share his experiences. He now works at the Sacramento Public Library, in the Sacramento Room. Tom is also co-author of *Images of America: Mather Field* and *Historic Photos of Sacramento* with James Scott, a library colleague.

The Coral Reef was everyone's favorite. It offered good food, was family friendly and the bar had top quality and original ingredients. It was open for forty years, had seven dining rooms and could feed hundreds at a time. John, Edwin and Elwood Maleville, who also owned the Coral Reef Lodge across the street, owned it.

Harry Holland was maître d' when I arrived, a funny old newspaperman, with a prodigious appetite for drink. My first memory of him was before

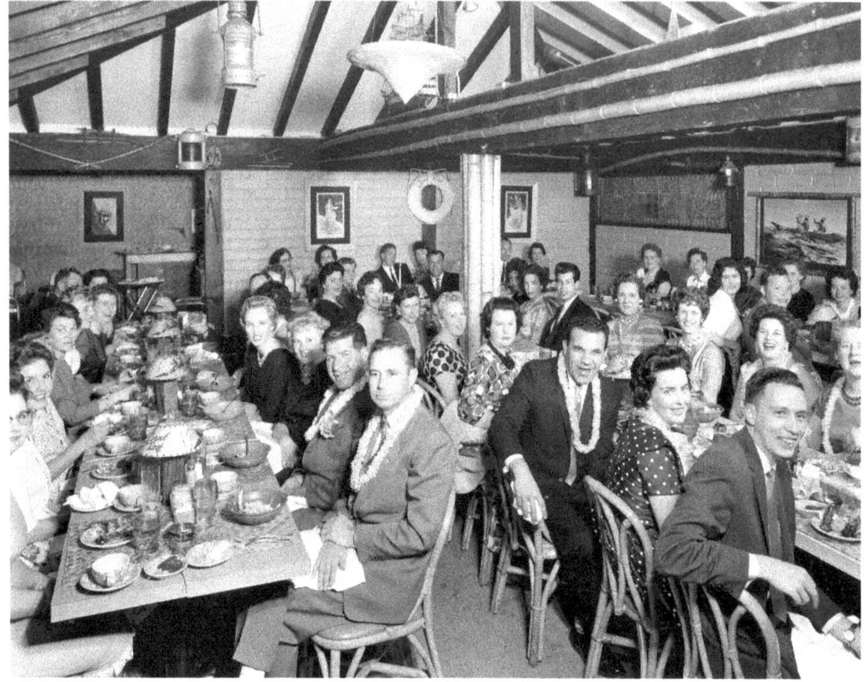

The Coral Reef had seven dining rooms, serving family dining in the Outrigger Room and large banquets in others. *Sacramento Public Library, Sacramento Room.*

I started to work there. My wife and I took her brother for his birthday (I think). I spotted a cockroach crawling along the side of the table. I caught the eye of a busboy and pointed, then he disappeared and Harry showed up at the table. "So, that's where he went to!" Harry said. "Please don't make a big deal out of it, then everyone will want one!"

I had been a fan of the food ever since my folks first brought me there to eat. I always enjoyed watching people react to their meals and surroundings. The place was full of props from the South Seas. Many of the people I served had played their part in the war and were familiar with the locales. There were no New Age folks and few hip people among the older clientele around the Reef. They had all served in World War II or Korea and were at least ten years older than me.

We had a lot of regular diners and drinkers, local celebrities like Betty Vasquez, Creighton Sanders, Tom La Brie and most of the families that settled and invested in the Town and Country/Country Club area, when big bands still played at nightspots later torn down or morphed into restaurants or car dealerships.

Everything came from bottles, no guns or dispensers. We offered a full bar from Pernod to Rock 'n Rye. We'd blend, mix, shake or pour everything from scratch. Mother's Day was one of our biggest, and we sold hundreds of Ramos, Silver or Golden Fizzes with egg white or yolk. We had some bartenders from Hawaii who worked there over the years, including a great guy who was a magician and did tricks at the bar. The most popular drinks were Mai Tai, Planters Punch, Lovers Cups, Singapore Sling and Fizzes for Mothers Day.

We had a lot of car salesmen, just like all the bars and cocktail lounges on Fulton, and they provided some amusement and lively times. Unless they were trying to impress someone, they were not big tippers. The prices for a beer and drink usually provided some wiggle room for a tip, so if a glass of wine or a bottle of beer was under $1 we could expect the small change to find its way into our tip jar, except for them. Some of our favorite ways to mess with the car salesmen was to have a dish of the stuff called "Slime" they sold at Toys R' Us. I'd dip their dime or quarter into the slime and then put it on their cocktail napkin or in the trough in the middle of the bar. A more drastic but equally satisfying way to deal with them was to put a dot of superglue on the back of the coin (usually a dime, change for a bottle of Heineken) and then put it on a napkin or some other surface and watch them try to slide it into their pocket.

The music consisted of a long tape of standard island music that never varied in all the time I worked there. "I want to go back to my little grass shack…" Tiny Bubbles and some tunes that still play a loop through my mind. The music that plays "From Here to Eternity" as Fatso Judson exits the Congress Club to meet his death at the hands of Pruitt is one I heard almost every night for years at the Coral Reef, and whenever that scene plays, I'm a ten-year-old boy watching the movie for the first time.

Pineapple Spare Ribs

2 pounds baby back ribs
1⅓ cups Heinz Ketchup
⅓ cup pineapple juice
⅓ cup molasses
Sliced ginger to flavor
Onion salt, salt and pepper

3 tablespoons soy sauce
1 fresh Hawaiian pineapple cut into rounds, then cubes
2 green peppers diced

Ask butcher to cut baby back ribs in half. Make sauce by heating everything but pineapple and green pepper. When mixed, add cut pineapple, green pepper and stir until well coated. Marinate spareribs in the sauce for at least two hours. Then put a flame under the pan and parboil the ribs for about 10 minutes. Add water if the sauce starts to go dry. Put into a roasting pan and bake in the oven for about 30 minutes. Then place under broil till the top of the ribs are browned.

MAI TAI

1 ounce light rum
½ ounce lime juice
½ ounce orange curacao
½ ounce orgeat syrup
1 ounce dark rum
Maraschino cherry and a paper umbrella for garnish

Pour all the ingredients except the dark rum into a shaker with ice cubes. Shake well. Strain into an old-fashioned glass half filled with ice. Top with the dark rum. Garnish.

AMERICO'S TRATTORIA ITALIANA

In 1977, Paul D'Alessandro and Jackson Leong, longtime friends from high school, opened Americo's Trattoria Italiana at the corner of Twentieth and Capitol and turned Sacramento Italian food on its ear.

Their secret weapon was Paul's family. Paul's mother, Lorraine Perry D'Alessandro, was the restaurant's first hostess. In 1959, she ran Lorraine's, a restaurant and catering business in the Elks Building. She started off small and eventually took over the entire banquet facilities. Her husband, Americo, read cookbooks voraciously and created new dishes for Lorraine to

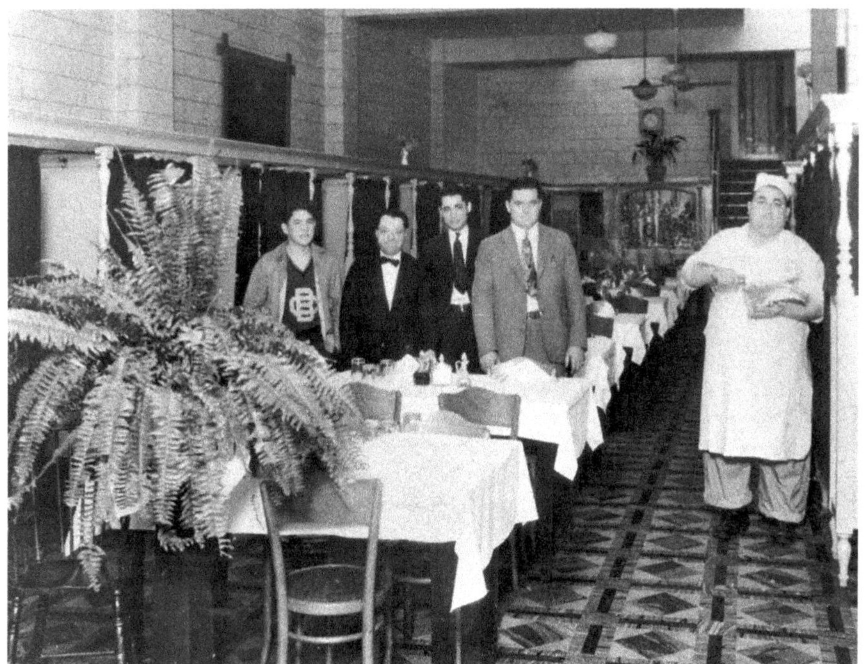

The Da Rosa Dining Room offered fine dining. The D'Alessandro family owned it and the popular Star. *Center for Sacramento History.*

try. "When Jackson was a kid, he always said he wanted to start a restaurant with my father, and he did," said Paul. Americo's father, grandfather and uncle owned the Star and Da Rosa Italian Restaurants, considered among the best in their day.

They envisioned a place that served home-style Italian cuisine at affordable prices. Paul and Jackson poured all their money into it. "I borrowed $5,000 from my parents," Paul said. "Jackson had inherited $5,000. We thought that would do it. It took another $25,000 each and second mortgages. Our friends stopped by to help us after work or took vacations from their jobs to help get it done on time. Without them we could never have afforded to open."

The architect, Rann Haight, was highly sought for his ability to create sophisticated open space. He was also the architect for the arena. "We took over a former machine shop and wanted to keep the high vaulted ceiling. We exposed the ductwork and put in industrial lights and brick partitions. To create warmth, we added lots of greenery, like the inside of a home patio, wood tables and bentwood chairs. Dick Morisawa, a former buddy of ours from high school, painted a surrealistic painting of Jackson as a

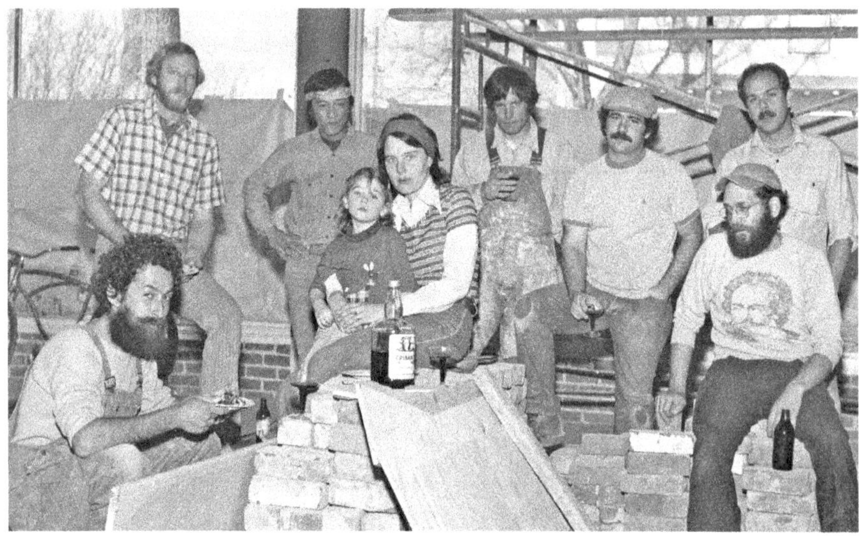

Lines formed to watch construction of Americo's and kept forming to get a table at this authentic Italian—not Italian American—spot. *Courtesy D'Alessandro family.*

contemplative Bacchus on the wall. We put window boxes on the outside. Our auntie planted basil and fresh herbs. Once, a policeman came by, very concerned because it seems there was marijuana growing, too."

They were the first to put calamari fritti and ossi buchi on the menu. The pastas were prepared in a windowed cubicle open to the view of diners. Complete dinners included minestrone; a plate of marinated antipasto with salami, olives, peppers and chickpeas; Muzio bread; and a crisp salad of hand-torn greens, finished with house dressing, a robust and unusually spicy Gorgonzola dressing.

A sizable portion of Americo's menu was devoted to veal, serving ossi buchi con risotto e funghi, veal shanks and saltimbocca alla romano. Desserts included zabaglione freddo; canolo, a rich dense and dark chocolate mousse; and torta sformata al formaggio, their house-made cheesecake.

The signature dish—fettuccini with asparagus, mushrooms and cream sauce, available only for a few months out of the year—was always better somehow when Americo made it. Maurice Read remembers Trish Mori as a particularly attentive and "always perky" waitress. He said the hostess "made you feel at ease even when you had a long wait. There wasn't really a bar, though there was a counter with wine and beer. Jackson Leong tended it, the first place you could order any wine by the glass and to serve real varietals by top-notch wineries."

Lorraine was diagnosed with cancer, Americo started working part time and Paul began dreading the long nights away from his kids. He took a job with a friend. The restaurant continued on for another ten years, even after the deaths of Lorraine and Jackson. When Ed Brown, who owned the adjacent Rubicon Brewing Co., and Chef Rick Mahon took over, they announced there would be no "immediate change in format," but Rick Mahon re-opened with a French country theme and called it the Waterboy, now one of Sacramento's premiere destination restaurants.

Paul missed the restaurant life. He, his daughter, a professional chef who trained at the CIA (Culinary Institute of America), and his wife, Bonnie, now run a restaurant called Tony's on the Lake in Coeur D'Alene, Idaho. The most popular item on their menu is Fettuccini All'Americo. "I guess running a restaurant is just in the blood," Paul says.

Fettuccini All'Americo

Courtesy of Toni D'Alessandro Lane

3 cups heavy cream
1 pound fettuccine
4 cups asparagus (once blanched and cut)
1 tablespoon butter
4 cups sliced mushrooms
4 tablespoons chopped fresh garlic
1 cup grated Parmigiano Reggiano (divided in half)
Salt and pepper to taste

Place cream in a heavy saucepan and bring to a boil. Turn down the heat to a simmer and reduce until thickened. Bring a large pot of water to a boil. Add salt to the water, to taste. Add fettuccine to boiling water, stirring the first few minutes or so to make sure it doesn't stick, and cook until al dente (10-12 minutes). Fill a shallow pan with water, large enough to hold asparagus. Boil. Add asparagus and blanch for about two to three minutes. Take out of water and plunge into a cold bath to keep the green color. Cut into chevrons (diagonal). Melt butter in a sauté pan. Add mushrooms and asparagus, just until hot. Add garlic and take off the fire. Drain pasta. Place in the bowl you plan to serve in the reduced cream. Add Parmesan and season with salt and pepper. Add the drained pasta. Toss. Place sautéed asparagus, mushrooms and garlic on top. Sprinkle with more cheese, salt and pepper.

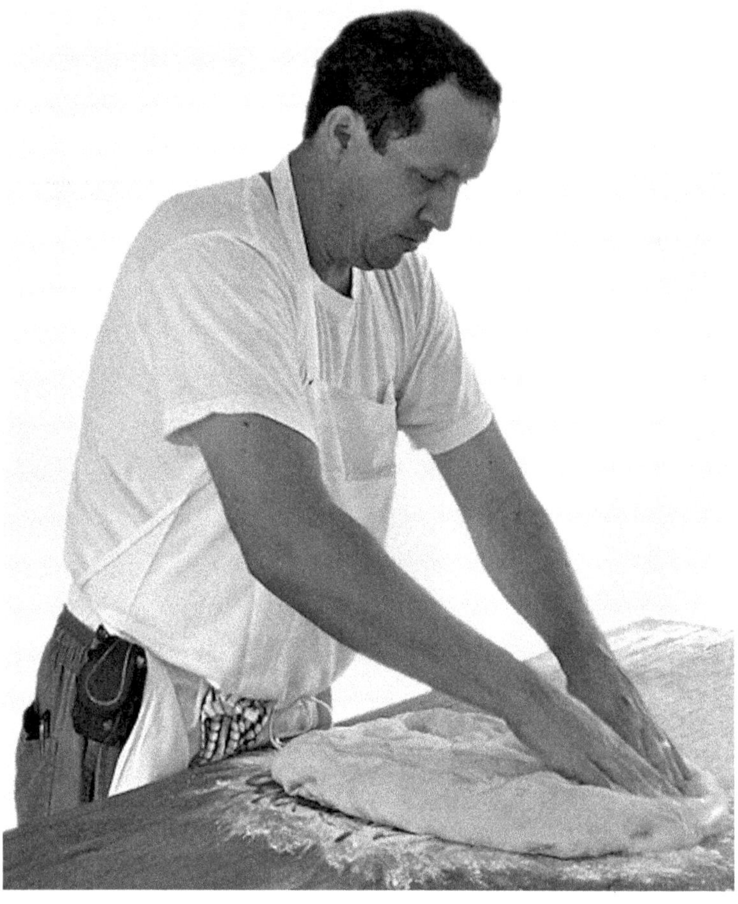

Americo's made its pastas from scratch. Paragary's Bar and Oven introduced wood-burning ovens for pizza. *Author's collection.*

WULFF'S FRENCH COUNTRY RESTAURANT

When Horace and Helen Wulff opened the doors to their French provincial restaurant, it was a breath of fresh air. Wulff's shunned haute cuisine for that of the French countryside. Lit for romance, the cloth and candles, red-tiled floors, tapestries, ladder-backed chairs and a beamed ceiling all contributed to the ambiance of a secluded French village.

Secluded it was, squeezed in behind a Swanson's Dry Cleaner and a power transmission tower.

Avid cooks and travelers, the Wulffs had cooked their way through Julia Child's books and television shows and traveled extensively throughout France. When Horace, an engineer at Aerojet, was laid off during an economic downturn, the decision to open a restaurant was a foregone conclusion.

They hired Chef Ann Shelton, who learned her craft by cooking with her mother, a respected and knowledgeable home cook. Untrained, nevertheless she won a bronze medal in the International Culinary Olympics at Frankfurt in 1980.

Wulff's had a tempting menu including braised duck, grilled lamb chops, sweetbreads, coquilles St. Jacques, filet of sole in almond butter sauce and rabbit in a rich wine sauce. Every meal was preceded by soup du jour and the house salad: butter lettuce topped with bay shrimp and a creamy tarragon, mustard and garlic dressing.

There were many reasons proffered for the decision to close. Horace Wulff said it was just time, as he was nearing seventy. He conceded that French food was going out of style. Not everyone could afford an hour and a half for lunch, and the lunch crowd had diminished.

Joan Alby, a regular, claims, "There isn't a dish Ann made I could recreate at home, even if I had a recipe. Curried lamb with crepes, crème caramel au Grand Marnier with raspberry sauce and especially her Choucroute Garnie. Long before bacon reigned supreme, she added a half cup of pork fat."

"It isn't just Wulff's I miss," she continued. "The Ram, Aldo's, Masque, Chinois East/West, Bon Appetit, Mace's, the Terrace and Lautrec…gone. I'm thankful there is a glimmer of French in Café Rolle and Rick Mahon's Waterboy, but oh how I wish right now for Wulff's pate Maison with coarse rabbit and cornichons."

Wulff's House Dressing

Courtesy of Joan Alby

⅓ cup tarragon vinegar
1 teaspoon salt
½ teaspoon black pepper
½ teaspoon dry mustard

1 teaspoon Worcestershire sauce
1 cup olive oil
1 clove garlic

Mix everything but garlic together. Whisk. Add garlic cloves. Store in refrigerator for at least two hours. Remove garlic cloves before serving. Serve with a salad that has shrimp in it!

Open for Business

Remembrance of things past is not necessarily the remembrance of things as they were.
—Marcel Proust

There is no denying that Sacramento food fashions changed over the years. Oysters, caviar, mussels and lobster used to be poor people's food. Now they're delicacies. In the past, we ate out sparingly, cooking most meals at home. The average Sacramentan now eats out four or five times a week. And 40 percent of the time that meal is eaten in the car or at a fast food establishment.

Since we began writing this book, many of Sacramento's long-established and well-loved restaurants have closed. In fact, we're worried that one or two on our "still around" list might be gone soon.

It's not possible for this book to cover every place that contributed to Sacramento's restaurant scene, or to detail more than a handful of restaurants. Although—nominally—this book is about lost restaurants, there are a few comfortably notable places that have been around for decades, which we just couldn't ignore. Weathered walls, worn floors, old-fashioned décor and time-honored traditions still give us a brief glimpse into the texture, character and life of places we can only mourn.

A RIVER RUNS THROUGH IT

The river's languid flow and a simpler way of life informed the menu of two of the Delta's most idiosyncratic eateries. Both were famous for offering diners a very limited menu. Tony's in Walnut Grove served Chicken Mornay, Veal Mornay and New York steak. Al the Wop's, just down the road in Locke, had four options. Steak—rare, medium rare, medium or well done.

Tony's sides were abundant: baked potato with sour cream and chives, half a loaf of garlic bread, Portuguese beans perfumed with cumin and linguica and a simple side of rice. Al's paired the steak, unadorned, with two thick slices of toasted French bread.

Don Burns, who recently retired from the Sacramento Public Library, reminiscences about working at Tony's circa 1971 and other experiences he had in the Delta.

> *I got a job working at Tony's in 1971, when I was sixteen, because my father was a fishing buddy of the cook, Smokey Dryden. When I was hired, Tony did not like to do W-2 forms, so he says, "Kid, you got a choice. Either I pay you minimum wage or a dime a customer and all the beer you can drink." Well, I took the latter of the two. My dad said, "Well, if you do a man's job, you drink a man's beer." I'm sixteen years old, drinking beer, driving thirty-two miles back to the house, on levee roads in the fog.*
>
> *Tony's was only doing dinners on Saturday and Sunday nights from 4:30 until about 10:30 or as late as midnight, depending on what kind of crowd came in. Tony's only served steaks and veal at a set price of fourteen dollars. The place would only seat about sixty. There were a lot people, when money was more plentiful, who would come up the Delta from the Bay Area and basically use their boats as floating hotels. They would dock on the river. It was only a hundred yards or so over the levee and into Tony's. There were quite a few other restaurants like that but it was always packed.*
>
> *Tony was about 5'6", not a really tall gentleman, but very gracious. Tony loved to come up to tables and ask, "How's your meal?" And then when they were served the entrees, the beans and the rice, he would do this presentation. "Let me show you how it's done. You take a little bit of the rice, and you take a little bit of the beans," and he had this special hot sauce that he cooked himself in the back room and he'd say, "Not one, not two, but three drops." It was almost like a science experiment, and to me, it was like a dinner show. And even though you might have seen him do it thirty times and you were a regular customer, you always played dumb*

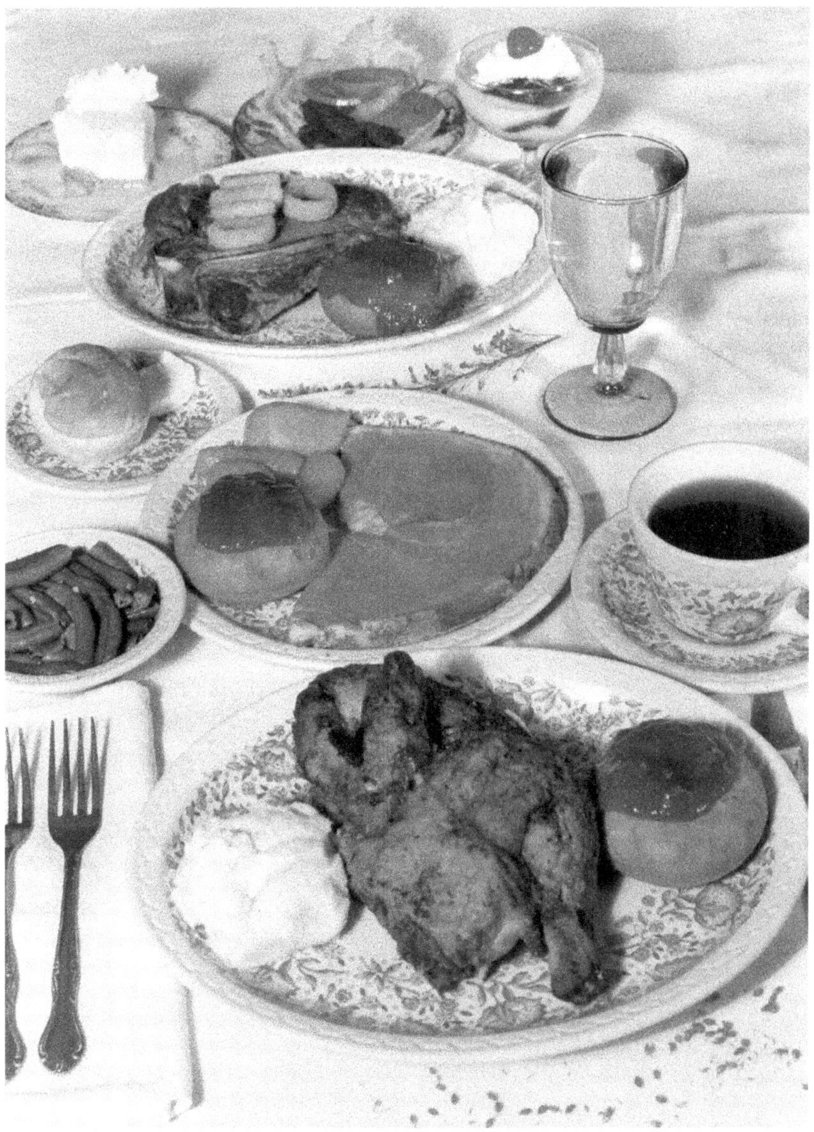

Many restaurants served limited menus. Dunlap's served chicken (smothered or not), ham and steak. *Center for Sacramento History.*

and said, "Tony, how do you make these beans taste so good? What's the combination?" and he would almost do this dance at the table.

Tony was quite a procrastinator. About five years before I started working there in 1971, he put up a Christmas display. There was a little mock chalet roof over the bar, and he had a reindeer and a little snowscape scene, mini-Christmas trees and such, so after Christmas he just left it up all year round.

Well, in the early eighties the famous movie director Rob Reiner was filming a movie at the University of the Pacific in Stockton. Part of the script called for a bar scene at Christmas, so he said, "Hey, not too far from here is a restaurant called Tony's. He's never taken down his Christmas display," so they filmed the inside of this bar scene because they didn't have to redecorate anything. He had movie stills that are printed on 8½-by-11 photopaper on the walls with John Cusack, the lead actor.

Al's Place, aka Al the Wop's

When he opened in 1934, Al Adami was the only white business owner in the Chinese town of Locke. Fresh out of prison (for running illegal hooch and the speakeasy at the Ryde Hotel), he converted a Chinese restaurant to a legal bar. A county ordinance instituted after Prohibition and lasting a few years forbade operating a bar without offering some food. To Al, steak—and only steak—would fit the bill. One night, a local farmer came in with some peanut butter and orange marmalade to complement Al's toasted bread, and it started a tradition.

Today, a jar of peanut butter is on each table. The orange marmalade has morphed to apricot jam. This story, which may be apocryphal, along with one about a trick with a dollar bill, is too good to ignore. Don Burns knows how the dollar bill trick is done. "The thing about Al's is they have dollar bills on the

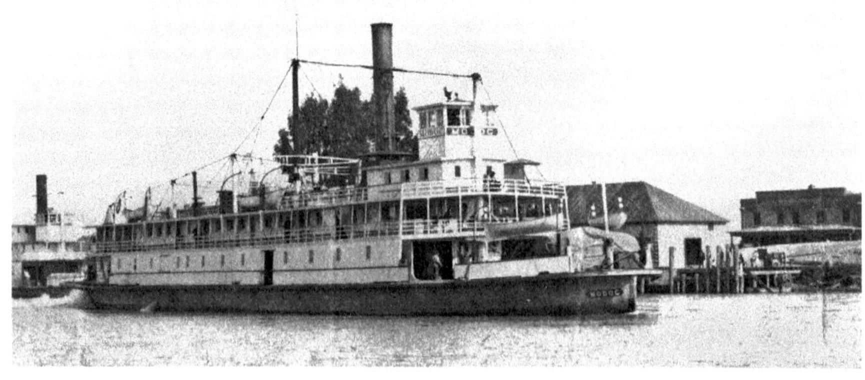

Steamboats ran from Sacramento, connecting Delta towns and San Francisco. *Author's collection.*

ceiling. Very tall ceiling, I think it's about thirty feet high. There's a special trick where you take a dollar bill and wrap it around a silver dollar, add a thumbtack and if you throw it up in a certain way it will stick. Well, during Chinese New Years, in the old days, they used to invite all the regular patrons and close down the bar for the public and throw a big old feed for themselves with the money they got from the ceiling. Times have changed, so now they donate all the money to the Chinese Benevolent Association in Locke."

Giusti's

In 1896 or so, Egisto Giusti became proprietor of the Ryde Hotel. The hotel, not much more than a shack, most likely offered a few rooms and board, as there weren't many eating places close by. Depending on what history you read, he sold out and built Giusti's in 1900 (or 1912), at Walnut Grove Road on the north fork of the Mokelumne River, as a family residence—and a toll station—for boats going downriver. In 1910 or 1915, he began serving drinks and dinners, a custom continued today by grandson Mark Morais, the third generation. Giusti's is the oldest restaurant continually operated by the same family in Sacramento County.

You get there by boat or by car, passing miles of pear orchards and grape arbors on twisty river roads. The weather-beaten sign and worn steps at the entry add to its charm. About 1,500 baseball and John Deere caps, stapled to the ceiling, are part of a tradition started by longtime bartender Mark Rogerson. Sometime in the 1970s, he decided to staple up caps patrons carelessly left behind on the off chance they might come back to retrieve them.

Don Burns remembers, "I went there as a kid, and they used to hang women's underwear on the bar. I think the ladies finally got tired of it."

Along the bar walls are dozens of photographs of devoted regulars and friends, such as *Perry Mason* author Erle Stanley Gardener and celebrities who could always depend on wine or heavier stuff from Egisto throughout Prohibition.

Lunch and dinner feature top-quality, local, in-season ingredients and family-style meals at reasonable prices. New York steak, wild local salmon in season, fried chicken, pasta, prime rib and a Wednesday night two-for-one lobster dinner. And, of course, Portuguese beans.

Giusti's Portuguese Beans

8 cups dried pinto beans
8 quarts water
4 15-ounce cans tomato sauce
2 to 3 pounds linguiça links, cut into fork-size pieces
1 pound bacon, cut into 1" pieces
1 bell pepper, seeded and diced
2 yellow onions, diced
Salt and pepper, to taste
6 bay leaves
2 cups granulated garlic
2 cups ground cumin
2 tablespoons red pepper flakes

Soak beans in water overnight. Next day, add all to a big stockpot, except bacon, bell pepper, onions and seasoning. Bring to a boil. Sauté bacon until crisp. Add bacon into pot, leaving fat in pan. In bacon fat, sauté bell pepper and onions until tender. Put all in bean pot. When boil starts, reduce to simmer. Add salt and pepper. Stir now and then so beans don't stick. Serve when beans are tender, approximately 2 to 3 hours. Correct seasoning, adding more salt and pepper, if needed.

Español

When you go to the Español on Folsom Boulevard, you step back in time. The Español began life in 1923, as a Basque restaurant serving sheepherders who lodged in boardinghouse quarters above it. City records indicate it emerged as early as 1919 as the Hotel Español, first owned by Victoriano Urrutia and then Castro Arrate and Mamerto Fernandez. Frank (Babe) Luigi and brother Mario bought it and relocated in 1952 to the site of the Commercial Hotel at Third and I Streets. Because of eminent domain, it had to move to its current location on Folsom Boulevard, in the center of what was then "Little Italy," in 1965. Karen Zito recalled in a 2010 interview that the boardinghouse was still operational in the 1950s. Boarders were served oxtail stew, lamb fries (testicles), tongue and tripe from original recipes. The restaurant focused on Italian food, served "Basque style." Huge tureens of minestrone soup were followed by platters chock-full of salad, pastas and meats, and then spumoni for dessert. Karen died, but her family still serves up family-style fare to all comers.

For some years, Español vied with other restaurants for the title of the oldest eatery in the city. The Rosemount Grill, Capitol Tamale Café and Hong King Lum have all closed. Now, it's down to Español or Frank Fat's, depending on whether you base this honor on opening date or same family ownership. Although primarily a bar, some people include the Old Ironsides, the first place to get a liquor license after Prohibition ended. To comply with liquor laws, it served lunch Monday through Friday—only one item per day. Club Pheasant in West Sacramento has been around almost as long, but technically, it is in another county.

Bob Miller, who painted all the watercolor illustrations used in this book, shared with us a story about the cannon in the original Español window. "In about 1928, a car from the Southern Pacific Depot jumped the tracks, ran across the street and into the Español. Of course, SP fixed it up, but the owner of the Español put a cannon in the window and said, 'Next time that happens, I'm going to blow up the guy.'"

Basque Spaghetti

Karen Zito recited this recipe, served to boarders, to the authors.

Kosher or sea salt
1 pound spaghetti
6 ounces Spanish hard chorizo, cut into quarter-inch slices
1 tablespoon butter
3 large cloves garlic, peeled and crushed
3 eggs, beaten
1½ cups grated aged Spanish cheese (manchego)
Salt and freshly ground black pepper to taste

Bring a pot of salted water to a boil. Add spaghetti and cook until al dente, 12 minutes. Meanwhile, heat the chorizo with butter and garlic until the sausage starts to brown. Add eggs and half the cheese and blend together. Drain pasta and put in a large bowl. Add the chorizo. Add the egg mixture. Toss until the pasta is well coated. Salt and pepper to taste. Add remaining cheese, mix again and serve while hot.

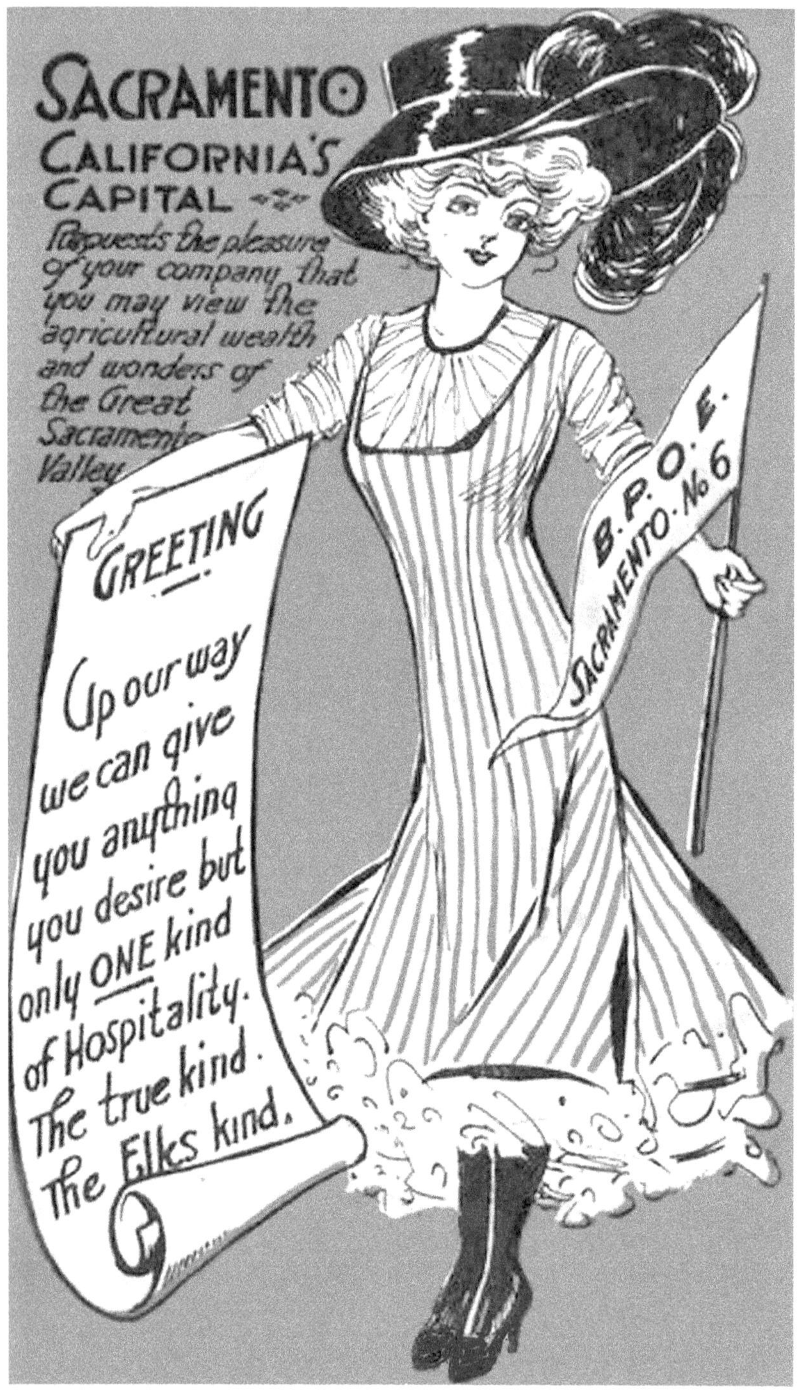

Elks Lodge, now on Riverside Boulevard, still serves breakfast on Sundays and banquets for members and guests. *Sacramento Public Library.*

PANCAKE CIRCUS

One of Sacramento's classic lost restaurants is not really lost at all but still cooking strongly. Al and Myrle Nahas established Pancake Circus, one of the "youngest" old restaurants around, with partner Bud Sheely at Twenty-first and Broadway as the Platter in 1961. Once a twenty-four-hour eatery, it specialized in pancakes and steaks. Sheely became the sole owner about 1971. Since then, it has gone through a succession of dedicated owners. Still, it's packed almost every day from early morning to 3:00 p.m., serving up old-fashioned diner fare, often to regulars who run restaurants of their own. Its special quality is the service of long-term staff and cooks, many who have been there much longer than the present owners.

Recently retired hostess Louise Gonsalves explains why Pancake Circus and the nearby Trails remain when other more prestigious places have vanished.

> *I think it's probably the interchange you have with people who come here, year after year. We're old school; most of us have been here a long time. We were taught: be polite and caring and interact with your customers. It wasn't a case of my name is Susie and I'll be your server today and I'm a clone that you get nowadays with no interaction. We know everyone by name, what they like to eat and the names of their kids. We have three generations coming here. I'm putting kids in the same highchairs I put their parents in.*
>
> *The other reason is our personal service. We're always willing to go the extra mile. We used to have a contract with the railroad running along Nineteenth Street. We had a custom menu to make it easy to order, prepare and deliver. The #1 steak sandwich came with French fries. We had a club sandwich, hamburger, a big half pounder because we were serving railroad men who wanted to EAT. Then we had a couple of omelets with pancakes. We had to tape everything down to make them secure. If they were having coffee, the Styrofoam cup lid had to be taped down really good to make sure the coffee didn't spill.*
>
> *The railway company would arrange to have a cab pick up the order for the taxi driver to drive to the exchange point near City College. The train*

would slow down, not stop, and the lookout would throw the boxes to the engineer as the train passed by. That's why everything had to be taped so the steak wouldn't go flying out of the box and the coffee wouldn't spill and the mashed potatoes wouldn't go bye-bye.

At the time, we were the closest to the Railroad Junction, who served good old-fashioned yummy "Mom's fill-my-tummy food." That's what it took to get the railroad guys coming.

The Hispanic heritage in this area is also strong. I remember one day this woman came in with her little granddaughter, and the granddaughter wanted the French burritos and we couldn't figure what she meant by French burritos. "You know, the burritos with the cheese inside and the strawberries on top, and whipped cream." She meant blintzes or French crepes but to her mind they were burritos.

Market Club

The Market Club is a hidden treasure just off Fifth and Broadway and is known for its eccentric food, hours and waitresses. To find it the first time, you'll need directions. It's really easy to get to. Drive past a row of fish companies, beer distributors and wholesale restaurant suppliers. Look for a row of dilapidated buildings and a weathered "Produce Market" sign. Turn right, not at the first gravel driveway, but the second, where you'll see an army of Produce Express delivery trucks. Try to avoid the water-filled potholes. Pick your own parking spot. It's on the left, with an old brick façade, under an air-conditioning unit that always drips water. Walk up the loading ramp to the dock, open the door and you're in another era.

Inside, a horseshoe-shaped Formica counter surrounded with very old stools faces paintings of golf scenes. The barely separate dining area is memorable for its talking deer's head, festooned with ribbons, and an autographed photo of Sab Shimono, a Sacramento boy who made good in Hollywood.

This "greasy spoon" opened in 1933, the same time as the Produce Market, a collective created by Asian farmers, so rumors that a speakeasy operated on the second floor cannot hold water, as Prohibition ended in 1932. Roy Tomita's family owned it for twenty-seven years. Current owners Jim and Mona Sakata took over with no previous restaurant experience. They trained for a year and kept the same menu. Jim sources ingredients from the markets next door, and his suppliers cut all the restaurant's meats to his specifications.

Opening at 5:30 a.m. to attract—and hold—an older crowd of state and produce workers who've been coming here for generations, the restaurant is closed by 1:00 p.m. and closed Mondays and Saturdays. On Sunday, Jim and Mona close by noon.

Breakfasts include fluffy pancakes, traditional bacon and eggs, Chicana omelets, Wienie Royale, SPAM, baloney and some tasty steaks, including a pork steak, breaded with panko crumbs, so big it almost falls off the plate.

Loyal customers often come after 11:00 to gorge on lunchtime specials: short ribs on Tuesday, broasted chicken on Wednesday, corned beef on Thursday and fried rice with egg on top on Sunday. Everyday dishes include hamburgers, steaks and sandwiches. The daily specials come with a homemade tomato beef soup, a small salad with ranch dressing (if they haven't run out of lettuce) and rolls and butter. Good, hot coffee is served, though occasionally it runs out—especially near closing time.

Just before we went to press, the Market Club closed permanently due to a family illness. Our favorite restaurant, it will be sorely missed.

Thanks for the Memories

This has been a wonderful journey. The history of eateries in the Sacramento area is filled with tastes and memories. Most of these tastes are gone…forever. Only memories remain, and they fade as we get older. The good news is that a few of the tastes are still here, but you have to travel fast to get to these places. Each year, more and more restaurants close. In fact, since starting this book, some half dozen of our favorites closed, and the Market Club has a sign on the door that reads: "Closed Indefinitely Due to Family Illness."

So, eat out and often. Thank the servers, cooks and owners who work their fingers to the bone to create a lasting memory for you. As author Kazuo Ishiguro said, "Memories, even your most precious ones, fade surprisingly quickly. But I don't go along with that. The memories I value most, I don't ever see them fading."

Lost Restaurants of Sacramento will continue under the auspices of We Are Where We Eat, a project that chronicles the stories of the people who grow, distribute, prepare and serve the food we eat. If you have stories of your own, go to our website, discoverwhereweeat.com; our blog, losteateries.blogspot.com; or email us at wearewhereweeat@me.com. Send us articles, stories, images, MP3 files or videos of your favorite places, past and present.

Bibliography

We made a conscious decision to cite almost all of our sources in the text rather than burden the reader with footnotes. Rest assured that we have done our best to note every interview, newspaper, book or article. If we missed anything, this bibliography should fill you in. If there are any omissions, we heartily apologize. Interviews are listed in our acknowledgements.

Books

Arellano, Gustavo. *Taco USA: How Mexican Food Conquered America*. New York: Scribner, 2012.

Avella, Steven M. *The Good Life*. Charleston, SC: Arcadia Publishing, 2008.

———. *Sacramento: Indomitable City*. Charleston, SC: Arcadia Publishing, 1993.

Bancroft, Hubert Howe. *California Inter Pocula*. San Francisco: History Company Publishers, 1888.

Barber & Baker, Engravers. *Sacramento Illustrated*. San Francisco: Monson & Valentine, Steam Book and Job Printers, 1855.

Burg, William. *Sacramento's K Street, Where Our City Was Born*. Charleston, SC: The History Press, 2012.

———. *Then and Now: Sacramento*. Charleston, SC: Arcadia Publishing, 2007.

Caesar, Clarence. "*An Historical Overview of the Development of Sacramento's Black Community, 1850–1853*." Master's thesis, California State University–Sacramento, 1985.

California Historical Society. *From Sutter's Fort to Capital City*. San Francisco: self-published, 1973.

Carver, MaryAnn Burk. *What It Used To Be Like: Portrait of My Marriage to Raymond Carver*. New York: St. Martins Press, 2006.

Choy, Philip. *Canton Footprints*. Sacramento: Chinese American Council of Sacramento, 2008.

Conlin, Joseph R. *Bacon, Beans and Galantines: Food and Foodways on the Western Mining Frontier*. Reno: University of Nevada Press, 1986.

Dana, Julian. *The Sacramento: River of Gold*. New York: Farrar & Reinhart, 1939.

———. *Sutter of California*. New York: Blue Ribbon Books, Halcyon House Edition, 1938.

Davis, Hon. Winfield J. *An Illustrated History of Sacramento County California*. Chicago: Lewis Publishing Co., 1890.

Galarza, Ernesto. *Barrio Boy*. Notre Dame, IN: University of Notre Dame, 1971.

Hess, John L. and Karen. *The Tastes of America*. New York: Grossman Publishing, 1977.

Hingston, Edward Peron. *The Genial Showman, reminiscences of the life of 'Artemus Ward.'* London: Chandos and Willis, 1881.

Hooker, Richard J. *Food and Drink in America, A History*. Indianapolis, IN: Bobs Merrill, 1981.

Hurtado, Albert. *John Sutter: A Life on the North American Frontier*. Norman: University of Oklahoma Press, 2006.

Jakle, John A., and Keith A. Sculle. *Fast Foods: Roadside Restaurants in the Automobile Age.* Baltimore: Johns Hopkins University Press, 1999.

Jones, Evan. *American Food: The Gastronomic Story*. New York: Dutton, 1975.

Kelley, John. "*The Chronology of Sutter's Fort.*" Legacy of John Sutter papers, Sutter's Fort State Historic Park Archives.

Kibbey, Mead B., ed. *J. Horace Culver's Sacramento City Directory for the Year 1851.* Sacramento: California State Library Foundation, 2000.

———. *Samuel Colville's Sacramento Directory for the Year 1853–54.* Sacramento: California State Library Foundation, 2000.

Lender, Mark Edward, and James Kirby Martin. *Drinking in America: A History*. New York: Free Press, 1982.

Lucetti, Cathy Lee. *Home on the Range: A Culinary History of the American West.* New York: Villard, 1993.

MacGowan, Joseph. *A History of the Sacramento Valley*, Vol. 1–3. New York: Lewis Historical Publishing, 1961.

———. *The Sacramento Waterfront 1849–1875.* Sacramento: Sacramento Museum and History Division, 1976.

Maeda, Wayne. *Changing Dreams and Treasured Memories: A Story of Japanese Americans in the Sacramento Region.* Sacramento: Sacramento Japanese American Citizens League, 2000.

Mariani, John. *America Eats Out.* New York: William Morrow, 1991.

———. *Dictionary of American Food and Drink.* New York: Harper Collins, 1994.

New Yorker. "Cafeteria," August 1988.

Pillsbury, Richard. *From Boarding House to Bistro: American Restaurants Then and Now*. Cambridge MA: Von Win Hyman, 1990.

Pitti, Edith, and Mary Praetzellis. *History of the Golden Eagle Hotel: 1851–1874*. Santa Rosa, CA: Sonoma State University, 1980.

Ranhofer, Charles. *The Epicurean*. New York: Dover Publication, 1971.

Root, Waverly, and Richard de Rochement. *Eating in America*. New York: William Morrow and Company, 1976.

Sacramento County Historical Society. *Golden Notes*. Editions from 1953 to 2011.

Severson, Thor. *Sacramento, An Illustrated History: 1839 to 1874*. Sacramento: California Historical Society, bicentennial reprint edition 1975.

Shaw, Myrtle Lord. *A Sacramento Saga*. Sacramento: Sacramento Chamber of Commerce, 1946.

Smith, Andrew. *Eating History*. New York: Columbia University Press, 2009.

———. *Encyclopedia of Junk Food and Fast Food*. Westport, CT: Greenwood Press, 2006.

———. *Hamburger: A Global History*. London: Reaction Books, 2008.

Tom, Lawrence. *Sacramento's Chinatown*. Charleston, SC: Arcadia Publishing, 2010.

Tripoldi, Tony. *Requiem for Torchy: The Life of a Gambler*. IUniverse, 2009.

Weiss, Melford S. *Valley City: A Chinese Community in America*. Cambridge, MA: Schenkman, 1974.

Willis, William L. *History of Sacramento County, California*. Los Angeles: Historic Record, 1913.

Zollinger, J. Peter. *Sutter: The Man and his Empire*. Gloucester, MA: Peter Smith, 1967.

Magazines

Life Magazine. April 30, 1945.
Popular Mechanics. October 1922.
Vibe. August 20, 2000.

Newspapers

Newspaper anecdotes provided the backbone for much of this book. All works are cited in the text. The California Digital Newspaper Collection in Riverside California allowed us to work at home and not get distracted. This reference can be found at: cdnc.ucr.edu.

Alta California (1849)
Placer Times
Sacramento Bee (1857 to 2000, with special thanks to Elaine Corn, Bob Sylva, Gwen Schoen, Carlos Alcala, Dixie Reed, Mike Dunne and Rick Kushman—all no longer with the paper. Allen Pierlioni, Steve Magagnini and Gloria Glyer are still on staff. All provided context and enjoyable reading, as have other food columnists since our first subscription in 1955.)
Sacramento Daily Union, Sacramento Union (1851 to 1956)
Sacramento Observer (Specifically, "Success Was No Stranger," an interview with George Dunlap, November 8–14, 1973)
Southern Hospitality Dished Up
Suttertown News (With kind permission of Tim Holt, the publisher.)
Valley Community Newspapers

Websites

Lawrence Fox's "Virtual Museum of Sutter's Fort." http://score.rims.k12.ca.us/activity/suttersfort/.

Jan Whitaker has written extensively on hotels and restaurants, including many fine books. Her website, however, is a gold mine. She kindly provided information for us and allowed us to use her articles for background material and to give context to our story.

http://restaurant-ingthroughhistory.com.

Online Services

California Digital Newspaper Collection (cdnc.ucr.edu)
Calisphere (calisphere.universityofcalifornia.edu)
Hathitrust (hathitrust.org)
Library of Congress (www.loc.gov)

Libraries and Historical Societies

California Historical Society
California State Library
Los Angeles Public Library
Sacramento County Historical Society
Sacramento Public Library
Sacramento River Delta Historical Society

Index

U

V

W

Z

About the Authors and Illustrator

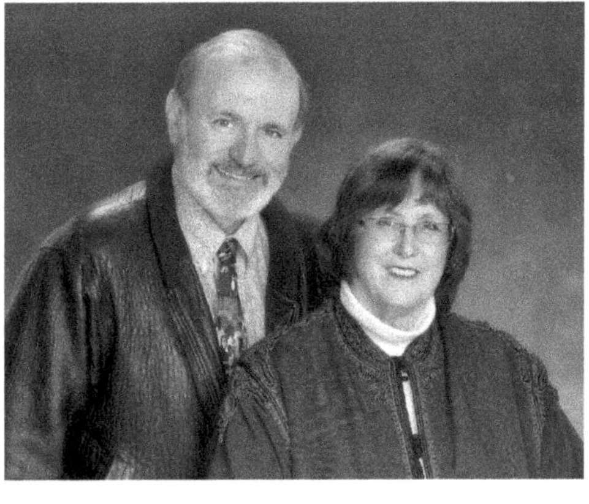

Maryellen and Keith Burns, siblings, started eating out in Sacramento in 1955. Maryellen is director of *We Are Where We Eat*, a Sacramento foodways alliance that chronicles Sacramento's food stories. A writer, editor, teacher, food sleuth and former caterer, she serves on the boards of the Sacramento County Historical Society and I Street Press and is a member of the Culinary Historians of Northern California, Slow Food and other food, wine, history and art associations.

Keith is an author, publisher, film and television writer, director and producer, as well as an antiques, popular culture and entertainment industry consultant and appraiser. His bookstore (Books on Main) and site for ephemera (www.burnsbizarre.com) feature more than one million historic books, artifacts and ephemera. He spent many years as a columnist covering food, books and culture for publications throughout California. He's a member of the Directors Guild of America, Writers Guild of America and the Editors Guild.

Bob Miller, an illustrator, designer and advertising director, picked up a paintbrush to do a landscape on the side of an old wooden peach crate he found behind his father's barn in the 1940s and has painted and drawn ever since. He has exhibited widely in galleries and art fairs. His murals and whimsical drawings grace the promenade connecting Old Sacramento to the K Street Mall River Walk on the east side of the Sacramento River.

www.ingramcontent.com/pod-product-compliance
Lightning Source LLC
LaVergne TN
LVHW052340100826
845147LV00021B/1132